The Politics and Economics of the Transition Period

The Politics and Economics of the Transition Period

Nikolai Bukharin

Edited with an Introduction by
Kenneth J. Tarbuck

Translated by
Oliver Field

Routledge & Kegan Paul
London, Boston and Henley

86786

First published in 1979
by Routledge & Kegan Paul Ltd
39 Store Street, London WC1E 7DD,
Broadway House, Newtown Road,
Henley-on-Thames, Oxon RG9 1EN and
9 Park Street, Boston, Mass. 02108 USA
Set in 11-point Imprint on 12-point
and printed in Great Britain by
Morrison & Gibb Ltd
London and Edinburgh
This edition and translation

British Library Cataloguing in Publication Data

Bukharin, Nikolaĭ Ivanovich

The politics and economics of the transition period
1. Communism
I. Title   II. Tarbuck, Kenneth John
335   HX56   78–41064

ISBN 0 7100 0114 2

Contents

Contents

Preface

Certain problems presented themselves in the editing of this work, and these fell under four headings.

First, Bukharin's terse style sometimes leaves the precise meaning open, indeed he refers himself to his almost 'algebraic style' at one point. To try to partially overcome this problem I have occasionally interpolated remarks of my own. These remarks have been clearly marked off by the use of square brackets and the reader will be well aware of my incursions, and that they are wholly my own interpretations. Such incursions have been kept down to an absolute minimum and I hope they do not mar the flow of the work.

Second, there is the author's rather careless use of references, sometimes only giving abbreviated ones or giving no publishers or date of publication. This problem has been more difficult to resolve and on more than one occasion I have not been successful. This has meant that certain entries in the bibliography are not complete. In the notes and references only short entries are used, the full ones being incorporated in the bibliography. Since there was, inevitably, a certain overlap in the use of standard works between the author and myself I have combined all full references into one bibliography. I have also, where possible, given references to English translations of works quoted by Bukharin.

Third, there was an over-lavish use of emphases and quotation marks in the original text which most readers would have found cumbersome and detracting from the flow of the work. I have tried to reduce this overemphasis without, I hope, losing the particular flavour of Bukharin's style. In this respect it has often been necessary to reduce the emphasis from a whole sentence to one word which conveys the urgency which Bukharin wished to impart to his work. In this respect I have, where necessary, erred on the side of leniency in wielding the editorial function, since it was my wish to retain, as far as possible, the work in the form the author wrote it.

The fourth problem posed by Bukharin's text was the copious nature of the footnotes. In many instances these could have been included in the body of the text by a little judicious re-writing *on the part of the author*. Unfortunately, Bukharin – to our knowledge – was never able to produce a second edition of his work, when such rewriting could have been done. Although sorely tempted, I had to acknowledge that such work was beyond the brief of an editor and, therefore, have left the footnotes as in the Russian edition. I should, however, warn the reader not to skip the footnotes since they form an integral part of the work and often carry Bukharin's arguments a stage further than in the main body of the text.

In all these respects, the judgments and responsibility for making such changes that have been made in this English text are wholly mine.

I would like to take this opportunity to thank Professor Sidney Heitman, of Colorado State University, for his invaluable help in matters relating to material on or by Bukharin. Without his assistance my own work would have been that much more difficult. I would also like to thank my wife Marion for her unstinting efforts to ensure that I produced a finished work that was intelligible. My thanks also go to Professor F. Duchene of the Centre for Contemporary European Studies, Sussex University, who afforded me facilities to work undisturbed in a congenial atmosphere.

K.J.T.

The texts used for the translation of this edition are 'The Theory of the Dictatorship of the Proletariat', first published in a collection of articles *Oktiabr'skii pererorot i diktatura proletariata*, Moscow, 1919; and *The Economics of the Transition Period*: Part I *General Theory of the Transformation Process*, Communist Academy, Moscow, 1920. (Part II was never published.) Both texts are the first known publications.

Editor's Introduction

I

The two items brought together in this book complement each other and form a unity for those who wish to study particular aspects of the early period of the Bolshevik revolution. Moreover, these two items enable one to locate a certain point in the development of the theoretical conception of Bukharin. In so far as Bukharin was considered to be one of the major theorists of Bolshevism this book will also shed light upon how the Bolsheviks viewed themselves in this period.

The first item, *The Theory of the Dictatorship of the Proletariat*, written in 1919, is the shorter of the two and helps set the scene for the major piece, *The Economics of the Transition Period*, written in 1920.

II

The first essay is of particular interest from several points of view. It takes up and develops ideas on the state that Bukharin had first formulated in 'The Theory of the Imperialist State', which he wrote in 1916. However, at the time of writing this was not published in full. It appeared only in an abbreviated form, first in *Jügend-Internationale* no. 6, 1 December 1916, and then slightly later in *Arbeiter-Politik* no. 25, 9 December 1916. This article upon the imperialist state did not appear in full until 1925, when it was published in the journal *The Revolution is Right* (Moscow). The reason why only an abbreviated form appeared was that Lenin had rejected the original article for publication in the Bolshevik émigré press, because of its alleged 'semi-anarchist' ideas. However, Lenin subsequently adopted the main body of Bukharin's ideas on

1

the state, and incorporated them in *The State and Revolution*, which he wrote on the eve of the October revolution.[1]

The present article by Bukharin, on the dictatorship of the proletariat, is a continuation and development of ideas first formulated nearly four years previously. It is also one of the first major re-statements of these ideas since the October revolution. Before that date, i.e. 1917, the only living, concrete example of workers' power that Marxists had before them as a model had been the Paris Commune of 1871. In 1916 Bukharin had only been able to deal with the problem at the level of theory; here in the present work he was writing from actual experience, as a major participant in the creation and holding of Soviet power, i.e. the dictatorship of the proletariat.

Another aspect, which is most interesting in the light of sub-sequent developments in the Soviet Union, is the manner in which Bukharin extols the manifold forms of workers' power as evinced by the Soviets. Little or no mention is made of the party, either on the general level or on that of the particular experience of the Bolshevik Party. This is in striking contrast to the heavy emphasis placed upon the 'leading role of the party' which was to become the official Soviet dogma of the Stalin era. Those who are accustomed to the heavy emphasis placed upon the party as the organ of workers' power will find Bukharin's ideas refreshing and thought-provoking. It must be remembered that at the time this essay was written by Bukharin there were still other socialist parties active in the Soviets, albeit on a limited scale. Nor had anyone yet thought that the Bolsheviks should have a legal monopoly of political activity, and hence of power, despite their *de facto* position of almost single-party rule. All other parties were banned singly and for particular reasons, on an *ad hoc* basis without any attempt to formulate a theory of the one-party state. Such ideas only came later. It would be beyond the scope of this introduction to go into the reasons as to why the Bolsheviks felt compelled to ban all other parties, but the question is one that needs careful consideration.

III

The present text needs to be set in the context of its time and alongside much better-known pamphlets by Lenin, *The Proletarian*

Revolution and the Renegade Kautsky, and Trotsky, *Terrorism and Communism*. Bukharin's essay can be seen as fitting temporally between Lenin's work of 1918 and Trotsky's of 1920. In all three works the opponent singled out for the most vigorous attack was Karl Kautsky. This was not accidental, since Kautsky had occupied a unique place within the German Social Democratic Party and the Second International. It was an indication of Kautsky's prestige and authority within the international Marxist movement that three of the leading figures of the Russian revolution felt compelled to take up cudgels with him in the midst of the life-and-death struggle of the civil war then raging in Russia.

The reason why these three writers felt this need to challenge Kautsky was well located by Max Shachtman, when he wrote:

Karl Kautsky had known Karl Marx and Friedrich Engels in his youth. After their death, he became the principal literary executor of the two founders of modern socialism. His writings on a wide variety of subjects were regarded everywhere as classical statements of the socialist view.[2]

Apart from the very real practical need that the Bolsheviks had to win socialists away from Kautsky's views – he opposed the Bolsheviks – to their own ideas, and in the process form a new international, there also subsisted a psychological element. This later element can be seen as a revulsion against a father-figure, who it was felt – correctly – had deserted his own principles on a number of substantive issues. Both the urgency of the situation and this loss of filial faith added particular acrimony to all these essays.

Both Lenin's and Trotsky's works on this subject have been readily available in English for a number of years now. However, Bukharin's essay has never appeared in English before. There were two editions in the early 1920s, in Russian, printed in New York – aimed at the large Russian émigré population in the USA – and a subsequent edition in Moscow in 1924.[3] Therefore, the present edition makes available to the English reader an essay which will help them in the study of Bolshevism, Bukharin and the period.

IV

Bukharin's *The Economics of the Transition Period* holds a special place in his writings and in relation to the period in which it was written. Any study of the man and the period must take into account and locate this book. The work itself has carried on an almost subterranean existence in footnotes and references in many other works, yet it has been inaccessible for the non-specialist reader. It had only one Russian edition, in 1920, and one German edition in 1922. It was never reprinted in the author's lifetime. Because of this its title is relatively well known, its contents very much less so.

Although written in 1920 the book has, like much of Bukharin's writings, a freshness and relevance today that is remarkable. This quality is emphasized when one considers that, up to the time it was written, so very little had been written on the subject matter. Bukharin was a real pioneer in this respect and because of this the work has all the faults, as well as the merits, of such an enterprise. Before the Russian revolution of October 1917 very few Marxists were prepared to talk or write, in any other than the most general terms, on what the outline of the future socialist society would be like.[4] Of course, some writers, e.g. William Morris and Jack London, had projected their own particular vision of socialist society or the transition to it in the novel form, but they hardly rank as theorists in this respect. Bukharin, however, wrote his book on the basis of living experience within the revolution then in process. If he dared to predict, it was on the basis of the evidence around him. That he should prove wrong on a number of points should occasion no surprise. We should, however, acknowledge his intellectual audacity.

Alfred Rosmer gave an amusing, but enlightening, insight into Bukharin's character and role in 1920. When he attended the second congress of the Third International he spoke to Trotsky about Bukharin, and reported the following:

> Trotsky . . . said . . . 'Bukharin is always in front, but he's always looking over his shoulder to make sure Lenin isn't far behind.' When I got to know the two men well I got a visual image of these judgements – Lenin solid and stocky, advancing at an even pace, and the slight figure of Bukharin galloping off in front, but always needing Lenin's presence.[5]

Rosmer's anecdote gives us an idea as to the role that Bukharin played, not only in relation to Lenin, but also to the whole Bolshevik Party. He acted as the intellectual cavalry, seeking out new fields, harrying the enemy with his pen and probing into unknown territory.

This particular book represents a nodal point in Bukharin's own career. Up to and including 1920 Bukharin had consistently been on the left of the Bolshevik Party, and the present work was his last major offering before his subsequent evolution to the right of the party.[6] Yet any study of this book and of Bukharin's subsequent writings indicate more continuity than is usually allowed for by those commentators who have only a cursory knowledge of him. The thread of continuity was provided by his theory of equilibrium, which I will deal with later. If 1920 marked the high point of Bukharin's leftism, then it can be said to be equally true for the Bolsheviks as a whole, Lenin included. The rigours of the winter of 1920–1 and the Kronstadt rebellion stripped away the exuberance and illusions about 'war communism' for all but a tiny minority within the Bolshevik Party.

To fully understand the import of this book it is necessary to locate it in the historical period of which it is the product. Also it is necessary to constantly remember Bukharin's own caveat, that it was 'written in an almost algebraic formula'. This latter point will explain the rich complexity and compactness of the text, and also perhaps the quite different interpretations that it is possible to put upon certain passages.

V

What then was the period in which this work was written? It was one of civil war and revolution, following on from Russia's collapse during the First World War and the revolutions of February and October of 1917.

The imperialist war that had begun in August 1914 had thrown an intolerable burden upon Russian industry, its agriculture and transport system. Although there had been a considerable growth of Russian manufacturing industry between 1890 and 1914, taken as a whole it was quite inadequate to face the strains imposed by a modern industrial war. In terms of production and transport facilities Russia was far behind any of the other major participants in that war. Although much of the industrial production was carried out in large modern units, these were still only relatively small islands in an ocean of small-scale production and a backward agriculture.[7] Thus there was considerable unevenness within the Russian economy as a whole. In the first stages of the war production rose but, as the war dragged on, it declined rapidly. Food and raw materials' shortages reached famine proportions by the winter of 1916–17. The revolution of February 1917 further aggravated this situation and with it went further disruptions of industry. Therefore, by the time of the October revolution, when the Bolsheviks assumed power, the whole economy was in a state of chaos. Large areas of western Russia were under German occupation until the collapse of the Central Powers in November 1918. Since these occupied areas contained rich grain lands and the industrialized sectors of Poland, the food shortage in the towns and the goods famine in the countryside were further aggravated.

It was in this situation that the Bolsheviks assumed power. Until the start of the civil war, in the summer of 1918, there was an almost honeymoon-like period in which the Bolsheviks not only shared power with the Left Socialist Revolutionaries, but also attempted to obtain the collaboration of some sections of the bourgeoisie.[8] There were no immediate moves to take into state ownership the major manufacturing industries, although there was a vigorous campaign to extend workers' control, i.e. supervision of owners and managers by rank-and-file committees. The Bolsheviks, on the insistence of Lenin, moved with caution in relation to nationalization in this period. It is true that certain measures of nationalization had been undertaken in the first few months of the Soviet government, e.g. the Merchant Marine had been nationalized in January 1918 and the sugar industry in May of that year, but the main efforts had been directed towards the stabilization and regularization of the tottering economy on the existing basis of ownership.

Lenin's theme in this period was the need to install an efficient system of accounting and control, and to bring all factories back to full production as soon as possible, even if this meant employing former owners and managers at high salaries. The most radical measures had been initiated from below, by workers seizing factories and above all by the peasants dispossessing the land-owners and sharing out the land between themselves. This latter move was endorsed by the Soviet government, but it was an acknowledgment of an accomplished fact over which they had little or no control. The reason for the caution on the part of the Bolsheviks can be found in the expectation of an early revolution in Germany and other parts of Europe. They reasoned that if such an event occurred, particularly in Germany, the problems regarding the supply of industrial and processed goods would be solved, if not immediately, then at least fairly quickly.[9]

This policy was not without its critics, and the Left Communists – among whom was Bukharin – pressed for more and far-reaching measures against the capitalists. Such were the tolerant conditions still prevailing that the Left Communists were able to publish their own public journal – *Kommunist* – and Lenin had to argue policy questions with them publicly; just as had been the case over the Brest–Litovsk peace treaty.[10]

The situation changed radically in the summer of 1918. First, civil war began in earnest, and second, there was a fear of further German intervention. These threats came on top of sabotage and flight by the owners of industry, and these factors themselves led to further complications. There was a wave of factory seizures by workers' committees, very often on a local and fragmentary basis. These were followed by a Soviet government decree on 28 June 1918 which nationalized all branches of industry.[11] Later on, in November 1918, all internal and foreign trade was nationalized, the latter having little practical significance at that time since all foreign trade had by then ceased with those parts of the country in the hands of the Soviets. However, this state monopoly of foreign trade was to become of critical importance later on. The civil war reinforced the centrifugal tendencies at work within the economy and as Carr notes:

> the machinery of exchange and distribution established by recent decrees was quickly pushed aside; and for some time the most effective instruments in extracting grain from peasants were the 'iron detachments' of workers from the towns and factories reinforced by the local committees of poor peasants.[12]

Another source, and consequence, of the economic chaos was inflation: like all the belligerents in the war, part of the Russian expenditure on arms and munitions had been met by an increase in the note issue of the central bank. There had been a budget deficit ever since 1914, rising to 81 per cent of the budget in 1917.

The budget for the first half of 1918 had been estimated at 17.6 millard rubles expenditure, revenue at only 2.8 millard.[13] So, although the Bolsheviks did not start the inflationary process, they were unable to stop it either, this despite their wishes to do so in the first few months of Soviet rule.

Given this chaotic situation the Bolsheviks, when faced with the necessity to fight a civil war and foreign intervention, had to take urgent and drastic measures to supply the towns and the new Red Army. There was evolved – it would be wrong to say worked out or planned – a system for the production of war material and the provisioning of the towns which subordinated all else to survival. Victor Serge succinctly summarized the system of war communism that emerged as follows:

> War communism could be defined as follows: first, requisitioning in the countryside; second, strict rationing for the town population, who were classified into categories; third, complete 'socialization' of production and labour; fourth, an extremely complicated and chit-ridden system of distribution for the remaining stock of manufactured goods; fifth, a monopoly of power tending towards a single party and the suppression of all dissent; sixth, a state of siege and the Cheka.[14]

The first official step on the road to war communism came in May 1918 with a decree which conferred upon the Commissariat of Supply extraordinary powers for the collection of grain. This was the legal basis for the armed detachments of workers who were supposed to confiscate surplus grain and the hoards of grain speculators. This was later changed to requisitioning fixed amounts of grain, which went beyond taking surpluses. Thus began the process that eventually led to the peasants ceasing to sow grain, and ultimately to the New Economic Policy.

In the towns money soon ceased to circulate, workers were given rations, all state services were provided free, school meals were given to children free, even theatre tickets were distributed among factory workers free. Many Bolsheviks saw in all this the realization of their aims as communists, but the reality was far from what the founding fathers of Marxian socialism had envisaged as being communism or socialism.

It was in the feverish atmosphere of gun smoke and subsistence rations that Bukharin tried to peer ahead and formulate some theoretical propositions regarding the transition to socialism. Much of what he wrote was, essentially, a defence or even a celebration of war communism.

However, in the process he threw out innumerable ideas that were ahead of his time, and it is to these that I now want to turn.

VI

Bukharin takes as his starting point the *world* capitalist economy: 'contemporary capitalism is world capitalism, this means that capitalist relations of production dominate the whole world and connect all parts of our planet with a firm economic bond.' When he says this he is, essentially, enunciating one of the basic tenets of Bolshevism in its emphasis upon the internationalization of the class struggle in the epoch of imperialism. Moreover, this conception is an essential component in the Bolsheviks' perspective in which they set the Russian revolution. Despite his later support for the theory of 'socialism in one country' Bukharin was, at this stage, firmly convinced and clear in his own understanding that capitalism had indeed produced a world market, a world economy, a world social system and a world history.

These ideas were strengthened and elaborated later on in the book when Bukharin discussed the disintegration of the world capitalist system and the growth and development of transitional workers' states. He says: 'The dictatorship of the proletariat cannot triumph if the proletariat of different countries are isolated from each other. Therefore, during the course of the struggle, an adhesion, a bond, a cohesion, a union between all emerging, proletarian soviet republics is inevitable.' And 'For *the proletariat* its economic and political unity is a matter of life and death, since its partial victories (its dictatorships) express the overcoming of the disintegration' of the world capitalist system.

Furthermore, when examining the *world* dictatorship of the proletariat he says: 'The productive forces, distributed not according to national divisions, but according to the principle of economic rationality, develop at an unprecedented rate.' So, here he was not even thinking of *socialism* on a world scale, rather the preparatory stage, of the initial dictatorship of the proletariat achieving world hegemony.

9

These ideas were a long way from Bukharin's later espousal of 'socialism in one country'. Moreover, at this early period his ideas coincided with those of Lenin on this point. Lenin, in 1919, wrote:

> Only by appraising the role of the Soviets on a world scale can we achieve a correct understanding of the details of our internal life and a proper regulation of them. The job of construction is completely dependent on how soon the revolution will succeed in the more important European countries. Only after it succeeds there can we seriously get down to the job of construction.[15]

The point here is that these views were not peculiar to Lenin or Bukharin, but were generally held by the Bolsheviks at this time. Therefore, we can see that 'socialism in one country' was a revision of previously held views on the part of Bukharin, and decidedly retrograde.

The internationalization of the world economy and of capital has, of course, become much more delineated in terms of the international and multinational corporations that have developed since the end of the Second World War. Many of the tendencies that were only there in skeletal form when Bukharin wrote his work have now come to fruition, in a way that has a direct relationship to what he was writing about. We can now see the full flowering from the roots that are carefully dissected when Bukharin wrote about world economy being a living unity.[16] This itself poses problems for any discussion of transitional societies, for how can one talk about the transition to socialism whilst the major parts of this world economy, especially its most advanced industrial sectors, are still dominated by capitalist economic, political, social and personal relations? Most of the existing transitional societies overthrew capitalism when it was relatively weak and underdeveloped within the particular national boundaries. This being the case, these societies have been unable to stop themselves being drawn into the existing world economy, being partially shaped by it, and they have been stamped with certain features that stem from this subordinate relationship with the capitalist mode of production.

Bukharin was at pains to point out the difference between the simple sum of national economies in the world – which if viewed only in this manner would mean that there would be no *world* economy – and the concrete living complex of institutions which go to make up the totality which is greater than its constituent parts. He says: 'The presence of a special relationship – that is what makes a simple aggregate a real aggregate, but just such an aggregate excludes the concept of an arithmetical sum, because it is much greater and more complex than that sum.'

What Bukharin is stating here is the Marxist concept of the dialectics of unity and change. Given sufficient quantitative accretions of one or more factors in a given situation there will be induced a qualitative change. In this sense merely to take the arithmetical sum of factors in a society and presume that this gives us an understanding of that society would be wrong. For example, if one studies the development of international trade since the end of the Second World War it becomes clear that trade between the developed capitalist countries has expanded faster than trade between developed countries and the underdeveloped ones. Moreover, much of what passes for trade between countries is today the movement of products *within* international firms. These two factors are relatively new phenomena and therefore, when one is discussing the world economy and the development of international trade, one would have to examine each stage in its concrete empirical condition and ask how this or that element has altered the complexion of the totality.

The totality of society, although made up of the total factors, is one that is arrived at by an understanding of which ones are the determining ones and thus the ones that give rise to the particular character of that society.

This may appear to be a mere exercise in philosophical logic and as such out of place in a work of economic theory. However, from the point of view of a Marxist, it would be wrong to accept only the phenomena which appear on the surface, i.e. those that are immediately apparent, and thus ignore the causal influence and function of the determining factors in a relationship. A quite simple example of this can be given. At the height of the 'emergency' in Malaysia in the 1950s it was estimated that the cost to Britain far outweighed the financial return upon investments there. Thus 'logically' it was a foolish expenditure. But if one asks who paid such expenditures and who received the benefits, one gets a different answer to this apparently simple arithmetic problem. There was, of course, no abstract 'Britain' involved, but the concrete one of the capitalist British state. And whilst it was the

11

capitalist corporations which received the benefits by way of the remitted profits they did not by any means wholly pay for the upkeep of British forces in Malaysia. It was the British state which paid for this upkeep, and its revenue was, and is, mainly drawn from the British working class. Also the British economy as a whole benefited by the substantial amount of dollars which the Malaysian tin and rubber earnings added to the sterling area pool. So we can see that by an examination of the total situation it was possible to turn a 'loss' into a profit.

Bukharin was, therefore, at pains to point to the real aggregate of society, the totality, and show that this is different from a mere summation of its parts. And the concrete application of this epistemological method in the period in which Bukharin was writing was the Bolshevik revolution of 1917. It was only by grasping the *world* totality of capitalism that it was possible and justified for a small exploited minority – the Russian proletariat – to lead an *anti-capitalist* revolution in a backward, absolutist, semi-feudal country.

VII

Bukharin introduces an important distinction in attempting to outline his ideas on transitional societies. He says, about capitalism:

> This system is not a 'teleological unity', i.e. a consciously directed system with a definite plan. There is no such plan. Here there is not even a subject of the economic process. In the main, it is not a case here of 'society produces' but of 'production takes place in society'. And for this reason, people do not rule the product, instead the product rules the people.

But in a transitional society one of its hallmarks is precisely an attempt to develop a teleological unity – purposeful planning consciously guiding production for predetermined ends. The process of bringing the product under the rule of man is begun. Under capitalism production takes place within society – sometimes in spite of it – the very anarchy of capitalist relations of production militate against any attempt at real social planning. All experience points to the conclusion that what passes for planning in capitalist societies is merely a method of indicative *projections* for the economy as a whole. Even those parts of the economy which are under the direct control of the state – nationalized industries – cannot be planned in a purposeful manner, but are always *reacting* to market conditions.[17] In a socialist society production becomes a subjective as well as an objective process, it becomes a social process carried out by society for society. However, in a transitional society the planning process struggles with the law of value for mastery of the determination of the whole.

Like many Marxists of the period under review, Bukharin was fascinated by the attempts of the Imperial German government to organize production for total war. Because of this he tended to over-estimate the extent of this organization, and draw conclusions that were not justified at that time. He says:

> Finance capital has done away with anarchy of production
> within the major capitalist countries. Monopolistic alliances of
> employers, combined enterprises, and the penetration of
> banking capital into industry has created a new model of
> relations of production, transforming the unorganized
> commodity capitalist system into finance capitalist *organization*
> . . . the exchange relation expressing the *social* division of
> labour . . . is replaced by a *technical* division of labour within
> an organized 'national economy'.

Clearly, Bukharin was projecting what was a war-time trend into the future, and seeing it as a permanent feature of capitalism. This was not to be. In all the major capitalist countries after both world wars there has been a dismantling of state control over the economy, even if there was never a complete return to the pre-war situations. However, the *tendency* towards monopolization and centralization has been deepened and extended since Bukharin wrote the above. He was obviously correct to point out the importance of such a development. In this we can see the simultaneous development of two levels of thought by Bukharin: on the one level he was fully expecting the victory of the proletarian revolution on a world scale, and at the other level he was projecting the continuing survival and development of capitalism and trying to grapple with the problems posed by this latter contingency.

In discussing economic phenomena under capitalism Bukharin points out that all such manifestations are market ones, since capitalism knows no other type or relationship. But, 'this does not

13

mean, however, that every economic phenomenon is a market one'. This is very pertinent to any consideration of an economy of the transition period. The only economics that capitalism recognizes are precisely those of the market place.[18] Yet, given different situations, different phenomena can become economic factors without becoming market ones. We come across the most outstanding example of this within capitalist society itself, through the unpaid labour of house-bound women. There they labour, unpaid, in cooking, cleaning, rearing children, etc., i.e. producing new labour power for the market. But in no way can their activities be said to be related to the market. This should not be construed as meaning that such labour by women is not useful, it *is* and also very *necessary* labour for the functioning of the capitalist system.

This leads us to the general consideration that, given the release of the self-activity and resourcefulness of the working class by revolution, one of the most potent factors in building a new society will not necessarily be given to quantification by the market mechanism. Therefore, the point that Bukharin was making, although contained in one short sentence, is crucial to an understanding of the economic process in a transitional society.

VIII

In chapter 2 Bukharin sets out, in rather abbreviated form, his theory of social equilibrium. He argues that any class society has contradictory elements within it; on the one hand there is the antagonism between the ruling class and the exploited majority over the production and division of the total and surplus product. On the other hand, there is the essential unity without which *no* society could exist. This means that there are impulses towards disequilibrium contesting with those phenomena which help to stabilize social equilibrium. The mechanism for maintaining this social equilibrium is the state, which he says employs all means 'from sheer coercion to the most complex ideological cobweb, to control the camp of its class opponents'.[19]

At first sight what Bukharin is saying seems to be very little different from the accepted Marxist view of the state as the repressive organ of the ruling class. However, Bukharin puts more emphasis upon the total unity and equilibrium of society than is usual. This leads him to view crisis, or crises, as stemming essentially from a *loss* of equilibrium, which may or *may not be* of such an order that new alignment of classes is necessary for a new equilibrium to be attained. This sets Bukharin apart from those who advanced what was an essentially linear concept of crisis, for within his approach is the possibility that society may achieve a new equilibrium at a point other than the optimum desired by any of the parties involved. In much the same way that Keynes argued that there were a number of equilibrium levels for capitalist economies *other* than that of full employment, so, too, does Bukharin posit that disequilibrium may lead to a new equilibrium which is either a stalemate or a new and quite unexpected situation. This is particularly important when one comes to examine Soviet society from the mid-1920s onward. In this respect Bukharin's views are not so laden with catastrophism that vulgarized versions of Marxism were, and still are.

Bukharin, in 1920, thought the imperialist war of 1914–18 had been the product of a world-wide disequilibrium of the capitalist system and this in turn had pushed the disequilibrium to a point where collapse was in process (not that he was alone in this view).

On the question of the particular laws of motion that different modes of production and societies have, he says: 'every phase of historical development and every model of relations of production . . . conform to its own specific laws.' Going on to say: 'this is the same basis for the classification of state. Every production model has a corresponding state model, and to every state model corresponds a quite definite model of war.' Bukharin gives examples of slave-owning economies, colonial wars of mercantile capitalism and, of course, capitalist imperialism. Finally he says: 'the same thing happens when a socialist dictatorial power wages war.'

In this latter point he is clearly advancing a theoretical justification for the decision, taken by the Bolsheviks, to take the Russo-Polish War of 1920 into Poland and attempt to stimulate revolution there. There were differences within the Bolshevik leadership as to the advisability of this venture, Lenin and the majority of the leadership taking an optimistic view of the possibility of arousing the Polish workers to revolutionary action. The minority, which included Trotsky and most of the Bolshevik leaders who were of Polish origin, wanted the Red Army to halt its offensive at the Russo-Polish border, thus making it clear that there were no designs upon Polish national integrity. Bukharin went along with the majority and brought forward his theoretical formula which had a direct relationship to the then current situation.

In the event the Red Army was defeated in its attempt to capture Warsaw and with this defeat were dashed the Bolshevik hopes of stimulating the Polish workers to action. With this defeat also ended any hope of carrying revolution into central Europe on the point of a bayonet; it was to be twenty-five years later that such an event happened and then in circumstances quite different from those originally envisaged.

Nevertheless, there can be little doubt about the validity of the general proposition that Bukharin was advancing, i.e. that different social systems or different classes developed their own style of warfare. The American revolution of 1776 developed new methods of warfare when faced with the British army. Also the French revolution saw the development of the *levée en masse* as opposed to the small professional armies of the absolutist states who attacked it. During the Russian civil war the Red Army organized an independent cavalry army as opposed to the more normal usage of such troops. And, although it was the German army in the Second World War which made the most dramatic and successful use of air-borne troops (in the Crete campaign), the idea for such methods originated with the Red Army. The theory of the original conception for the use of air-borne troops was that they should link up with partisans or aid workers' risings in capitalist countries in revolutionary situations.[20] Many other examples of this general proposition may be found in military history.

Bukharin argues at some length that the tendency towards state capitalism had been speeded up under the impact of the First World War. By this he meant the unification of capitalist enterprises into ever larger units and the direct control of the economy by the state.[21] He takes this a step further when he argues that this process had been carried into the working class and its organizations, positing that 'the method of reorganization was the same method of subordination to the all-embracing bourgeois state', and that the workers' organizations 'were, in point of fact, statified by the imperialist state and they were reduced to a "workers' department" in the military machine'. As a description of the reality of the situation during the two world wars this was broadly true, especially of the trade unions. Moreover, in those countries which had fascist regimes it is indubitable that the workers' organizations *were* destroyed and replaced by departments of state. One has only to recall the Nazi Labour Front to understand this. Also, there can be little doubt that since Bukharin wrote on this question the tendency towards the statification of the trade unions has become more pronounced in all major capitalist countries. The various attempts to curtail trade unions' rights and to draw them into the machinery for implementing 'incomes' policies in various countries, all lend substance to Bukharin's views, or at least to their basic premise.

However, remembering Bukharin's own caveat, we must also recognize that the workers' organizations cannot be *wholly* absorbed by the state unless they are emasculated or smashed outright. Even to this day, after generations of 'responsible' leadership, these organizations still continue to have an independent existence and carry on real struggles. In this, as in all social theorems, it must be remembered that they are only tendencies and are not immutable nor do they develop with linear precision along one particular road.

IX

Bukharin introduced a quite new and novel concept when he discussed the effects of war production upon an economy. He pointed out the *illusory* growth of the gross national product to which a war economy gave rise, and this in fact masked a *decline*. Although it will be easily grasped that war destroys large amounts of material means of consumption and means of production, he went further and analysed its effect upon the forces of production and the accumulation of capital. He introduced a concept which he termed 'expanded negative reproduction'.

Before passing directly on to discuss this concept it would be as well to understand what Bukharin defined as the productive forces in an economy.

By productive forces of society we shall mean *the aggregate of the means of production and labour power*. Thus, it will be the aggregate of various kinds of machines, raw materials, fuel and so on *in natura*, on the one hand and on the other hand the sum total of the various kinds of labour power *in natura*.

Here we see a quite broad concatenation of factors with which society maintains itself and expands its wealth. And since labour power itself is a part of these productive forces its maintenance and expansion is a vital ingredient. For, Bukharin argues, capitalism must have an equilibrium that is dynamic, and since this equilibrium implies a constant state of flux, it is possible to precipitate disequilibrium in a downward direction. He says:

> The viewpoint of the development of the productive forces coincides with the viewpoint of *reproduction*: the development of the productive forces corresponds to expanded reproduction . . . their collapse finds expression in the fact that an ever-decreasing share of recurrently consumed products is being produced. In this last instance we have social regression.

In this view Bukharin was directly challenging the 'truly monstrous theoretical constructions that draw the conclusion about the *beneficial*(!) influence of war on "national economic" life'. Also, by implication he was challenging the views of Rosa Luxemburg (and all who since followed her in this respect) in her assumption that armaments were a field for the creation and realization of surplus value. Bukharin argues that 'war production has an altogether different significance; a gun does not become transformed into an element of the productive cycle; gunpowder is shot into the air and does not crop up in a different guise in the next cycle at all'. Pointing out that, when arms' production and war reaches a certain point, when larger and larger quantities of material goods and labour power are sucked into this process, it will begin to destroy the very basis of production itself. Thus, 'what we have here is not expanded reproduction, but an ever-increasing *under-production*. Such a process can be designated expanded negative reproduction. This is what war is, considered from an economic point of view.'[22] What Bukharin was doing was to describe the actual situation in Soviet Russia during the period of war communism and the civil war. The gigantic military effort was sucking out of the economy, not only surplus products, but the very means of replacing the means of consumption and means of production. In 1920 the Red Army consumed one quarter of the available wheat in Soviet-held territories.[23] Moreover, it was also draining the working class: in 1917 there had been three million workers employed in Russian industry, by the winter of 1920–1 the number had declined to

1,480,000.[24] And by 1921 the population of Moscow had declined by one half and that of Petrograd by two-thirds.[25] This was a situation which could only have lasted a short time longer before complete collapse ensued.

Bukharin was equally clear about the effects of expanded negative reproduction even before such a catastrophic situation was reached. One phenomenon associated with both world wars has been inflation:

> The huge quantity of accumulated securities are tokens, the realization of which lies wholly in the future and depends on the one hand on the conditions of capitalist reproduction and on the other hand on the very existence of the capitalist system. It is clear that a colossal flood of notes in their very varied forms may become absolutely incommensurate with the real labour process. . . . This expanded negative reproduction runs parallel to the accumulation of paper values.

Here we can see *some* of the roots of the inflationary spiral which has engulfed the capitalist world in the 1970s. The Keynesian practitioners have become puzzled by the effects of their prescriptions for economic health. What they, and most others, forget is that most government spending is unproductive, in the Marxist sense, and therefore is a deduction from the total surplus value that is socially produced. This may have beneficial effects on an economy at a low level of economic activity, with surplus capacity, but once the cycle begins its upward swing it will *retard* capital accumulation and the increase in real wealth.

Bukharin was well aware of these factors, years ahead of his contemporaries, and indeed of those who followed him. He was also aware of the dangers inherent in the process, because 'the process of reproduction is not only a process of reproduction of the material elements of production, but also a process of the *reproduction of the very relations of production*'. Given the regression of reproduction then there will be a loosening, an *atrophy* of these *relations*, not merely of reproduction but of all class relations. Thus, with it, expanded negative reproduction carries the seeds of revolution.[26]

The process of expanded negative reproduction, then, reacts upon the political and social equilibrium, and should it be pushed too far this in turn will react back upon the productive forces,

19

giving a further twist to the downward spiral. Bukharin argues that just as there is a period of political disintegration, so too will there be a period of technical and productive collapse. Moreover, he argues that this is historically inevitable. This means that there is an inevitable reduction of the productive forces and 'in this way the process of expanded negative reproduction is *extraordinarily speeded up*!' What we have posited here is a series of reciprocal acts which reinforce each other; there is in effect a multiplier effect in a downward direction, but one that has escaped all control. Is this historically inevitable?

The inevitability lies not in any absolute criteria, but depends upon the configuration of circumstances. Looking at what happened in France in 1968 one can see that equilibrium was disrupted, but not sufficiently to precipitate a catastrophic decline in the productive forces such as to lead to expanded negative reproduction. On the contrary, the massive social turmoil of that year only acted as a 'hiccup' on the productive forces. Even the overthrow of the fascist régime in Portugal and the ensuing long period of instability only led to a decline of production but not a decline of the productive forces in the sense in which Bukharin writes. Taking another example, that of Cuba, we can see that the economic blockade imposed by US imperialism after 1960 did serious damage to the Cuban economy and, in fact, speeded up the political and social disequilibrium which ended by the complete overthrow of capitalism on the island and the establishment of a new equilibrium, but of a non-capitalist nature.[27] Had the position been reversed, i.e. had Cuba entered its anti-capitalist revolution *after* such an event in the USA, the disruption to the Cuban economy would have probably been much less than it actually was. However, the situation in Cuba did not reach the catastrophic proportions of that in Soviet Russia.

The historical evidence that has accumulated since Bukharin wrote his work points to the correctness of his more general proposition, i.e. that when a social transformation takes place, such as one that unseats a ruling class, then some decline in *production* is inevitable. But it would be wrong to assume that this process *inevitably* leads to a decline in the productive *forces* nor is it inevitable that the decline in production – such as it may be – will assume a catastrophic character.

X

In any period of rapid social and economic change most observers concentrate upon the decay of the old and the birth of the new; and, of course, in a period of revolution all these phenomena are considerably heightened. But, along with the upheavals, changes, decay and birth of new forms, there subsists much which remains from the previous period. There remains the thread of continuity. Bukharin was quite explicit in this:

> The new society cannot appear like a *deus ex machina*. Its elements *arise within the old*, and since it is here a question of phenomena of an economic order, then the elements of the new society must be sought in the *relations of production* of the old.

It is this explicit recognition of the inevitability of this transition period which marks Bukharin, and other Marxists, off from the utopians. It is impossible to wake up one fine morning in a socialist wonderland, free from all the taints and traces of capitalism with its reified relations. Between all major periods of development in human activity, and its socialization, we find such transitional periods, in which the elements of the old jostle those of the new. The old sometimes subsists in a debilitated form, the new sometimes arriving in a bastardized form; each one struggling for mastery. Such a period of transition between capitalism and communism will not be of short duration. Bukharin predicts that it is one 'which embraces a whole enormous epoch'.

But the crucial difference in this respect is that the previous social system – capitalism – was created spontaneously, behind the backs of the participants. Communism must be built consciously, it cannot develop as islands amid a sea of capitalism, nor by sleight of hand in the hope of dazzling the bourgeoisie so that they do not notice they are being expropriated. Moreover, just as capitalism developed in a multi-form manner, according to the historical and localized particularities, so too will socialism in its initial stages. To suppose that, particularly in the transition period, there can be only *one* form, *one* road, *one* model, is to fly in the face of historical evidence.

It will have been noted that up to now there has been an emphasis upon the period preceding and immediately following a

21

proletarian revolution. In fact Bukharin tended to telescope two distinct problems, i.e. the transition from bourgeois power to proletarian power on the one hand and the transition from capitalism as a mode of production to that of communism as a mode of production on the other hand. This has led to some confusion since, although these two aspects are, of course, related, they pose rather different questions begging to be answered.

Bukharin was not alone in this ambiguity. In classical Marxist writings there was the custom of referring to post-capitalist society as the lower phase of communism or as socialism, which would develop into communism proper. Although Marx and Engels made few references to any specific or detailed aspects of post-capitalist society in its initial stages, they made sufficient for us to know what their general concepts were. Some of Marx's most specific statements occur in the *Critique of the Gotha Programme*; about the intermediary stage he says:

> What we have here is a communist society, not as it developed on its own foundations, but, on the contrary as it *emerges* from capitalist society; which thus in every respect, economically, morally and intellectually, still stamped with the birthmarks of the old society from whose womb it emerges.[28]

and further on:

> Between capitalist and communist society lies the period of the revolutionary transformation of one into the other. There corresponds to this also a political traditional period in which the state can be nothing but *the revolutionary dictatorship of the proletariat*.[29]

However, what Marx and indeed most Marxists expected was that a socialist revolution would occur in an advanced capitalist country, and rapidly spread to one or more other such countries. Hence, when they spoke about socialism being the lower phase of communism they envisaged a society that had *already* reached a high level in the development of the productive forces, and a high level of culture.[30] Moreover, although they did not expect a simultaneous revolution in the advanced capitalist countries, it was expected that after a revolution had occurred in several such countries there would be an integration of their respective economies, giving rise to an even faster growth than would be possible with separate development. Trotsky threw some light on this question, when he wrote in 1936:

> By the lowest stage of communism Marx meant, at any rate, a society which from the very beginning stands higher in its economic development than the most advanced capitalism. Theoretically such a conception is flawless, for taken *on a world scale* communism, even in its first incipient stage, means a higher level of development than that of bourgeois society. . . . Whoever tries now to mechanically apply the universal conception of Marx to the particular case of the Soviet Union at the given stage of its development, will be entangled at once in hopeless contradictions. . . . The present Soviet Union does not stand above the world level of economy, but is trying to catch up to the capitalist countries . . . this designation [socialism] obviously does not apply to the Soviet Union, which today is considerably poorer in technique, culture and the good things of life than the capitalist countries. It would be truer, therefore, to name the present Soviet regime in all its contradictions, not a socialist regime, but a *preparatory* regime transitional from capitalism to socialism.[31]

Such an approach will enable one to correctly locate a number of Bukharin's references to the transitional economy. He makes a number of statements regarding the differences between capitalism and socialism. He tells us that political economy will disappear as a science, since political economy is specific to capitalism. Surplus value will be replaced by surplus product. Commodities will disappear, there will only be products and, since no commodities, no value. Prices under socialism will be arbitrary or even imaginary, the money system will collapse. Wage labour will disappear and so there will be no wages; workers will receive a 'socio-labour ration'.

In most of these assumptions Bukharin was formally correct, *if* one accepts Marx's definition of socialism or as Trotsky rephrased it. But when writing the present work Bukharin mistook a number of phenomena which had the *formal* appearance of belonging to a socialist régime, but which in fact were rooted in the extreme disequilibrium of the period of war communism. Commodities had disappeared, not because of material abundance but because of the extreme scarcity of use values then prevailing. Goods were not exchanged, this is true, they were requisitioned by the state. For the same reason wages were replaced by rations, not the socio-labour ration of the future, but rationing under famine conditions, i.e. it was the antithesis of the abolition of wages under socialism. Money disappeared since it was useless because of the goods famine and galloping inflation, not because its functions had been superseded by the planning of abundance. In other words, these phenomena were indications of a negative disequilibrium not a positive, to use Bukharin's own vocabulary, and this disequilibrium had reached the stage of expanded negative reproduction. Many of the phenomena that seemed to have disappeared in the period of war communism were to spring up again, with renewed vigour, after the introduction of the New Economic Policy in 1921. The present work, although still occasionally referred to, no longer served as a guide in the post-1921 period. Trotsky's definition was one that accorded more closely with reality.

However, many of the basic theoretical propositions of Bukharin's work still retain their validity. The fact that the so-called socialist countries, even today, fall short of classical Marxist conceptions of socialism is an indication of the long road still to be travelled. The road itself is not permanently fixed, since the longer capitalism survives in its main advanced centres, the further transitional societies have to march to catch up with them, let alone surpass them. Moreover, the longer capitalism survives the greater the distortions engendered within the system both globally and nationally. The longer these conditions subsist the greater are the distortions engendered within the existing post-capitalist societies, for they are being pulled along the road to a 'consumerist' society of the capitalist model. The *world* economy remains and this is still one dominated by capitalism, therefore no particular section can totally escape being incorporated into this real aggregate.

XI

One further aspect remains to be dealt with. Bukharin's insistence upon the destructive character of the transition from capitalist power to proletarian power should not be lightly put aside. The attempt, by many who profess to be Marxists, to project a peaceful transition to proletarian power is not merely wrong historically, but they are of positive harm to those they 'lead'. Such theories erode the necessary will to action in times of crisis. The net result is to assist the bourgeoisie in re-establishing *their* equilibrium, as for example France in 1968 or, on a more catastrophic scale, Chile in 1973. Furthermore, such 'theories' sow the seeds of demoralization by pretending that socialism can be built without any sacrifice. Bukharin was quite uncompromising in his honesty on this question. In this he stands in sharp contrast to the soporific utterances of many latter-day 'Marxists'.

Moreover, as can be seen from the last chapter of this book, Bukharin was fully cognizant of the interrelationship between the problems of revolution and the reconstruction that follows:

> the world revolutionary process begins with the partial systems of the world economy which are on the lowest level, where the victory of the proletariat is easier but the crystallization of the new relations harder; the speed with which the revolution ensues is inversely proportional to the maturity of the capitalist relations and the height of the model of the revolution.

Subsequent experience seems to have borne out his views in this respect. Those countries which can be considered transitional societies have all displayed this process to some degree or other. The lower the level of capitalism has been before the overturn of class relationships on a national scale, the harder has been the task of socialist construction. To this we can add that precisely because not one *major* capitalist country has, up to now, been subject to this process, this itself has also retarded the development of the existing transitional societies. In this we can see the working of the law of uneven and combined development as a real historical tendency, for on a world scale we have a combination of advanced capitalism and backward 'socialism'. Here we return to the starting point of Bukharin's theoretical exegesis of the transition period, namely the *world* economy and system which has its own dynamics and history. Only when capitalism becomes a subordinate and dwindling part of this totality will socialism be able to exhibit that dynamism that Bukharin and other classical Marxists expected.

K.J.T.

Part I

The Theory of the Dictatorship of the Proletariat[1]

Foreword

In the final analysis *any* theory has practical roots, but if this is true of science it is even more true of the social sciences. They are a driving force of which everyone is aware and this clearly affects Marx's position that 'a theory also gains in strength, if it attracts the masses'.

But for a theory to set the masses on the right course, it must itself be the right theory. And for a theory to be correct it must satisfy certain general 'methodological' requirements. One such requirement for socio-theoretical constructions is that of *historicity*. This means that it is essential to understand the special and unique features of any period of social development. The senseless repetitions of 'eternal truths', the rancid rumination befitting the scholarly cows of liberalism are downright sickening to the spirit of genuine social science.

However, neither bourgeois scholars nor the empty wind-bags from the 'living corpses' of the abortive Second International are able to assimilate what is in essence a highly revolutionary, dialectical viewpoint. Kautsky is a typical specimen of this school.

With the onset of the age of imperialism, when history presented the working class with the task, first, of *understanding* the new chain of events and, second, of *responding* to it in some way or other, Kautsky completely lost his head and the pitiful babble, the innocent (and, at the same time poisonous) pink water with which he sprinkled the German proletariat, proved in theory a prostitution of Marxism and in practice led to complete apostasy. He completely misunderstood the *nature* of the imperialist epoch, its specific character. He regarded imperialism as a mere historical accident, a kind of 'sin' of capitalist development and a pathological phenomenon which could be cured by the exorcisms and formulae of the arbitration courts and disarmament – formulae borrowed from pathetic bourgeois pacifism. The result is well known: it was Kautsky who threatened the workers with a 'hostile invasion' and blessed the policy of the SPD [Social Democratic Party of Germany] – base policy of 'defending' a robber bourgeois fatherland.

Now, once again a *new* historical era is beginning. The curve of imperialist development, which had been consistently rising, is beginning to fall catastrophically. The epoch of the *decay* of capitalism is coming and it will be followed directly by the *dictatorship of the proletariat*, born amidst the pangs of civil war.

For cowardly and base souls this is a period of even greater 'discomfort', when everything deteriorates, everything old, corrupt and obsolete, where there can be no place for the theory or practice of the Buridanov donkey and where it is necessary to make a choice and *act*. And once again we see that Kautsky, who spent the war indulging – though in moderation – in licking the boots of generals and preaching 'caution', is now engaged in the noble task of attacking the Bolsheviks and pouring slops on to the Soviet Republic, since this meets with the approval of the authorities. If we exclude his – *sit venia verbo* – 'views' logically, we again reveal his complete inability to analyse the question historically, to approach it, not from the standpoint of trite phrases, but from the standpoint of revolutionary dialectics.

The Soviet Republic – the greatest achievement of the proletariat – must be considered as a form of dictatorship of the proletariat, as a special form of *state power*, which is inevitable in a certain historical period, whether Messrs Dan, Kerensky, Kautsky and the SPD want it or not. But in order to understand the historical validity of the dictatorship of the proletariat, it is first essential to ventilate the question of the state in general.

I A General Theory of the State

Even if we stick to the platitudes of purely theoretical appraisals, it is noticeable what a huge, retrograde step many 'outstanding' thinkers took during the war in just this field. What was earlier, and deservedly, designated impudent, idle talk now appears to be of paramount value in today's market of militant 'studies'. Grown men prattle like two year olds. The inarticulate sounds which the Scheidemann-ites [SPD] and the Dan-ites of the world now make are the best proof of this. So the reader should not complain about us, if to begin with we endeavour to recall some 'forgotten' words. There are an infinite number of different definitions of the state. We shall disregard all those theories which regard the state as possessing some kind of theological or metaphysical essence, 'a super-intelligent origin', 'realization of a spiritual concept' and so forth. Nor are we interested in the numerous theories of the lawyers, who examine the matter from the narrow standpoint of formalistic, legal dogmatism, and go round in a vicious circle defining the state in terms of the law and the law in terms of the state. Such theories do not impart any positive knowledge because they lack a sociological foundation, they are suspended in thin air. The state can only be understood as a social phenomenon. A sociological theory is, therefore, essential and Marxism provides just such a theory.

From the Marxist viewpoint the state is the most common organization of the ruling class, the basic function of which is to defend and extend the conditions of exploitation of the enslaved classes. The state is a relationship between people, and moreover – since we are talking about classes – it is a relationship of supremacy, power and enslavement. It is true, as long ago as 2500 BC the famous Babylonian code of Hammerabi declared that 'the aim of a ruler is to safeguard the law of the land and to destroy what is wicked and evil so that the strong may not harm the weak'.[2] In its essence, this idyllic, high sounding nonsense is still being handed to us in all seriousness, even now.[3] This 'truth' is analogous to the assertion that the aim of the employers' associations is to increase workers' wages. In reality, in so far as there is a consciously regulated organization of state power, in so far as one can, therefore, speak of the formulation of *aims* (which already presupposes a certain degree of social and state development) these aims are determined by the interests of the ruling classes and *only by them*. So-called 'generally useful functions' are merely the condition *sine qua non*, the necessary conditions for the state to exist, just as the aim of any bourgeois economic organization (and this is the aspect we would emphasize: *the aims* of the organization) is not production as such, or in itself, but the acquisition of profit and super-profit, although *without* production human society could not survive. The 'socially useful' functions of the bourgeois state are, therefore, the conditions for the most protracted and successful exploitation of the oppressed classes, primarily the proletariat. Two factors determine the evolution of these functions: first, the direct personal interests of the ruling classes (without railways the development of capitalism is impossible – hence the building of the railways; excessive degeneracy in a nation deprives the state of its necessary human military material [i.e. conscripts] – hence sanitary measures etc); in the second place, considerations of strategy against the oppressed (so-called concessions under pressure from below) – where the lesser evil, from the governing strata's angle, is preferred. In both cases the principle of an economy of 'strength' operates with a view to creating the best conditions for the exploitation process. The interests of the ruling class, which are merely concealed behind the pseudonym of the interests of 'the nation', 'the whole', 'the people' and so on, are the governing principle behind the behaviour of the state authority. The state is everywhere the organization 'of the most powerful, economically ruling class, which thanks to the state becomes the politically ruling class too, thereby acquiring for itself new means for the control and exploitation of the enslaved class'.[4]

As the generalized reorganization of the ruling classes, the state comes into being in a process of social differentiation. It is the product of a *class* society. In its turn, the process of social stratification is the derivative of economic development and by no means the simple result of naked force on the part of conquering groups of foreign origin, as some economists and sociologists (e.g. Gumplovitch and Oppenheimer), who in substance merely repeat the notorious Dühring on this point. This is how Franz Oppenheimer defines 'the historical state': '*In form*', he writes, 'it is a legal institution, imposed on the conquered group by the victorious group. *In content* it is the systematic exploitation of the subordinate group.'[5] 'Classes are, and can only be, created by political means.'[6] Thus, according to Oppenheimer, the classes are merely modified groups of victors and vanquished, and not the legitimate child of economic development at all. Their emergence is associated *exclusively* with 'non-economic factors'. In this theory of 'the origins of classes' and the state only one thing is correct – that actual history is a history of robbery and violence. But this is not the end of the matter for, in reality, neither 'legal institutions' nor a certain type of production relations can come into being and *hold their ground* if, in the economic development of a given society, there is insufficient soil for them. In particular, the basis for the emergence of classes and their consolidation as the main social category is economic differentiation with the growth of the *division of labour and private property*.[7]

Logically, the formation of classes by no means presupposes conquest, and history gives us instances of the formation of classes without conquest, such as the formation of the state in North America. Certainly, North American feudalism and the supremacy of the landed aristocracy is generally under-estimated as an embryo.[8] However, the evolution of capitalist relations in America is completely misunderstood from the standpoint of the 'pure theory of conquest'.

The apparent radicalism of analogous theoretical constructions has highly apologist roots, for here the assault is directed not at the foundations of a commodity economy – private property – but only as the monopolistic form of the latter, as though this monopolistically modified form were not the logical and historical sequel to the elementary form of a simple commodity economy. As a matter of fact, the state, like the classes, 'is by no means a force imposed on society from without . . . it is, on the contrary, a product of this society at a certain stage of its development'.[9]

If the characteristic attribute of a state, its 'essence', is to be seen in the fact that it is the universal organization of the ruling class, then the truth is that the state is an historical category. Such was the view of Marx and Engels. Just as capital, according to Marx, is not a thing, namely the means of production as such, but a social relationship, expressed in things, the 'essence' of the state lies not in its technical-administrative role, but in the *relation* of the state, which is concealed beneath that administrative-technical shell.[10] But since this relation of the state is an expression of the class structure of society, the state will therefore disappear with the disappearance of classes. Thus the state not only has an historical beginning but an historical end too. 'Even radical and revolutionary politicians,' wrote Marx as he exposed the narrow viewpoint of his contemporaries, 'look for the root of the evil not in the nature (Wesen) of the state but in a definite form of the state, which they wish to replace with another state form.'[11] Even more decisively Engels said: 'All socialists are agreed that the state, and with it political power (Autoritat), will disappear by virtue of the coming social revolution, in other words, that social functions will lose their political significance and become simple administrative functions watching over social interests.'[12]

In *Anti-Dühring*, Engels declares that the state must 'die off' (absterben). In *The Origin of the Family*, he relegates the state to the future society's museum of antiquities 'along with the bronze axe and the spinning wheel'. These quotations (and they could, of course, have been augmented) are not random: on the contrary. The specific features of the Marxist method are apparent here, a method which regards social phenomena, not as eternal and immutable categories, but as transient phenomena, which arise and disappear at definite stages of social development. Thus this is not a question of terminology, as some critics would have it, just as there is no terminological dispute in the argument: is a savage's stick capital or simply a stick?[13] For Marx, the critical yardstick, the logical fundamental division, was the difference in the *types of relations between people*, and not fetishistically misconstrued 'outward appearances'. Strictly speaking, Marx's object was to understand social development as a process of uninterrupted change in these types (socio-economic structures), and this is also how he approached the question of the state as the *political* expression of a broad economic category, in a *class* society. And just as bourgeois economists, whose viewpoint is static and unhistorical, cannot understand Marx's specific viewpoint on economic categories, neither can bourgeois lawyers and sociologists understand the Marxist view of the state. 'Marx's theory,' said Gumplovitch, for example, 'contains a new, and to a considerable extent, correct understanding of the state.' But . . . 'the terrible mistake of socialism is rooted in his belief that the state will make itself superfluous.'[14] That's what the 'radical' Gumplovitch has to say. His colleagues cannot now (*ex officio*) understand Marx.[15]

Thus a communist society is a *stateless* society because it is a *classless* society. But if communism denies the state, then what does the conquest of state power by the proletariat signify? What is meant by the dictatorship of the working class, which Marxists have discussed and do still discuss so much? The answer to this question is given below.

2 The Necessity of the Dictatorship of the Proletariat

A small preliminary observation: to what limits the apostasy of one-time socialists can go is clear from the special pamphlet Kautsky published against the Bolsheviks (*Die Diktatur des Proletariats*).

In this elaboration of his renunciatory thought we find, amongst other things, such truly classic passages as 'Here (i.e. for the justification of their dictatorship N.I.B.) they (the Bolsheviks) opportunely remembered a *remark* about the dictatorship of the proletariat which Marx *once* made in 1875 *in one of his letters*.'[16] For Kautsky, the entire doctrine of the dictatorship, which Marx himself saw as the *basis* for the theory of revolution, was reduced to an empty, chance remark 'in one of his letters'! No wonder Kautsky regarded the theory of the dictatorship of the proletariat as a '*new*' theory.

This 'new' theory, however, can be found almost in its entirety in Marx's work. Marx clearly recognized the need for a *temporary* state organization of the working class, its dictatorship. He also saw the inevitability of an entire *historical* period, the specific characteristics of which will distinguish it from both the capitalist period and the communist period with its rationally constructed stateless society.

The characteristics of this era lie in the fact that, having smashed the state organization of the bourgeoisie, the proletariat is obliged to reckon with its continued resistance in various forms. And precisely in order to overcome this resistance, there must be a strong, firm, comprehensive and, therefore, *state* organization of the working class.

Marx raised the issue of the dictatorship of the proletariat in more abstract terms than concrete reality does. In his analysis of capitalist production, he took capitalist economy in its 'pure' form, i.e. in a form uncomplicated by any vestiges of the old [feudal] relations of production, or any national peculiarities and so on, and he treats the question of the dictatorship of the working class in just the same way, as a question of the workers' dictatorship in general, that is to say a dictatorship which destroys capitalism in its pure form. And there was no other way to consider the question if he was to do it in abstract, theoretical terms, i.e. if he was to give the broadest algebraic formula for the dictatorship.

Experience in the social struggle now permits concrete definition of the question along the most diverse lines. And first and foremost this experience indicates the need for a decisive, indeed, *iron* dictatorship of the working masses.

The socialist revolution, that *forcible* upheaval which was long ago discussed in the *Communist Manifesto*, cannot be instantly accomplished throughout the world at the wave of a conductor's baton. Life is much more involved and complicated than 'dull theory'. The capitalist jacket will not split everywhere at once but will unravel in those places where the fabric of the bourgeois state is weakest. And here the victorious proletariat will be faced with the problem of repulsing an external enemy, foreign imperialism, whose whole process of development inevitably incites it to destroy the state organization of the proletariat.

One of comrade Lenin's greatest merits is that he was the first person in the Marxist camp to raise the question of the *revolutionary wars* of the proletariat.[17] And yet this is one of the most important problems of our epoch. It is clear that a mighty world revolution will embrace both defensive and offensive wars on the part of the victorious proletariat; defensive in order to repulse the advancing imperialists, and offensive in order to deal the final blow to the retreating bourgeoisie, to incite as yet oppressed peoples to rebellion, to liberate and set free the colonies and to consolidate the conquests of the proletariat.

Modern capitalism is *world* capitalism. However, this world capitalism is not an organized unit, but an anarchic system of state-capitalist trusts in all-out conflict.[18] Nevertheless it is a world-wide system, whose components are linked together. This is precisely why the European war became a *world* war. On the other hand the relative fractionalism of the world economy, combined with the different location of the imperialist states, provoked a world war which did not break out simultaneously, but was a process which gradually drew one capitalist country after another into the war. Italy, Rumania and America entered the war significantly later but, as soon as America did enter, it became a war that embraced both hemispheres, i.e. a *world* war.

World revolution develops in a similar way. It is a process of capitalist degeneration and proletarian rebellion, where one country follows another. During this period the most diverse factors are strangely interwoven: imperialist wars, national-separatist uprisings, internal civil wars and finally class wars between the state-organized bourgeoisie (imperialist states) and the state-organized proletariat (soviet republics).

However, the further events spread, the more apparent the factor of *class* war becomes. The celebrated 'union of nation', which bourgeois pacifists have kept dinning into our ears, all these 'leagues of nations' and other rubbish, which the class traitorous gangs [reformist socialists] slavishly repeat, are in actual fact nothing less than an attempt to create a holy alliance of *capitalist* states with the object of *jointly stifling* socialist revolts.[19] Marx was correct in pointing out that a revolutionary party unites the counter-revolutionary party. And this is true of the world revolution of the proletariat; the world revolutionary process or, as it is rightly called today 'world Bolshevism', unites the forces of international capital. Such an external situation is bound to have enormous internal significance. Were it not for the presence of imperialist forces outside, the vanquished native bourgeoisie, overthrown in open class conflict, could not hope for a bourgeois restoration. The process of de-classing the bourgeoisie would go ahead more or less speedily and with it would disappear the need for a special organization to repress the bourgeoisie, for a state organization of the proletariat, its dictatorship.

However, the true state of affairs is just the reverse. The bourgeoisie, already overthrown and in one or some two or three countries still has huge reserves in the shape of foreign capital. And it follows from this that its resistance is protracted. The experience of the Russian revolution brilliantly confirms this. Sabotage, conspiracies, revolts, the organization of Kulak uprisings, and of bands led by former generals, the Czechoslovak venture, innumerable 'governments' in outlying districts supported by foreign bayonets and purses and finally punitive expeditions and campaigns against the Soviet Union on the part of the entire capitalist world – these are phenomena of one and the same order.

Two conclusions can and must be drawn from this inevitable course of historical events: first, we are faced with a whole *period* of bitter struggle to the death; second, for this period to pass as quickly as possible, a regime of dictatorship by an *armed* proletariat is essential. A tactical rule can be inferred from a scientifically applied prognosis for which all the data exist.

Of course, everything on earth can be called into question. There are pitiful sophists, whose purpose in life lies in endless scholastic fluctuations between the empty and the vacant. Just such a one is Kautsky. He was unable to understand the significance of imperialism and now he cannot understand the meaning of the ensuing phases, the epoch of socialist revolution and the dictatorship of the proletariat. 'I expect,' writes this so-called workers' leader,

> that the forms taken by the social revolution of the proletariat
> will be quite distinct from those of the bourgeois revolution;
> that the proletarian revolution, in contrast to the bourgeois,
> will fight with 'peaceful methods' of economic, legislative and
> moral order, wherever democracy is rooted.[20]

Of course it is impossible to argue with renegades who have gone in for so much re-education, that they see democracy in Taft's jackboots.

But there is an example of a truly democratic country before our very eyes, where democracy has really taken root, and that is Finland. And the example of this one country shows that civil war in more 'cultured' countries is bound to be even more brutal and ruthless, ruling out all grounds for 'peaceful' and 'legislative' (!!) means.

Kautsky tries to prove that by dictatorship Marx meant not dictatorship but something quite different for, so he says, the word 'dictatorship' can only refer to an individual and not to a class. But one has only to quote Engels, who saw very well what a dictatorship of the proletariat must be, to realize how far Kautsky has retreated from Marxism. Engels wrote against the anarchists:

> Have these people ever seen a revolution? A revolution is
> undoubtedly the most authoritarian thing imaginable. A
> revolution is an act in which part of the population imposes its
> will on the other part by means of *guns, bayonets and cannons,*
> i.e. extremely authoritarian means. *And the victorious party*
> *must maintain its supremacy by the fear which its weapons inspire*
> *in reactionaries.* If the Paris Commune had not been supported
> by the authority of an armed populace against the bourgeoisie,

would it have lasted more than a day? Do we not, on the
contrary, have a right to *censure* the Commune *for not
exercising its authority enough*? (Here one should translate it as
'its power' 'autoriata' N.I.B.)[21]

Both Engels and Marx clearly understood the impending situation.
Now that this opinion has been confirmed by experience, to talk
of 'peaceful' and 'legislative' ways is simply ridiculous. The
revolutionary epoch which has just begun demands an appropriate
orientation. If this is an era of unprecedented *class struggles*
developing into *class wars*, then it is quite natural that the political
form of working-class rule should have a peculiarly military
character. There must be a new form of power, the dictatorial
power of a class which is 'storming the heavens', as Marx described
the Paris Commune.

According to Kautsky, Marx was not writing about 'a form of
government' but about 'an actual situation', when he wrote about
the dictatorship. In fact Marx was writing about something *greater*
than 'a form of government'; he was describing a new, and distinctive *type of state*. On the very same page where Kautsky 'refutes
the theses on dictatorship written by the author of these lines',[22]
he cites a quotation from Marx, which says that the Commune was
'finally, an overt *political form*' of proletarian dictatorship, and not
an accidental 'situation'. Thus an entire historical period separates
communism and capitalism. During this time state power will still
be maintained in the shape of the proletarian dictatorship, where
the proletariat is the *ruling class* which, before it disappears as a
class, must crush all its enemies, re-educate the bourgeoisie and
remake the world in its own image.

3 The Collapse of Democracy and the Dictatorship of the Proletariat

One of the central problems of major practical significance is that of the relationship between democracy and the workers' dictatorship.

Marxists do not invent a purely rationalistic model of the forms of government, they grasp the basic trends and confirm their aims to these. And this is the only way to approach the question of the dictatorship. One must bear in mind here the fact that political form is a superstructural relationship erected *between* the classes. And this political shell inevitably shatters if it is not supported by a correlative class structure. We made a general assessment above of the coming epoch; it is one of ever-increasing civil war which turns into organized class war. Therefore, the first question we must ask is whether civil war is compatible with democratic forms, or not.

But one short remark as a preliminary. Our opponents, who include Kautsky, interpret democracy as something which already exists. But this is a deliberate *lie*. There is no democratic state in existence right now. What exists now in Europe, America and Japan is the dictatorship of finance capital and this is the point of departure for developments.

So the question must be put like this: *is it possible in an age of civil war to organize the proletariat in the forms of the old bourgeois democracy, which have been destroyed everywhere by finance capital?* Democracy, in so far as we mean by this word a definite political system, was hitherto one of the forms – the most refined form – of bourgeois supremacy. What was the fundamental prerequisite of the democratic system? It consisted in the availability of a series of 'fictions', which were exceedingly skilfully used for the systematic deception of the masses. One such basic fiction was the concept of 'the popular will' or 'the nation' and 'the whole'. The entire system of democratic institutions rests upon populism. It is not difficult to grasp the class implications of populist norms. It is clear that in reality there are classes with conflicting and irreconcilable interests and there is really no question of a 'popular' will, which would unite both workers and capitalists. But the bourgeoisie needs, and *must* have, the fiction of 'the nation'. The bourgeoisie is a ruling minority, in order to keep the masses under control it must speak in the name of 'the entire nation', for it cannot *openly* speak on behalf of a small group. This is how the fetish of the popular will originates and the bourgeoisie puts itself forward as the *nation*, as the 'country', and the bourgeois state organization as a 'fatherland' common to all.

The proletarian revolution is, however, a breach of the civil peace – it is civil war. And civil war reveals the true physiognomy of a society split into classes. The national fetish is destroyed in the fire of civil war and the classes take their places, weapons in hand, on either side of the revolutionary barricades. It is not surprising, therefore, that in the process of the proletariat's revolutionary struggle, all these forms, establishments and institutions which bore the semblance of being 'national' inevitably collapse. Once again this is an unavoidable and historically absolutely inevitable process, whether individuals, groups or even certain intermediate classes want it or not. For civil war has its own intrinsic logic and, once it is set in motion, so is the process of collapse of the old forms, whereby the bourgeoisie ruled in the name of all society.

These considerations, which some comrades advanced even before the October revolution, have now once again been confirmed. Wherever we look we see the same phenomenon: 'national', 'popular democratic' institutions are *inconceivable* and given the correlation of forces they are *impossible*.

Let us take one of the main constituent parts of any state power – the army. To any non-utopist it is clear that a national army is inconceivable now. The proletariat cannot allow the bourgeoisie into its army and so the Soviet Republic organizes a workers' and peasants' *red* army. But for the bourgeoisie, too, it becomes increasingly dangerous to allow conscripted workers and peasants into its army. It is therefore obliged to organize a *white guard*. Where it tries to organize a 'national' military apparatus, led by bourgeois counter-revolutionaries (cf. 'the people's army' of the Czechoslovak–White Guard forces), the apparatus is inevitably demoralized and perishes, for its formation in *present* times is inherently contradictory. The same thing happens in all spheres of activity, including economics; in the factory the 'inter-class' co-existence of bourgeois and proletariat becomes impossible; general housing committees break down and are replaced by the housing committees of the *poor*; general village soviets are de-

stroyed and replaced by committees of *poor peasants*; in the municipalities people who confront each other in the streets, weapons in
hand, cannot live side by side and the municipalities are replaced
by sections of working-class soviets. The Constituent Assembly
ceases to exist for the same reasons; the old parliaments explode
along with any 'national' constitution.

Of course, one could claim that there is a logical error in this
reasoning, that it is all just *petitio principii* and that instead of
proving the rightfulness of the Bolsheviks' actions, we are merely
describing these actions. But this is not the case. Our enemies,
ardent supporters of 'Dumas' and 'Constituent Assemblies', up-
hold general democratic formulae in words alone. For instead of a
Constituent Assembly, there is only the one correct, i.e. *class*,
viewpoint expressed in the moiety represented in such bodies. In
all the dumas etc. of Siberia and 'Czechoslovakia' it has been
solemnly declared that there is universal suffrage, *but there is no
place for the representatives of the anti-state parties*, i.e. the Bolsheviks, and hence the working class.

It would be ridiculous to think that these are all accidental,
'pathological' phenomena. In fact, what is happening here is the
disintegration of something which could only be united on one
condition: namely, in a situation where the proletariat is hypno-
tized by bourgeois ideology, where it is not yet conscious of itself
as a class destined to overthrow the bourgeoisie and where it
regards itself as a part, not able to change the whole. The complete
and decisive victory of the proletariat, its *world-wide* victory, will
ultimately restore the unity of society on a new basis, that of de-
classing society altogether. Then absolute, state-less communism
will be a reality. But until that time we are in for a hard struggle
which can be reconciled only with the form of a dictatorship. If the
working class wins, then it will be a dictatorship of the workers; if
the bourgeoisie wins, it will be a dictatorship of the bourgeoisie
and its generals.

One can also approach the question from a somewhat different
standpoint, although it amounts to the same thing in the end. It is
possible to isolate the basic class forces and examine just who will
hold power. In 1905–6 Kautsky described the Russian revolution
not as a bourgeois revolution but as something 'unique'; now,
twelve years after the build-up of finance capital in Russia, he
describes the hundred times more mature October revolution as

43

a bourgeois revolution. But if, as Kautsky maintains, historical development proceeds in the same direction as Kautsky's own development, i.e. *backwards*, then the bourgeoisie is bound to be in power. But the bourgeoisie wants a military dictatorship of generals, which the proletariat is absolutely against. The petty bourgeoisie, the intelligentsia and so on cannot hold power – that is the ABC for Marxists. The peasantry is now separated out – a revolution is taking place in the countryside – but no one stratum of the peasantry can play an independent role. That leaves only the proletariat. However, the power of the proletariat enrages not only the upper bourgeoisie, but also the 'middle estate'. None the less, the proletariat is sufficiently strong, leading the poor peasants in its wake, to smash its enemies. The only possible outcome in this situation is the dictatorship of the proletariat.

Traitors to socialism most of all fear 'unrest'. Such a one is Kautsky. He was preaching 'peaceful' capitalism, when this capitalism was killing tens of millions on the battlefields. Now he is preaching 'peaceful' revolution to keep the proletariat from rising against capital. In all seriousness he writes about the 'security and peace', which are necessary for the revolutionary work of construction, and that is why he protests so vigorously against 'frightful' *civil* war. The craving for narrow-minded tranquility is the prerequisite for his criticism, which is truly monstrous apostasy. Democracy, i.e. that form of *bourgeois* supremacy, which would be the best protection against rebellion by the proletariat – this is his ultimate ideal.

That this is the case is clear if only from one remark: 'In the fight for political rights, modern democracy is born and the proletariat matures; at the same time a new factor emerges: *the protection of the minority, of opposition* within the state. Democracy stands for majority rule. But to no less an extent it means the protection of the minority.'[23] And that is why, according to Kautsky, democracy is now essential.

One has only to look at this splendid reasoning to see that Kautsky understands absolutely nothing about current events. Is it really possible to advise the Russian proletariat to safeguard the rights 'of the minority', i.e. the rights *of the counter-revolution*, which the good Kautsky mildly calls 'the opposition'? To safeguard the rights of the Czechoslovaks, the Tsar's okranniki [secret police], speculators, priests and all those who oppose the proletariat with bombs and revolvers – to do this is to be either a fool or a political charlatan. But this is what must be done according to a stupid petty bourgeois who is seeking to reconcile the classes, but does not understand that, once it has dealt with the proletariat, the upper bourgeoisie – whom he supports – will also devour him, its assistant.[24]

Any state is an instrument of force. At times of acute class struggle, this instrument is bound to have a particularly telling effect. Therefore, in an era of civil war, the model of state power is bound to be dictatorial. But this definition is a formal one. What is important is the *class* character of state power, and so long as state power is in the hands of the proletariat it will inevitably take on the character of a dictatorship, until its victory world-wide.[25] The proletariat not only refuses all 'freedoms' to the bourgeoisie, it employs the most drastic repressive measures against it, closing down its press and its organizations, breaking its sabotage by force and so on, just as the bourgeoisie did in its time through the agents of the landowner–tsarist regime. *But in return the proletariat gives the broadest freedom to the toiling masses, in deed and not only in name.* This point must be strongly emphasized. All 'democratic freedoms' are *formal and purely declarative* in character. Such for example is the democratic 'equality of all before the law'. This 'equality' is wonderfully personified in the formal 'equality' between the seller of the worker's labour-power and its buyer, the capitalist. This is a hypocritical equality which conceals the actual enslavement of the worker. Equality is proclaimed but in point of fact *actual* economic inequality reduces the formal equality to an empty spectre. The freedom of the press and so on, granted by bourgeois democracy to the workers, is not much better. They proclaim 'freedom' but the workers cannot realize it; the actual monopoly in paper, printing-works, machines, etc. on the part of the capitalist class, reduces the working-class press virtually to nothing. This resembles the methods of American censorship, which often does not simply suppress workers' papers, but 'only' forbids the post to distribute them and thus stifles the formal 'freedom of the press' completely.

The same thing happens with workers' meetings; the workers are granted the 'right' to assemble but are not given *premises* for this purpose, and street meetings are forbidden on the grounds of 'freedom for the traffic'.

The dictatorship of the working class destroys the formal equality of the *classes*, but by the same token frees the working class from material enslavement. 'The freedom of contract' disappears together with 'free trade'. But this violation of the 'freedoms' of the capitalist class gives a guarantee of *real freedom* to the toiling masses.

The centre of gravity shifts to *these* guarantees. The soviet government does not simply proclaim freedom of assembly for the workers, it allocates all the best halls in town, the palaces and theatres for workers' meetings and working-class organizations. It does not simply proclaim the freedom of the workers' press, it places at the disposal of the workers' organizations all the paper, printing-works and presses by commandeering and confiscating them from their former capitalist owners. A simple calculation of the buildings occupied by workers' and peasants' organizations – party, soviet, professional, factory, works, club, cultural and educational, literary and so on – which *never* were so numerous, will prove just *what* soviet power is doing for the real freedom and true emancipation of the toiling masses.

It is utterly characteristic of Kautsky that in his criticism of our theses he infamously cuts short the quotation just at the point where it speaks of *these* guarantees for the working class. Kautsky dismissed the essential part, in order to deceive the proletariat yet again. It remains for us to examine one more question here – why the communists were formerly in favour of bourgeois democracy, but now oppose it. This is not difficult to understand, if you take the Marxist point of view, which repudiates all and every absolute. It is an historical viewpoint. So it is perfectly clear, *a priori*, that the specific slogans and aims of the movement are wholly dependent on the *character of the epoch* in which the fighting proletariat has to operate.

The past era was one of gathering strength and preparing for revolution. The *present* era is one of the *revolution itself*, and this fundamental distinction also gives rise to profound differences in the concrete slogans and aims of the movement.

The proletariat needed democracy in the past because it was as yet unable to think about dictatorship in real terms. It needed freedom for the *workers'* press, *workers'* meetings, *workers'* unions, etc. At the time the *capitalist* press, the black *capitalist* associations and the assemblies of lock-out men were injurious to it, but the proletariat did not have the strength to demand the dissolution of the bourgeois organizations; for this it would have needed to over-throw the bourgeoisie. Democracy was valuable in so far as it helped the proletariat to climb a step higher in its consciousness, but the proletariat was *forced* to present its *class* demands in a 'democratic' form. It was forced to demand, not freedom of assembly for *workers*, but freedom of assembly in general (hence, freedom of assembly for the counter-revolution), freedom of the press in general (and hence for the Black-hundred press too), etc. But there is no need to make a virtue of necessity. Now that the time has come for a direct assault on the capitalist fortress and the suppression of the exploiters, only a miserable petty bourgeois can be content with arguments about 'the protection of the minority'.[26]

4 Soviet Power as a Form of Proletarian Dictatorship

We have already observed that the protracted nature of a lengthy civil war demands not simply individual measures against the bourgeoisie but also an appropriate *state* organization. We examined this organization solely as a *dictatorship*, i.e. a form of authority which expresses the class-repressive nature of this power more strongly.

Now we must clarify the features of the proletarian dictatorship as a completely *new* type of state.

The unavoidability of a new type of state was well understood by Marx and Engels, and for this reason, therefore, they did not dwell on the conquest of the *bourgeois* state (including democracy, citizen Kautsky) but on the explosion (Sprengung) and smashing (Zerbrechen) of the state machine. They treated the 'state non-sense' and the 'people's state' (Volksstaat), with which the opportunists were so concerned, with great insight.[27]

What determines the features of the new type of state? They are contingent upon two causes.

In the first place, the proletarian state is a dictatorship of the majority over the minority of a country, whilst every other dictatorship was the dictatorship by a small group.[28] In the second place, the aim of every previous state power was to preserve and consolidate the process of *exploitation*. Conversely it is quite clear that the majority cannot live at the expense of small groups and the proletariat cannot exploit the bourgeoisie. The aim of the proletarian dictatorship is to *break the old relations of production and to organize new relations in the sphere of social economics*, the 'dictatorial infringement' (Marx) of the rights of private property. The fundamental purpose of the dictatorship of the proletariat lies in the fact that it is a means of *economic* revolution.

If the state power of the proletariat is a means of economic revolution, then clearly 'economics' and 'politics' should merge into one. We also get such a merger under the dictatorship of finance capital in its classical, final, form, that of state capitalism. But the dictatorship of the proletariat turns all the relations of the

48

old world upside down – in other words, the *political* dictatorship of the working class must inevitably entail its *economic* dictatorship too.

Everything that has been said so far exemplifies first and foremost the characteristic of soviet power that it is *the power of the mass organizations of the proletariat and the rural poor*. In the 'democracy', so beloved of Kautsky, the participation of the workers and the poor peasants in the life of the state rested on the fact that once in four years he dropped a voting paper into a ballot box and then went away to sleep. Here, again, the bourgeois deception of the masses, by systematically hammering into their heads various *illusions*, is crystal clear. The workers are apparently taking part in the government of the state but in *fact* they are completely *isolated* from any participation at all in the running of the state. The bourgeoisie cannot tolerate such participation but, under certain conditions, it must create this fiction. That is why any form of government by a minority, be it a feudal-landowner, merchant-capitalist or finance-capitalist state, is bound to be bureaucratic. Whatever the circumstances it is always isolated from the masses, and they from it.

In the soviet republic we have something completely different. The *soviets* are a direct class organization. They are not reserved institutions, for the right to recall every deputy has been implemented; they are the masses themselves in the person of their delegates, in the person of the workers, soldiers and peasants. But it is not just a question of the soviets alone which form, so to speak, the apex of the whole state apparatus. No. *All* the workers' organizations become a part of the apparatus of power. There is not one mass organization that is not, at the same time, an organ of power. The workers' trade unions are the most important organs of economic dictatorship, controlling production and distribution, determining working conditions, playing a major role in the central institution of the economic dictatorship – the Supreme Council of National Economic – and actually directing the work of the Commissariat of Labour. The factory and workshop committees are lower cells of state control; the committees of poor peasants are one of the most important organs of local power and at the same time of the distributive apparatus of the country, and the workers' co-operatives are the same sort of cells. They all partake in working out all kinds of projects, decisions and resolutions, which then pass through the central apparatus – the Central Executive Committee or the Council of People's Commissars.

In one of his most remarkable pamphlets, comrade Lenin wrote that the task of the proletarian dictatorship lies in training every cook to run the state.[29] And this was in no way paradoxical. Through the organizations of the proletarian town and the rural poor – organizations which are more and more capturing the hearts of the masses – these masses who once feared even to think of their power, are beginning to *work* as organs of this power. There has never been a state anywhere that was so close to the masses. The soviet republic is virtually a huge organization of the very masses.

We would also emphasize, here, the *other* side of the coin – namely that it is not only a *workers'* organization, for the most part, but also a *working* organization. In 'democratic republics' the supreme organ is the parliament; which translates into Russian as 'a talking shop'. Power is divided into legislative and executive branches. By dint of sending the workers' representatives to parliament once every four years, the fiction is yet again created that the workers are participating in the *work* of the state. But in actual fact, not even the representatives do this, for they just talk. A special bureaucratic caste controls all the work.

In the soviet republic, the legislative and executive power is combined. All its organs, from top to bottom, are *working* bodies connected with the mass organizations, relying on them and through them involving all the masses in the act of building socialism.

In this way all workers' organizations become *ruling* organizations. Their functional significance changes. It could not be otherwise in the period of the proletarian dictatorship, when the working class is master of the situation and the state itself is a *workers'* organization.

One would have to be as hopelessly stupid as our Mensheviks or Kautsky, to protest against the transformation of the soviets into organs of power. Their 'theory' is like the story of the white bullock. Let the soviets become the organs of struggle against the ruling bourgeoisie. But what then, when they have triumphed? Then let them disband themselves as organs of power, and they begin the fight anew, so as . . . not to dare to triumph.

But the opposition to the power of the soviets, to the fact that the trade unions would become 'fiscal' institutions and so on, has another side to it. Neither Kautsky, nor the Mensheviks want *the mass organizations* to govern the state and take an *active* part in the state construction. Thus, whatever they may declare, they are for a combination of 'talking shop' plus a *bureaucracy alienated from the masses*. Their horizons do not extend beyond this old rubbish. Thus the soviet form of the state is the *self-government of the masses*, where every workers' organization is a component part of the whole apparatus. The organizational threads stretch out from central bodies of power to the local organizations in the most varied directions and from them to the masses themselves in all their immediacy. This bond, these organizational threads, never break. They are the normal way of soviet life. This is what *fundamentally* distinguishes the Soviet Republic from all other forms of state life.

The connection between politics and economics, between 'the management of people' and the 'management of things', is expressed in the closest possible co-operation between the economic and political organizations of the masses, but also in the fact that even elections to the soviets are held by given production units: factories, plants, mines and villages, in the place of work and struggle and not by purely artificial, territorial districts. This is how a permanent living bond is created between the representative bodies, the workers' deputies, and those who elect them, i.e. the masses themselves, united in their joint work and concentrated by the technology of large-scale production.

The initiative of the masses is the *fundamental* principle behind the entire development of soviet power. And it suffices to examine the role played by the workers of Petersburg, Moscow and other towns in organizing the Red Army, enthusiastically sending thousands of comrades to the Front, organizers, agitators and fighters, who remade the army and put it on its feet, or to look at the workers who increased their ability and educated themselves in various types of soviet economic institutions, to realize what a colossal step forward Russia has taken since the time of the October victory.[30]

The future belongs to the soviets; not even their enemies can deny this. But they are badly mistaken when they think that foreign soviets will confine themselves to servile tasks.

The soviets are the perfect form of proletarian dictatorship discovered by the Russian revolution. And if this is the case – as it undoubtedly is – then we are standing on the threshold of a transformation of the old robber states of the bourgeoisie into organizations of proletarian dictatorship. The Third International about which so many have spoken and written about will come. It will be *The International Soviet Socialist Republic*.

Part II

The Economics of the Transition Period

Foreword

The object of this work is to demolish common, vulgar and quasi-Marxist ideas about the nature of the Zusammenbruch (collapse) of capitalism predicted by the great authors of scientific communism and the nature of the process of transforming a capitalist society into a communist one. He who imagines the revolution of the proletariat to be a peaceful transition of power from one set of hands to another, and the revolution in the relations of production to be a change in the leadership of the organizational apparatus, he, who pictures the classic model of a proletarian revolution *in this way*, will recoil in horror from the tragedy mankind endures throughout the world. Amidst the smoking, charred ruins and the roar of civil war, he will be unable to discern the grand and stately outlines of the future society. He will remain forever a pitiful, ordinary man, whose intellect is as timid as his politics. He will impute his own weakness to the revolution, inventing all sorts of definitions for it, save its true one as a revolution of the proletariat.

Life's bitter experience has proved Marx to be correct, when he declared: 'We say to the workers, you will have to endure fifteen, twenty, fifty years of civil war and national hostilities, not only to change the social system, but also to change yourselves.'

In both its state and its production structure, the old society is splitting up and disintegrating, down to its lowest layers, right to the very depths. Never before has there been such a mighty collapse. But without it there could be no revolution of the proletariat – the proletariat which is building the foundations of the future society out of these disintegrating elements in a new relationship, new combinations and in accordance with new principles. And is building it, moreover, as the class subject, as an organized force which has a plan and the supreme will to implement that plan, whatever the obstacles. Mankind is paying a terrible price for the defects of the capitalist system, and only a class such as the proletariat, the Promethean class, will be able to bear the unprecedented torments of the transition period on its shoulders in order, finally, to light the lamp of communist society.

I shall also attempt in this work to analyse the fundamental traits of the transition period. 'I propose to publish a second part in the future, which will be a concrete, descriptive work on modern Russian economics. The need for such a summary is enormous and sufficient material has accumulated, which will need to be examined and theoretically interpreted.

The author's watchword was to reason things out fully, without fear of the conclusions. Unfortunately, there was no time to expound this work in popular terms and that is why it had to be written in almost algebraic formulae. The author will consider his task accomplished if those, whose thoughts were beginning to take analogous shape, formulate them definitively, and if those, who believed in naïve and reformist-type illusions, will at least reflect that the matter is much more complex than it appears in the vulgar pamphlets of the renegade period.

It is unnecessary to expiate on the fact that the author's guideline was Marx's method, the cognitive value of which has only now reached its full and titanic height.

N. I. Bukharin

Chapter I
The Structure of World Capitalism

Theoretical political economy is the study of a social economy based upon the production of *commodities*, i.e. the study of an *unorganized* social economy. Only in a society where production is anarchic, and likewise the distribution of goods, do the economic factors governing the life of the community manifest themselves in the form of 'natural' and 'spontaneous' laws independent of the will of individuals and collective bodies, laws which function with the same blind necessity as the force of gravity, 'when your house collapses about your ears'.[1] Marx was the first to record this specific feature of commodity production and his studies on commodity fetishism are a brilliant sociological introduction to theoretical political economy, which establishes the latter as an historically limited discipline.[2] Indeed, as soon as we take an organized social economy, all the basic 'problems' of political economy disappear: problems of value, price, profit and so on. Here 'relations between people' are not expressed as 'relations between things', and the social economy is regulated not by the blind forces of the market and competition, but by a consciously followed plan. In this case, there can be a certain system of analysis on the one hand, or a system of norms on the other, but there will be no room for a science which studies the blind laws of the market, since there will be no market. Thus the end of a capitalist commodity society will also see the end of political economy.

So, political economy is the study of a *commodity* economy.

This being so, a commodity-producing society is by no means the simple sum of its individual economic activities. In his polemic against Bastiat, Rodbertus brilliantly expressed the existence of a special economic environment, a special relationship which he called 'economic intercourse'. If we were faced with the simple sum of its economic activities there would be no society. This 'sum' is a purely logical unity and by no means a real, living complex.

Pure theory is not concerned with the extent of a given social economy and its spatial characteristics. It was for just this reason that Marx so scoffed at the term 'the national economy' selected by patriotic German professors. In the same way the question of who emerges as the subject of an individual economy is a comparatively minor one for abstract theory. What is of prime importance is the model of the relationship between these economies, namely, the model of an *unorganized* exchange relation. Conversely, all these questions do have enormous significance for a more concrete analysis, which is not restricted to extrapolating general laws.

Contemporary capitalism is world capitalism. This means that the capitalist relations of production dominate the entire world and connect all the parts of our planet with a firm economic bond. Nowadays the concrete manifestation of the social economy is a world economy. The world economy is a *real* living unity. Therefore, such definitions of it as that of the latest research worker, Dr Karl Tyszka,[3] are completely untrue. Tyszka writes:

> Just as a national economy is made up of the sum of the economic activities of the individuals of one nation, whether these activities be individual or co-operative, in the same way the *world economy is the sum of the national economies*. [And] The sum of the national economies, which are considerably influenced by the situation on the world market, makes up the world economy.

The first definition does not accord with the second; the second contains an inherent contradiction, since notion of a simple sum excludes an organic relationship. A sum of crabs in a basket is not a real unity, and likewise the number of babies born in a year 'united' in a statistical 'aggregate' does not represent a real unity either. The existence of a special *relationship* is what turns a simple aggregate into a real one. But this sort of aggregate excludes the concept of an arithmetical sum, because it is much greater and more complex than that sum.

So long as society produces commodities and not products, it will be an *unorganized* unity. The social nature of labour and the process of production becomes apparent here in the continuous exchange of commodities and in the fluctuations of market prices. This social nature of labour is nowhere manifested more clearly and simply, however, than in the case where we have a purposive social *organization* of labour.

A commodity society is a system with a particular model of relations, which determines the highly specific categories of the commodity world. This system is not a 'teleological unity', i.e. a consciously directed system with a definite plan. There is no plan. Here the economic process does not even have a *subject*. It is not a case of 'society produces' but of 'production takes place in society'. And for this very reason the people do not rule the product, instead the product rules the people and the 'spontaneous force' of economic development exceeds the limits of what is desirable. If the *whole* of society, under the commodity, and hence capitalist, mode of production, is blind, if the whole does not represent a teleological unity, then the same applies to its individual parts. Society is made up of interlinked parts and in a commodity society it is these parts which are the economic subject, the system is impersonal, blind and thus irrational.

This irrationality is also the fundamental precondition for the existence of political economy but this is just what the majority of bourgeois economists fail to understand. Thus according to Harms,[4] there would be no world economy, if there were no international trade agreements. Kobatsch[5] on the whole believes that a world economy does not exist as yet and that there will not be one until there is a world state. Kalver talks about a 'world market economy'. Throughout the entire polemic between Harms and Diehl,[6] there is not even a hint of the correct formulation of the problem. Efforts to find some kind of control mechanism as the determining characteristic of the economy stem directly from an utterly false impression of the nature of the capitalist social organism. To substantiate their study they are looking for a principle which kills that study.

The question now arises: just what are the consciously functioning parts of the world capitalist economy? In theory one can conceive of world capitalism as a system of individual, private enterprises, but the structure of modern capitalism is such that the economic subjects are the collective capitalist organizations – 'the state capitalist trusts'.[7]

Finance capital did away with the anarchy in production within the major capitalist countries. Monopolistic employers' associations, combined enterprises, and the penetration of banking capital into industry created a new model of production relations, which transformed the unorganized commodity capitalist system into a finance capitalist *organization*. The unorganized relationship of one enterprise with another, through buying and selling, has to a considerable extent been replaced by an organized relationship through the 'controlled holding' of shares, 'participation' and 'financing', which find personal expression in the 'Dirigenten' of the banks, industry, the enterprises and trusts. By the same token, the exchange relation expressing the *social* division of labour and the separation of the socio-production organization into independent capitalist enterprises is replaced by a *technical* division of labour within an organized 'national economy'.

The fragmented nature of capitalist production, however its anarchic character, far exceeds the bounds of the social division of labour. Division of labour was always understood to mean the disintegration of aggregate labour into different 'jobs'.[8] In particular the social division of labour was, and is, understood to mean the division of labour between separate enterprises. Although they are 'independent' of each other, capitalist enterprises need each other, for one branch of production supplies the raw materials, subsidiary means and so forth for another.

However, one should not confuse the *two* things: the fragmentation of social labour, which *arises from* the fact of the social division of labour on the one hand, and the fragmentation of social labour, which negates this very division of labour on the one hand. Separate commodity producers do not exist simply because there are different forms of labour. Within the limits of each separate *branch* of production, even of the more specialized and small-scale production divisions, there exists simultaneously a considerable number of independent commodity producers. In other words, the anarchic structure of a commodity society manifests itself in the separate existence of 'enterprises'. These 'enterprises', in their turn, stand in various relationships to each other: either they are bound to each *other* by buying and selling (heterogeneous enterprises), or they are in competition with each other (homogeneous enterprises). The master of a tailor's workshop is connected with the cloth manufacturer in that he buys cloth from him, but with regard to another such master, he is a competitor in no way bound to him by exchange transaction. The simultaneous existence of a tailoring and a cloth enterprise is an expression of the social division of labour, whilst the co-existence of several tailoring enterprises does not express any social division of labour.

Very serious attention must be paid to this distinction. Usually, the anarchy of capitalist production is seen in the light of market competition and of that alone. Now, we can see that market competition expresses only *one* part, only one model of the 'life' of separate commodity producers, i.e. that model of relations which is not connected with the division of social labour.

Nevertheless, owing to the interdependence of *all* the parts of the social economy the *heterogeneous* enterprises also wage a struggle amongst themselves. A capitalist society is one which produces surplus value. On the other hand the distribution process is one of *dividing* the surplus value between the subjects of the capitalist economy and not every enterprise realizes that surplus value which it produces. The most elementary law of capitalism – the striving of profit rates to reach the same level – already distorts this simplicity of relations.[9] The picture is even further complicated by the formation of every possible kind of capitalist monopoly. Hence, it is clear that the struggle for the division of surplus value between individual economic subjects (individual or co-operative) must be of a different nature. We shall, therefore, distinguish three types of competition.

1 By horizontal competition we mean competition between homogeneous enterprises. Here the anarchy manifest in competition does not rest on any social division.

2 By vertical competition we mean the struggle between heterogeneous enterprises, whose existence expresses the fact of the social division of labour.

3 Finally, by combined (complex) competition we mean the struggle that is waged by combined enterprises, i.e. capitalist units which amalgamate various branches of production, i.e. which transform the *social* division of labour into a *technical* division.

The criterion for differentiating these types of competition is the type of enterprise which, in turn, is based on one or another relationship to the social division of labour, i.e. to one of the fundamental production relations of the commodity world.

This differentiation also gives rise to the differentiation in the methods of competition. Indeed, it is quite clear that, whereas horizontal competition can operate on the market with low prices (the classical type of competition), with vertical competition, the low price method must give way to other means. And indeed we see that methods of direct pressure on the part of capital do start to play a major role here, with the *boycott* first and foremost as its most elementary form.

This change in the methods of competition is to a great extent still being charted, as the struggle begins to break out of the sphere of the relations of the market, even though the initial stimulus was the market relationship. *Price* is a *universal* category of a commodity society and therefore *any* upset in the balance is manifested in a definite movement in prices. The category of *profit* is inconceivable without the category of price. In short, every economic phenomenon of the capitalist world is, in some way or other, bound up with price and, hence, the market. This does not mean, however, that every economic phenomenon is a market phenomenon. It is the same with competition. Up to now, the chief consideration has been of *market* competition, which was characteristic of the pattern of horizontal competition in general, but competition, i.e. the struggle between capitalist enterprises, can also be waged outside the market in the strict sense of the word. Such, for example, is the struggle for spheres of capital investment, i.e. for the very opportunity to expand the production process. In this case, too, it is clear that other methods of struggle will be used than those of the classical case of horizontal market competition.

Now, we must return to modern world capitalism.

We have already observed that the units which make up the system of the modern world economy are not the individual enterprises, but indicate complexes, state capitalist trusts. Certainly, world relations do exist between the separate enterprises of different countries and the model of these relations in any one instance may be directly opposed to the model by which these countries relate to each other; but still, recently, relations between entire complexes are becoming predominant. The capitalist 'national economy' has changed from an *irrational* system into a *rational* organization, from a non-subject economy into an economic subject. This transformation has been made possible by the growth of finance capitalism and the cohesion between the economic and the political organizations of the bourgeoisie. At the same time, neither the anarchy of capitalist production in general, nor the competition of capitalist commodity producers, have been in any way destroyed. Not only do these phenomena still exist, they have even intensified by being reproduced within the framework of a *world* economy. The world economic system is as blind, irrational and without a subject as was the former system of national economy.

Now, the commodity economy does not disappear for good, even though within a country it either dies off or is considerably curtailed by being replaced with organized distribution. Having ceased to be 'national' the commodity market, in fact, merely becomes a world market. The same process is observable here as when two or more heterogeneous enterprises merge into one combined entity, where the raw materials are processed into the half-finished product and then into the finished product, and where the movement of products is not attended by a corresponding opposite movement of a monetary equivalent: 'economic wealth' *within* a combined enterprise circulates not as commodities but as products which become commodities only in so far as they are thrown beyond the bounds of the combined entity. In just the same way, a product for which there is organized distribution within a country is a commodity in so far as its existence is bound up with that of the world market. The difference – in comparison with a national economy – is only in the breadth of the economic system and in the character of the component parts of the system.

The special character of the state capitalist trusts also explains a special type of competition. A state capitalist trust is virtually a huge combined enterprise. Being in opposition to each other, these trusts are rivals not only as units producing one and the same 'world commodity', but also as parts of a divided social world labour, as units which are economically *complementary*. Hence their struggle is carried on simultaneously along both horizontal *and* vertical lines: this struggle is complex competition.

The transition to a system of finance capitalism constantly reinforced the process whereby simple market, horizontal, competition was transformed into complex competition. Since the method of struggle corresponds to the type of competition, this was inevitably followed by the 'aggravation' of relations on the world market. Methods of *direct* pressure accompany vertical and horizontal competition, therefore the system of world finance capital inevitably involves an *armed struggle* between imperialist rivals. And *here* lies the fundamental roots of imperialism.

The struggle of the finance capital state organizations is the clearest expression of the contradictions and anarchy of the capitalist mode of production where labour, socialized on a world scale, clashes with the 'national' state subjects of appropriation. The conflict between the development of the productive forces and the capitalist relations of production must – so long as the whole system does not blow up – temporarily reduce the productive forces so that the next cycle of their development might then begin in the very same capitalist carapace. This destruction of the productive forces constitutes the *conditio sine qua non* of capitalist development and from this point of view crises, the costs of competition and – a particular instance of those costs – wars are the inevitable *faux frais* of capitalist reproduction. A temporary equilibrium can be achieved, strictly speaking, in two ways: in the first place, by a direct reduction of the productive forces, expressed in a destruction of values; and, in the second place, by a partial abolition of the conflict between the constituent elements of the economic system. This latter is expressed in the centralization of capital. The centralization of capital devours competition, but, on the other hand, it continuously reproduces this competition on an expanded basis. It abolishes the anarchy of *small* productive units but it subsequently aggravates the anarchic relations between *large*-scale productive bodies. Conflicts in the economic system disappear in one place, only to reappear on an even greater scale in another. They turn into conflicts between fundamental parts of a huge *world* mechanism.

The centralization of capital proceeds along the same three basic lines which competition takes: there is either horizontal centralization, where the absorption of homogeneous enterprises takes place, or vertical centralization where the absorption of alien enterprises takes place and, finally, combined centralization, when combinations of different elements take place or a complex and simple enterprise combine. In a world economy the centralization of capital is expressed in imperialist annexations which can likewise be distinguished along the three fundamental lines of competition.[10]

War results in the same phenomena that we see resulting from a crisis; side by side with the destruction of the productive forces go the abolition of small and medium-sized world groupings (the death of the individual states) and the rise of even greater combinations, which grow at the expense of the groups which perish.

The relations of production of the capitalist world do not, however, amount to the same thing as the relations between 'commodity producers', i.e. the relations between individual capitalists or their alliances (syndicates, trusts and states). Contemporary world economy is not only a commodity economy but also a *capitalist* commodity economy. The contradiction between the various parts of the economy lie in two main areas: that of the anarchic relationship between enterprises and of the anarchic structure of society, as a *class* society. In other words, what we have here are both 'pure economic contradictions and 'social' contradictions. Clearly, the first category of relations has a direct influence on the second. The destruction of the productive forces and the process of capitalist centralization greatly aggravate the contradictions between the classes and, given a certain combination of both factors, the collapse of the entire system ensues, beginning with the organizationally weakest links of that system. And this is the start of the communist revolution.

Chapter 2
Economics, State Power and War

The 1914–18 war raised the question of state power point-blank. If in the pre-war period views flourished – even in the Marxist camp, which were fairly heavily coloured with a Manchester hue – from the moment the imperialist state threw tens of millions of people on to the stage of history and instantly revealed its colossal significance as an *economic* factor, the analysis of state power became a matter for theoretical and practical discussions.

The life of the all-embracing state organizations, not the life of society, but the life of the *state*, was highlighted. Hobbes wrote in his *Leviathan*[1] that there is no power which can compare with the power of the state, but his *Leviathan* would turn out to be a puppy in comparison with the enormous strength displayed by the state apparatus of finance capital.

In a class society, war is waged by the state organization. In a capitalist society, the contradictory economic structure of society ultimately leads to an acute crisis in its political structure. It takes two basic directions: the anarchy of world capitalism, the contradiction between social world labour and 'national' state appropriations, is expressed in the clash between state organizations of capital, in capitalist wars. On the other hand, the contradiction between classes of a capitalist society, tremendously aggravated by the development of the first contradiction, leads to revolution. In both cases the question of particular state organizations is resolved;

war gives rise to realignments of forces on the same basis and the model of state power and its social content is retained; revolution changes the very basis of the state organization by putting new classes into power and giving birth to a new type of state entity.

Questions of war and state power are, therefore, the most critical questions of our epoch and demand solution. We are primarily concerned with them here in purely theoretical terms.

Marxism examines the relationship and interdependencies of all social phenomena, where every concatenation of events forms a link in the chain of causes maintaining, developing or, conversely, destroying a certain model of relations of production, a certain economic structure of society. We must examine both war and state power from this point of view.[2] Every class society is a mechanism which produces surplus product and acts on the instructions of one part of that society. This surplus product can take the form of value (as in a capitalist economy) or remain simply as product (as in a slave-owning society). In both these cases, however, we have a process of exploitation. Let us now pose a very general question: how is this process of exploitation possible? How can a system exist which harbours such a colossal, inherent contradiction? In what way can a society which is essentially composed of *two* societies (classes) represent a relative unity? In other words: how is it possible to preserve a relative social equilibrium and stability in a social system which is based on the division of the social whole?

The answer is clear: for such a society to exist there must be some additional factor which *rivets* that divided society together and represses (in a 'coarse' physical sense and a 'subtle' ideological sense) the opposition of the oppressed classes. In short, in order to preserve the system it is essential to have an *organization* which can control not only things but, more important, *people*. And such an organization is the *state*.

However, it should not be supposed that the state is something which stands *above* society and above *classes*. There are no supra-class elements in society. On the contrary, as we have seen above, the basic function of the state – in the case of minority rule – is to preserve, consolidate and expand the process of exploitation. Hence, it is clear that the state organization is *exclusively* an organization of the ruling *class* or, as Engels wrote, 'the state is the organisation of the propertied classes for their defence against the propertyless classes'.[3] This circumstance must be particularly emphasized. Actually, a relatively expedient solution for the entire socially contradictory system could theoretically be achieved in two ways: either by the existence of a 'third force', reconciling the classes, smoothing out the contradictions and promoting continual compromises; or by the existence of an organization from one of the camps, which uses every method, from brute force to the most complex ideological cobweb, to control the camp of its class opponents. What happens in reality is the second solution to the problem, i.e. the presence of an organization of the ruling classes. The majority of even Marxist-type systems advances the first, 'harmonious' theory of the state.

As a matter of fact this 'theoretical' wisdom is to be found as far back as the code of the Babylonian King Hammerabi who declared that the 'aim of a ruler is to safeguard of the law of the land and to destroy what is wicked and evil, so that the strong may not harm the weak'.[4] The most 'serious' argument in favour of this venerable 'theory' is the existence of the so-called general useful functions of state power; the building of railways and hospitals, factory legislation, insurance, etc.

In an impartial analysis, however, it appears that these functions of state power by no means preclude its purely class character. They are either the essential condition for extending the very process of exploitation (railways), or they protect other interests of the ruling classes (sanitary measures), or else they are strategic concessions to the class enemy.[5] The aim of a trust or syndicate is to increase profits and not to feed the people or give them work. However, to get this increase, it must engage in production and hire workers, to whom in some cases (during strikes etc.) it makes concessions, while never for a moment ceasing to be an employers', as the German workers express it, 'scharfmacherische' organization. These 'generally useful' functions are merely the *essential* condition for the process of exploitation.

The most characteristic trait of the state organization of the ruling class, the one that distinguishes it from the class's other organizations, is its universality. The state organization is the most wide-spread class organization, where all its strength is focused, where the instruments of mechanical pressure and repression[6] are concentrated and where the ruling class is organized as a *class* and not as a part or small group of that class. For this reason then,

certain activities, for example 'economic' activity since it embraces
the whole class, inevitably take on a 'political' character; blows
aimed here are not directed against an individual group but against
the class as a whole, and hence against its state power.

A state is a definite human organization. Thus it expresses not
the technical relationship of people to nature, but the *social*
relationships of people to each other, of some people to others. It
would be quite wrong to look for the 'essence' of a state in its
technical and organizational definitions, e.g. in the fact that it has
a centralized apparatus. For the abstract concept of centralization
may presuppose diametrically opposite models of social relations,
but it is precisely in the model of these social relations that the crux
of the matter lies. 'A negro is a negro, a person from a black race.
But he only became a slave under certain conditions.' The means
of production are always means of production. This is a technical
concept. But it is only in certain conditions that these means of
production become capital; this happens when a certain social
relationship of a very specific type starts to materialize within them
– the type which constitutes the so-called 'essence' of capital:
'capital is not a thing, but a social relationship' (Marx).

For Marx, all social phenomena are historical and it is precisely
in their historical determinacy that he looks for their essential
characteristic. There is nothing surprising, therefore, in the fact
that the state, from the Marxist point of view, is a wholly historical category, namely, a category of a class society. What is
essential in a state is not that it is a centralized apparatus, but that
this centralized apparatus embodies a certain relationship between
the classes, to wit, the relationship of the state, power, enslavement
and oppression. The apparatus will disappear together with the
disappearance of the classes and with the class state in its final
form – the dictatorship of the proletariat.[7]

Among bourgeois researchers it is Gumplovicz and Oppenheimer, under the strong influence of Dühring, who come closest
to the truth. Oppenheimer defines 'the historical state' in the
following manner: '*In form* the state is a legal institution, imposed
on the conquered group by the victorious group. In content it is
the systematic economic exploitation of the subordinate group.'[8]
Leaving aside the question of conquest and the fact that the origin
of the classes in themselves is ascribed solely to 'non-economic
pressure',[9] we must acknowledge that Oppenheimer's formulation

regarding 'economic exploitation' is essentially correct (which does not prevent the author in other works from feeling moved to lavish compliments on the 'classless' Prussian civil servant).

From the above analysis of state power its character can be clearly seen as a 'super-structure' upon an economic basis. As with every 'super-structure', it is not simply a bell-glass covering economic life, but an active force, a working organization which consolidates in every way possible the production basis on which it arose.

We must now raise another question, that of war, and it must be approached from the same angle from which we approached the question of state power. What place does war occupy in the stream of social life? And since social life is first and foremost a process of reproduction and change in the social relations of production, what role exactly does war play in this?

It is easier to answer this question now. You see, it is not 'the people', nor 'nations' who wage war: war is waged by *states*, using the living strength of their 'people' on the battlefields, just as they use them in the factories, plants or mines. The *army*, that instrument which is set in motion when war commences, is the most essential part of the state apparatus. Here we would observe in passing that the whole social edifice is notable for the peculiar monism of its architecture. All its parts are in one and the same 'style'. Just as people are placed in a certain hierarchical order, in the relations of production – an order which corresponds to the class groupings – so too in the state apparatus in general and in the army in particular this social hierarchy is reflected.

However, if war is a function of the state, is state power *in actu*, and if, on the other hand, the state itself as an apparatus, is the means of strengthening and expanding certain relations of production, then clearly this is the principal 'task' of war too. The struggle between states is a manifestation of the struggle between certain bases of production personified by the ruling class of these states. Every production structure has an equivalent model of state power and hence an equivalent model of war. We are not interested here in the technical and organizational side of military matters (although that too is determined by general technical and economic conditions), what interests us is the social significance of this phenomenon. In order to answer the question about the 'essence' of war, it must be treated to the same historical analysis as the question of the state. Then we shall get a similar answer, namely, that war, from the sociological standpoint, is the means of reproducing those relations of production, on the basis of which it arose.

The state is a 'non-economic' factor. Nevertheless, it has colossal economic significance. Similarly, war, too, as a function of state power and a 'non-economic' factor, is one of the key factors of the economic process.[10] The question will have to be treated in greater detail in a subsequent theoretical analysis. The social process is not just the expansion of a certain production structure, it is also a process of *replacing* some forms, some modes of production and economic structures by others. But this replacement of its bases is also accompanied by an inevitable replacement of their state carapace. New relations of production burst the old political integument.

Every phase of historical development and every model of relations of production, however, conforms to its own specific laws. In order to understand any epoch in theory, one must take it in all its peculiarities and analyse those characteristics which make it an epoch, i.e. which create a special model of relations, above all the relations of production. If, by using this method, we can lay bare the laws of social development, then clearly we should also examine wars in the same way, in view of the cohesiveness of all the manifestations of social life.

The foregoing affords a basis for the *classification* of wars. It is the same basis as we used for the classification of states. Every production model has a corresponding state model, and to every state model there corresponds a specific model of war.

Let us take some examples. Take a slave-owning economy. In this instance the state means the state of the slave owners and a war by this state is merely a means for expanding the slave-owning system, for expanding the reproduction of the slave-holding relations of production. The so-called colonial wars of Spain, Holland, France, etc., were the wars of the merchant–capitalist states; their social role amounted to the expansion of the merchant–capitalist relations of production, which were later transformed into the relations of industrial capitalism. When industrial capital and its state organizations engaged in the struggle for markets, wars began to subordinate the 'underdeveloped' world to the rule of capital. Finally, when the capitalist mode of production donned the jacket

71

of finance capitalism, there immediately appeared on the scene a special model of state power, which was the robber imperialist state with its centralized military apparatus; and the social role of war came to lie in extending the spheres of supremacy of finance capital, with its trusts and bank consortia.

The same thing happens when a dictatorial socialist power wages a war. When the workers' state goes to war it strives to expand and consolidate the economic basis on which it arose, i.e. the socialist relations of production (hence, by the way, even an offensive revolutionary socialist war is clearly permissible in principle). Again an entirely new model of state power is in keeping with production which is undergoing a process of socialization. The model of power is as much unlike all previous ones as the socialist mode of production is unlike all former modes of production, which are based on the private economic relations of property. Therefore, the social significance of a war waged by a workers' dictatorship differs in principle from the wars of all previous epochs.

A socialist war is a *class* war and must be distinguished from a simple civil war, which is not a war in the strict sense of the word, since it is not a war between *state* organizations. In a class war, *both* sides are organized in a state power, on the one side the state of finance capital and on the other the state of the proletariat.

We have taken all these phenomena in their pure form. In reality, of course, matters are much more complicated. Modern world economy, despite the huge centralization of capital, nevertheless presents a fairly motley picture. And even the world war, alongside its purely imperialistic elements, had a number of other elements interspersed in the general background, such as the national chauvinism of the minor nations, which are now – for an historical second – becoming independent bourgeois state units. However, it is not, if one may express it thus, this state petty bourgeoisie which will decide the fortunes of the world, it is the relationship between the giants of imperialism and, in the final analysis, the struggle between the giants of the class war which will decide them.

Chapter 3
The Collapse of the Capitalist System

The clash between the various parts of the world capitalist system, which were an expression of the conflict between the growth of the productive forces of that system and its anarchistic productive structure was, as we have seen, a conflict of the state-capitalist trusts. The objective need which has been highlighted by history, is for the organization of the world economy, i.e. the conversion of a *non-subject* world economic system into an economic *subject*, an organization which functions according to a plan, a 'teleological unity', an organized system. Imperialism attempted to solve this problem by its own methods. This has been formulated, not altogether accurately, by H. von Beckerath:

> Since free competition refused to act as a regulator of economic
> life, in the end a cry goes up for organisation. A rallying
> process takes place and a general struggle for industrial
> markets is waged. This is how the struggle arises between
> nationally united economic masses, a struggle of an ever-
> increasing political nature which subsequently culminates in a
> titanic political clash between nations contending for industrial
> commodity markets.[1]

The solution to the problem proved to be beyond the power of imperialism and the military crisis led a crisis throughout the entire system. Within the narrow limits of individual state-capitalist trusts, however, the first stage of the war was one of internal re-organization of the capitalist relations of production in the direction of planning and organizing the *partial*, fragmented systems which were fighting amongst themselves.

It is easy to understand and trace the fundamental causes of this reorganization, which was aimed at abolishing the internal pro-duction anarchy through the statification of the economic functions. Organizationally and technically this reorganization was made considerably easier by the extremely rapid dying-out of the middle groups. War had the effect of a gigantic crisis in this respect. With the sum of produced surplus value diminishing, this value con-tracted and accumulated in the (socially, technically and economic-ally) stronger productive units. The process of centralization of capital was greatly speeded up, and this accelerated centralization constituted the 'negative' condition of a new form of capitalist relations. The *positive* reasons for statification were the require-ments of war, as a huge organizational process. The scope of this war, its technology, the complexity of the internal relations of the military apparatus, the colossal demand for the products of industry and agriculture, which the military organization im-mediately made and, finally, the decisive significance of the out-come of military operations for the classes in command – all these made the complete mastery of the anarchy within the contending partial systems a matter of immediate attention. Military successes, other things being equal, were directly proportionate to the economic organization of the state capitalist trusts.

The causes, mentioned above, were greatly aggravated by the shortage of a number of products, particularly of raw materials, a shortage which came to light immediately after the breakdown of international relations and which only increased the general exhaustion and impoverishment.[2] Clearly, this shortage called for the most economical, and hence rationalized and organized distri-bution. And since the process of distribution is one of the phases of the general process of reproduction, it stands to reason that the organization of distribution led, inevitably, to a greater or lesser degree of organization in the production process proper. It is not difficult to see that the capitalist class as a whole (and dynamically this means the representatives of finance capital), profited a great deal from this centralization. Only the extremely naïve regarded this as a violation of the sacred rights of property. In actual fact there wasn't the faintest whiff of any 'expropriation of the expropriators', since everything was centralized in the hands of the *finance-capitalist* state organization and not some 'third' force.

Opposition, for the most part, came only from the circles of the *backward* strata of the bourgeoisie, primarily the representatives of merchant, capital and commercial speculation. The organization of production and distribution in point of fact eliminates commerce in general and commercial speculation in particular; consequently, it cuts off commercial profit and speculative 'differential profit'.[3] In so far as this organization of production and distribution does take place, it does violate 'the sacred rights' of just these very categories, but it would be ridiculous to think that the 'rights' of the capitalist class as a whole are thereby destroyed. What actually happens is merely a redistribution of the surplus value in favour of the finance-capitalist groups and the transformation of commercial profit into dividend or interest paid by the *state* bank. Hence, there is no abolition of surplus value here, only a change in the *form* of part of this surplus value. *This* is the very essence of the state-capitalist organization as far as the questions of income categories and the distribution of surplus value are concerned. As for the diminishing share of surplus value accruing to the capitalist class and an increase of value going to the workers, as an assurance against revolution, this is a secondary matter and does not play an important role.[4] The mathematical limit to this trend is the conversion of the entire 'national economy' into a completely united *combined trust*, where all the separate 'enterprises' have ceased to be enterprises and become merely separate workshops, branches of this trust where, consequently, the *social* division of labour has turned into the *technical* division of labour and where the entire economy has become a completely united enterprise belonging to the appropriate group of the world bourgeoisie.

The general organizational principle behind this form of capitalism is the subordination of all the economic (and not merely the economic) organizations of the bourgeoisie, to its state. The reason for this is clear. Let us consider a whole range of bourgeois organizations: the state, syndicates, cartels and trusts; entrepreneurial alliances, co-operatives, bank consortia, scientific societies, organized bourgeois journalism and hundreds of other organizations. In theory it is clear that the maximum stability of the entire system will be achieved by combining, connecting and coordinating all these organizations. Which organization should be on top? This is also clear: the most important, most powerful and comprehensive. State power is just such an organization. The entire power of the class is concentrated in the state organization of the bourgeoisie. Hence, the remaining organizations, primarily economic, and all sorts of others, are bound to be jointly subordinated to it. They are all 'militarized'. They all turn into branches and departments of a united, *universal* organization. Only under these conditions does the entire system achieve maximum stability. In this way a new model of state power comes into being, the classical model of an *imperialist* state, resting on the *state-capitalist* relations of production. Here economics fuse organizationally with politics, the economic power of the bourgeoisie is directly combined with its political power, the state ceases to be the simple guardian of the process of exploitation and becomes a direct, collective-capitalist exploiter, openly opposed to the proletariat.[5] The development of state power here reveals its dialectical nature: state power came into being as the primary and sole form of the organization of the ruling class; it subsequently became one of many organizations of the bourgeoisie, finally it once more became essentially a single organization, *having absorbed all the others.*[6]

The state-capitalist relations of production are, logically and historically, an extension of finance-capitalist relations, and represent the culmination of them. It is no wonder, therefore, that the starting point of their development was those organisational forms, already provided by finance capital, i.e. the syndicates, trusts and banks. The trusts, as private, monopolistic organizations unifying production, not only commercially, but also technically, are superseded by *state* monopolies, as are the trust-like syndicates and cartels. The cartelization process is accelerated under pressure from the state, and so-called compulsory syndicates and cartels are created. The transitional model is a mixed enterprise, where the state is joint owner of a syndicate and the major shareholder in a joint-stock company, etc. and where the finance capitalist relation between state and private enterprise takes the form of so-called 'participation'. These are the most important forms as regards the reorganization of the relations of production, but they are by no means the only ones. A number of less vital changes are also relevant: state regulation and control of the production process (compulsory production and rate fixing, control of manufacturing methods and the internal technical and production structure in general); the regulation of distribution (compulsory deliveries and acceptance, the organization of state supplies, state warehouses, price fixing, rationing, etc.).[7] The banks, too, have a special and extremely important role to play in the organization: they pay deposits into the *state* bank, and the state bank, for its part, centralizes huge sums (suffice to mention war loans alone) and invests them in war industry. Since to a considerable extent these deposits represent periodic releases of capital, their organized 'investment' by the state bank signifies the virtual subordination of industry to the state bank and the transformation of owners' profit into interest paid out by the bank. So, in this way too, capitalist relations of production are transformed into state-capitalist relations of production and different types of capitalist incomes are levelled out, by being converted into a peculiar 'dividend' paid out by the one collective-capitalist enterprise, the one joint-stock company and trust which is the imperialist state.[8]

The models of organizational relationships take various concrete forms which differ according to their function: there, too, we have *planned* organization, whereby new and stable productive and technical units are created (an example of this may be seen in the compulsory trusts which centralize a number of former production combines, state monopolies and so on), and simple 'control' (for example, the compulsory sale and receipt). Finally, there is also the even lower element in the organization process – the introduction of norms[9] – of which price-fixing will serve as an example. It would be a mistake, however, to ignore the fact that the general tendency of 'state capitalist' development, which accelerates the trend of finance capitalism, is in the direction of advanced organization models which create stable, productive and technical groupings. The organization process need not necessarily *begin* with the production and technical side at all; the subjective aim of its activities may be, say, a pure *commercial* calculation rather than organizational, but nevertheless the objective, final result may be the creation of new productive and technical systems.

This phenomenon was apparent in the era of finance capitalism: the syndicates originally arose as commercial combines dealing on the market but, none the less, subsequent development led to the creation of trust-like cartels and then to the creation of real trusts, i.e. combines which were not merely commercial but also productive and technical. Or, to take another example, the penetration of banking capital into industry led to the consolidation of enterprises (to the creation of mergers and integrated trusts, etc.). So in these instances the process of organization spread from the sphere of circulation to that of production: this happens because the circulation process is a component part of the general overall process, i.e. the process of reproduction, whose parts and phases must all conform to its laws.[10]

Thus, *the reorganization of the relations of finance capitalism was a move towards a universal state-capitalist organization, with the abolition of the commodity market, the transformation of money into an accounting unit, production organized on a national scale and the subordination of the entire 'national economic' mechanism to the aim of world competition, i.e. primarily of war.*

In the analysis above we examined the organizational forms whereby the capitalist structure of individual countries adapts itself to the new conditions of life under general world capitalism. But we examined all the changes from the point of view of overcoming anarchy in *production*. Now, we must say a few words about *social* anarchy. The sum total of the relations of production embraces not only relations between people, in different organizations there also exists another aspect to the relation of production: we are talking about the relations between *classes*. Hence, there had to be reorganization along these lines, too, for otherwise the whole system would have proved to be highly unstable and short-lived. The requirements of the war had a colossal role to play here, too, for the mobilization of the workers and their minds for war was as necessary a precondition for waging an imperialist war as the mobilization of material production.

The process of overcoming the anarchy in production started with elements of organization which had already been set up by finance capitalism. Likewise, the process of social reorganization had to be based on those factors which had been established by earlier development. The *physical* organisational forms already existed in the shape of the *workers' organizations*: the trade unions, socialist parties and, to some extent, the co-operatives, with all their additional and subsidiary apparatuses. The *ideological* forms consisted in the singular mentality of workers' patriotism, which was partly a metamorphosis of vestiges of an old petty-bourgeois mentality and partly a product of the relative and temporary, personal interests of the working class in imperialist politics. Finally, the method of reorganization was the same method of joint subordination to an *all-embracing* bourgeois state. The treachery of the socialist parties and the trade unions was expressed in the fact that they entered the service of the bourgeois state, that they were in fact statified by this imperialist state and reduced to 'workers' departments' in the military machine. The statification of these organizations had its ideological counterpart in the peculiar bourgeois statification of the proletarian mentality, which was expressed in the wide-spread dissemination and recognition, even in proletarian circles, of the theory of so-called 'civil peace'. Of course, alongside these methods, those of direct, physical pressure and suppression continued to be developed, i.e. *openly repressive* measures.

These were the means used to secure maximum stability for the partial capitalist systems in the circumstances created by the great imperialist war, whereby the balance of the entire world system of capitalist society had been drastically upset.

For our analysis to touch upon all the basic trends towards organization in the capitalist system, we ought to mention the syndicates of *state*-capitalist trusts, special syndicates of the 'second order', the components of which are the state-capitalist trusts. Such are state 'coalitions' and the 'League of Nations'. The preconditions for these organizations were created by finance-capitalist relations, by the sum total of mutual 'participation'. The war intensified this process of syndicalization of the state-capitalist trusts; 'all-union' workers' conferences were, by the way, a manifestation of the same tendency. Here the trend towards organizations extends beyond the borders of an individual country. Consequently, these efforts by the capitalist world represented the highest manifestation of the organizing process.

These processes all took place in conditions of colossal *destruction* of the productive forces. The structural reorganization was accompanied by a regression of the productive forces. It was this, in the final analysis, which led to the inevitable collapse of the entire system. Hence, we are faced with the problem of tracing the fundamental impact of the destruction process.

By the productive forces of society we mean the *sum total* of the means of production and the labour force. Thus, on the one hand, it means the sum total of various kinds of machines, raw materials, fuel, etc. *in natura*, and, on the other hand, the sum total of the various kinds of manpower *in natura* (that of the metal workers, technicians, textile workers, etc., i.e. manpower of different kinds and skills).[11] Development of the productive forces is the basis for human development in general and so it is necessary to examine every fact of social life with this in mind. The position of the development of the productive forces is closely related to that of reproduction: the growth of the productive forces corresponds with expanded reproduction, when static they correspond with simple reproduction and their decline is expressed in the fact that an ever-diminishing share of periodically consumed products is replaced. In this last instance we have social regression.

The reproduction approach is virtually obligatory in any economic analysis, but it is doubly so for the economist who studies critical epochs and transitional phases of development. Indeed, in so-called normal times, the periodic recurrence of production cycles is taken for granted. Of course, specific problems do arise here, too, particularly for a capitalist society but, on the whole, a more or less smooth course of events may be assumed. The critical epochs, on the contrary, place every subsequent cycle of production in doubt. Hence the reproduction viewpoint is the *only* methodologically correct approach, since it analyses the conditions for the recurrence of production cycles, i.e. the conditions of *dynamic* equilibrium in the social system. [As Rosa Luxemburg said:]

> The literal meaning of the word 'reproduction' is repetition, renewal of the process of production. At first sight it may be difficult to see in what respect the idea of reproduction differs from that of repetition which we can all understand – why such a new and unfamiliar term should be required. But in the sort of *repetition* which we shall consider, in the continual *recurrence* of the process of production, there are certain distinctive features [emphasis by N.I.B.].[12]

The physiocrats understood this in actual fact perfectly well, but it has been substantially forgotten by the 'erudite' liveried lackeys of imperialism.

This is why the initial phase of the war gave birth to truly monstrous theoretical constructions that drew the conclusion about the *beneficial*(!) influence of war on 'national economic' life, a conclusion drawn from the fact of war profits, 'prosperity' of war industry and the increased share prices of metallurgical, chemical and other industries.

Let us look at the *real* process of reproduction, when the whole economic system comes under the banner of war, i.e. the productive forces have been redistributed in favour of war industry and work for the army in general. As a rule, labour expended on the needs of war is designated unproductive, from the economic point of view. What does this mean? It is easy to see exactly what it means when we analyse its influence on the *conditions* of reproduction. The normal process of production creates means of production and means of consumption. These are the two most important branches of the entire social economy. Clearly, the means of production enter the system of social labour in each case. Their production is the condition for reproduction. By and large, the same thing occurs with the production of the means of consumption. These means of consumption do not just disappear, without leaving any trace, for subsequent cycles of the production process. For consumption is *basically* a special process in the production of labour power. And labour power, too, is an essential condition for the process of reproduction. Consequently, production of both the means of production and the means of consumption turns out products which form the necessary conditions for the reproduction process, without which it could not take place.

Military production has an altogether different significance: a gun is not transformed into an element of a new production cycle: gunpowder is shot into the air and does not appear in a different guise in the next cycle at all. Quite the reverse. The economic effect of these elements *in actu* has a purely negative value, although it should not be supposed that economic significance is necessarily connected with a definite aspect of use value and the material form of the product.

If we take means of consumption which are supplied to the army, we shall observe the same phenomenon here. The means of consumption do not create labour power, since soldiers do not feature in the production process; they have been withdrawn from it and placed *outside* of it. So, for as long as the war continues, a considerable part of the means of consumption will serve not as means of production of labour power, but as the means of production of a specific 'soldier power', which has no role to play in the production process. Consequently, in conjunction with war the process of reproduction takes on a distorted, regressive and *negative* character; that is to say with every subsequent production cycle, the real production basis gets increasingly narrower and 'development' takes place not in an expanding but in a constantly narrowing spiral.

Another important circumstance to be noted here is that the army creates a colossal demand for its upkeep, but does not give any labour equivalent. Hence, not only does it not produce, it actually *takes away*; in other words, there is a *twofold* deduction here from the accumulation fund. This circumstance is the most important destructive factor. In addition to this, one should note the direct military destruction (the roads blown up, the towns torn down, etc.) as well as a large amount of indirect destruction (the de-skilling of the labour force etc.). Thus it is clear that the real bases of social production get narrower with every cycle of production of social capital. What we have in this case is not expanded reproduction, but ever-increasing *under-production*. This process may be called *expanded negative reproduction*, and this is what war is from the economic point of view.

So, what is really taking place is expanded negative reproduction and this process should be distinguished from its fetishistically distorted, capitalist expression on paper, for the monstrous theory about the positive impact of war is based upon the confusion of these two processes – the material–labour process on the one hand and the formal process on the other. Indeed, it follows from the foregoing that the form of capitalist income tends to become interest paid out in state securities under the state capitalist system. These securities, to a considerable extent, represent the right to *future* real value. At the same time, they can be in circulation and can even be accumulated in huge quantities. But their availability is one thing, the actual possibility of realizing them is another. In so far as the realization of value as profit does take place in the process of war, it may signify either the 'corrosion' of constant capital or the realization of a diminishing sum of surplus value, with its redistribution in favour of the major capitalist groups. The huge quantity of accumulated paper values are tokens, the realization of which lies wholly in the future and depends, on the one hand, on the conditions of capitalist reproduction and, on the other hand, on the very existence of the capitalist system. Clearly, the huge flood of bits of paper in various forms may become totally incommensurate with the real labour process, and in the conditions of a *capitalist* structure, this will be one of the indications of its collapse. Thus, negative expanded reproduction runs parallel to the accumulation of paper values.

From what has been said so far, the futility of 'expenditure' and the unfavourable appraisal of the destructive aspect of the process does not necessarily follow from the *capitalist* standpoint. Any capitalist crisis is a temporary destruction of the productive forces, but from the point of view of the capitalist system it must be evaluated by looking beyond the limits of a *few* production cycles, for in the final analysis a crisis extends the limits for subsequent development of the system. And the same thing applies to war. Let us suppose that the world war had ended in its second year, with the victory of one of the coalitions. Doubtless, in such a situation, after a period of destruction, the capitalist system would have had a good chance of putting itself right; having healed its 'wounds', i.e. having renewed the parts of constant capital which had been demolished and destroyed, the capitalist mode of production would have had the opportunity for further growth and on a higher and more centralized form than before. Hence, *what, from the point of view of direct military and para-military production cycles, seemed to be a pure loss, from the point of view of the general movement of the capitalist system on a large historical scale could prove to be a temporary reduction of the productive forces, which would be the cost of purchasing their further, and more powerful, growth.* In other words, we would be faced with a crisis – although unprecedented in its size and form – but certainly not with the *collapse* of the capitalist system, which would continue to develop, after a temporary hitch, in more organizationally perfected forms.

The question of *crisis* or *collapse* depends on the actual nature of the shock to the capitalist system, on its intensity and duration. Theoretically, it is clear that the process of expanded negative reproduction can carry on regardless only to a certain point, beyond which the decay and disintegration of the whole organism sets it. Let us proceed to analyse this question.

The process of reproduction is not only a process of reproducing the material elements of production, but also one which reproduces the very *relations* of production.[13] Expanded reproduction means expanded reproduction of existing relations of production; their scope and extent becomes greater; the existing mode of production is 'spread' with the internal reorganization of its component parts. The reproduction of the capitalist relations of production is a reproduction of their substance, in that the relationship between capital and wage labour is permanently maintained and expanded, but *within* this relationship the components of the productive structure are continuously changing. It is enough merely to point to the growth of the so-called 'new middle class'.

What takes place under expanded negative reproduction? To answer this question, we must dwell at some length on the question of the structure of society *as a whole*.

First of all, what are these 'relations of production' which we are discussing? Marx defined them as the relations between *people*, in the process of social labour and the distribution of the products of this labour. In concrete terms, in a capitalist society, this is where the relations between capitalists, experts, technicians, engineers, skilled and unskilled workers, merchants, bankers, usurers, etc. come in, and the relations between these elements are taken in their existing concatenations. Hence, the category of the relations of production is a universal one, applying to the social structure. Relations of a socio-class nature come in here (the relation of worker and capitalist), as do those of a different type (e.g. the relations between enterprises, the relations of collaboration, i.e. so-called simple co-operation and so on).[14] In connection with this, it should be noted that the relations of production are not something *distinct* from the *technical* organization of labour, in so far as we are talking about the relations within the direct labour process. In reality, the two are combined. A factory is not only a technical category but also an economic one,[15] for it is a complex of socio-labour relations of production. The factory hierarchy, under the command of capital, was cited by Marx as the model of capitalist relations of production. The *technical* elements (the labour power of the engineer, the manager, mechanic, craftsman, and unskilled worker) are at the same time elements of the *economic* organization and so long as they are assigned to a fixed social stratum they will have socio-class characteristics. And no wonder, after all, the classes primarily represent groups of people united by common conditions and a common role in the production process, with all its ensuing consequences for the process of distribution. The capitalist hierarchy in *production* is accompanied by a capitalist hierarchy in *distribution*; these are two sides of the same coin, inextricably linked and fused together.

The relations of production are the relations between people as components of a certain system. But it would be a gross simplification to equate a specific model of relations with these components. Society is not the *sum* of its components, nor is it the arithmetical sum of its components plus the relationships between them. For the social nexus cannot be set alongside the component parts. The physical distribution of people in the technical labour process and their functional role coalesce and congeal within the human components. In this way the social relationships are transformed and even become embodied in the internal structure of the components themselves, for the model of the social nexus lives in people's minds.

Thus, a particular social structure and a particular mode of production represents a specific model of relations; at the same time this model also creates its very components.

It is the relations of production which determine everything else. It is not hard to see why. If the relations of production were embodied in one model of the nexus, but the other relations (e.g. the state organization) were constructed according to a different model, then the system as a whole would be utterly unstable. Capitalist relations of production are inconceivable under the political rule of the working class, and socialist relations in production would be unthinkable under the political rule of capital. Consequently, every model of a society must inevitably be distinguished for the *monism* of its structure, which is the fundamental for the existence of any social system.

Capitalist society is particularly notable for this monism. The 'constitution' of the factory, the regiment and the government office is constructed to the *one* principle and the hierarchical model of the relations of production is expressed in an identical hierarchy of state power, the army, etc. At the top is the owning class, at the very bottom the class of the have-nots, and in the middle is the whole gradation of intermediate groups. The capitalist and the factory manager, the general and the minister or chief official-bureaucrat are all people of roughly the same class and the nature of their functions is similar, despite the difference in their spheres of activity. These functions have been assigned to them, and hence in addition to their technical character thay also have a clearly expressed *class* character. The engineer, officer and middle-grade official are, again, essentially people of the same class and their functions are of the same kind. The minor employee (the messenger, commissionaire, janitor), the worker and the soldier likewise occupy a similar position and the hierarchical class system establishes itself as a universal principle.

Capitalism is an antagonistic, contradictory system, but the class antagonism, which splits society into two fundamental classes is all-pervasive. Hence, the structure of capitalism is monistic antagonism, or antagonistic monism.

We have taken society as a system of component elements *in natura*. We must now follow this approach through consistently, for along with the reproduction approach it is a *categorical imperative* for any 'critical' epoch and, therefore, for any period of the decay of capitalism too. In 'normal' times, i.e. when conditions of mobile equilibrium prevail, it is possible to stay at the level of a fetishistic expression of social relations, since the times are stable and presuppose certain very real, *material* and socio-labour processes as their foundation. Monetary relations and categories of value, etc. are the universal categories of a capitalist economy and in 'normal' times we can conduct an analysis within these categories, since for 'normal' times, they are the norm: the law of value is the basic condition for the anarchic productive structure and the *conditio sine qua non* for the mobile equilibrium of the capitalist system.

It is quite different when the production system finds itself in 'abnormal' conditions. This means that conditions of mobile equilibrium do *not* obtain and, consequently, in methodological terms, it is totally inappropriate to conduct an analysis of value relations and categories of relations which are made a fetish of in general. On the contrary, the need here is to consider the natural form of things and of labour power, to keep an account in these units and to examine *society itself* as an organization of component elements in their natural and material character.[16]

Rudolf Goldscheid understood this truth perfectly, when he said

Generally speaking, the present war must first and foremost school us to one thing: *to more profound natural-economic thinking.* . . . Nearly all economic questions seem insoluble if they are considered exclusively from the monetary economic point of view, and *vice versa*, appear relatively simple from the natural economic point of view.[17]

The foregoing makes it clear why this is so: capitalist society has jumped out of its grooves and the categories of equilibrium cannot be commensurate with a 'critical' epoch.

So, the general question is now formulated thus: what happens to a social system in its natural form, a form of related natural components, in *conditions of expanded negative reproduction*?

In the formulae for labour value, we have the following series, $c+v+s$; $c+v+(s-x)$; $c+v$; $c+(v-x)$; $(c-y)+(v-nx)$ etc.; at the same time, value becomes incommensurate with price. Clearly, from the viewpoint of the capitalist system, the situation is not dangerous whilst the expansion of negative reproduction takes place at the expense of *s*. Beyond that point begins the 'corrosion' of fixed capital on the one hand and, on the other hand, under-consumption by the working class leads to instability in the functioning of labour power and its capacity in its *capital-generating* role, i.e. we have the destruction of the reproduction of labour power. This process is manifested in two ways, first, in pushing labour power out of the production process, and second, in lowering real wages, in under-production of the energy which generates labour power, de-skilling it, and, finally, severing the *relationship* between the lowest and highest components of the technical and productive hierarchy. The 'lowest' screws of the capitalist machine, if they do not receive sufficient 'lubricating oil', will come undone. The two main forms which this severance of relations take are:
1 their decay and *demoralization* (for example, absenteeism, a decline in labour discipline and, with office workers, inaccuracy, bribery, the violation of commercial customs and standards, etc.);
2 their *revolutionary* severance (mass refusal to work on the part of the workers, strikes, and all sorts of organized disobedience to the capitalist class).

This process of disintegration in capitalist relations can be observed at a certain level of expanded negative reproduction and, once begun, it takes hold in *all spheres* of the capitalist system. The capitalist-induced psychological habits of obedience to those in power, which had built up in the minds of the lowest elements, vanishes and their capitalist function becomes impossible. On the other hand, amongst the highest human elements of the system, where technical function coincides with class interests and the most important, fundamental class interest coincides with a stake in the preservation of the existing production system, the mentality [psychological nexus] of the struggle for its preservation is reinforced even further. The latent class struggle, which undermines the relations of production in a period of demoralization, breaks through to the surface as open revolutionary struggle in the period when the relations of the capitalist apparatus are violently *severed*. What takes place in production, *mutatis mutandis*, also occurs in the army and in the administrative state apparatus.

We have already seen that the process of collapse is absolutely inevitable once expanded negative reproduction has devoured the social surplus value(s). A theoretical analysis cannot establish with absolute accuracy exactly when and at which concrete, quantifiable figure characteristic of this process, the period of collapse will set in. This is a question of fact, not theory. The actual economic situation in Europe in 1918–20 clearly shows that this period of collapse has set in and that the *old* system of relations of production shows no signs of revival. Quite the reverse, the concrete facts all indicate that the elements of decomposition and the revolutionary severance of relations are progressing with every month that passes. In theory this is quite understandable, if you think about it. After all, a capitalist society, split into classes, can only exist when the mentality of civil peace has, so to speak, popular appeal, i.e. only when, and for as long as, the working class as a whole, the vital productive force of capitalist society, tacitly agrees to perform a *capitalist* function. Once this premise disappears, the continued existence of capitalist society becomes impossible.

Marxist revolutionary thought has firmly established that (in the political sphere) the transition of power from the bourgeoisie to the proletariat, a transition which is to be understood as a definite historical process, is manifested in the collapse of the old state machine, which breaks down into its component elements. The state is by no means an object which passes through the hands of the different classes, by inheritance, in accordance with venerable standards of bourgeois family law. 'The conquest of state power by the proletariat' is the *destruction* of the bourgeois system and the organization of a *new* state system, where the component elements of the old, disintegrated model of relations are in part destroyed and in part taken up into new concatenations, in a new model of relations.[18] That was the theory of Marx and Engels. The vast majority of quasi-socialist theorists, however, had and still do have a singularly primitive concept of 'the conquest of power': just change the 'leadership', 'the government' and the 'whole apparatus' is captured. Marx's revolutionary theory has now been proved in this sphere of relations and not only by abstract reasoning; it has been proved *empirically*.

The process of transforming the relations of production is by no means as easy as that. Here the notions which prevailed in the realm of the theory of political upheavals have turned out to be unusually tenacious. Typical in this respect is Hilferding's dissertation[19] on the fact that the seizure of the six banks ('the leadership') by the proletariat will give the latter command over the whole of industry, 'the whole apparatus'. It has been proven empirically that nothing of the kind occurs, for in reality the seizure of the banks only undermines the commanding power of capital. Why? The question is simply solved. Because the banks 'controlled' industry on the basis of specific credit and monetary relations. The model of this relationship was a model of credit relations, which just *caves in* on the seizure of the banks by the proletariat. After all we have said it is not hard, in theory, to understand the reasons for the collapse of the various sorts of hierarchical relations which arise in a capitalist society in conditions of expanded negative reproduction.

The process of decomposition and the subsequent revolutionary severance of capitalist relations is best exemplified by the army. The imperialist army is demoralized because – not to put too fine a point on it – 'discipline degenerates amongst the soldiers', i.e. the lowest link in the hierarchy can no longer serve as links in *this* particular hierarchy. The revolutionary severance of relations ensues with the mass, more or less, organized *disorganization* of the whole apparatus, which is the essential precondition for the victory of the new class. This disorganization also entails the collapse of the existing system. Thus, temporary 'anarchy' is objectively a completely unavoidable stage in the revolutionary process, which is expressed in the collapse of the old apparatus.

Roughly the same thing happens, too, with the technical and productive apparatus of a capitalist society. We saw that the relations of production are also technical relations and that the social hierarchy is also a technical one. Hence, it is absolutely clear that the decomposition and revolutionary severance of the social links of the system, which is the indicator of collapse, is the disintegration of the 'technical' apparatus of society, in so far as we mean the human technical organization of that society.

And, therefore, it is clear that to 'capture' the old economic apparatuses as a whole is impossible. Anarchy in production, or in Professor Grinevetsky's words, 'the revolutionary disintegration of industry',[20] is an historically inevitable stage, which no amount of lamentation can prevent. Certainly, from an absolute point of view, it would be an extraordinarily good thing if the revolution and collapse of the old relations of production were not accompanied by the disintegration of the technical and productive relations, but a sober assessment of the actual process, scientific analysis of them, shows us that the period of disintegration is historically inevitable and historically necessary.

The disintegration of the human technical hierarchy, which sets in at a certain stage of the process of expanded negative reproduction, has, in its turn, a profound effect on the state of the productive forces. They are closely bound up with the relations of production in a certain system of organized social labour. Hence, the disintegration of the 'apparatus' must inevitably be accompanied by a subsequent reduction in the productive forces. In this way, the process of expanded negative reproduction is greatly speeded up.

From the above analysis, it follows that any rebirth of industry (based upon disintegrating, capitalist relations), which is the dream of the *utopists* of capitalism, is impossible. The *only* way out lies in the fact that the lowest links of the system, the basic productive forces of capitalist society, the working class, will occupy the ruling position in the organization of social labour. Therefore, the construction of communism is the precondition for social rebirth.[21]

In theory, of course, this has not yet been proved by the realization of communism. The question of its preconditions and the probability of realizing it is one which is not logically related to the question of the collapse of capitalism. In theory, further decay is conceivable with the death of civilization and a return to the primitive forms of medieval semi-natural economy; in short, the picture which Anatole France draws at the end of his book *The*

Island of Penguins. For the time being, we shall leave the question to one side, in order to investigate it later. At present, however, we can assert that the restoration of the *old* capitalist system is impossible. The components of the technical and productive apparatus (the human elements) must be taken up in a *new* concatenation and united in a new type of relationship, for the development of society to be possible. Thus, *mankind is faced with a dilemma*: 'the death of civilization or communism', and there is no other alternative.

Assuming that after a number of productive cycles, the productive forces start to increase, one fundamental precondition is essential: the growth of socialist relations of production (advancing towards communism). In this case, the 'cost' of revolution (both the interruption in the labour process and the direct expenditure of social energy in the process of civil war) will be the price at which human society buys itself the opportunity of further growth.

The communist revolution of the proletariat, like every other revolution, is accompanied by a *reduction* in the productive forces (civil war), more especially when it is on the gigantic scale of modern class wars, where the bourgeoisie and the proletariat are organized into a state power. (Economically, and from the point of view of the next production cycle, the revolution has a purely negative value.) However, as we have already seen from the example of crises and capitalist wars, any judgment based on such a viewpoint is a limited one: it is necessary to elucidate the role of this particular phenomenon by starting from the *subsequent* cycles of reproduction on their *broad historical scale*. Then the cost of revolution and the civil war will be seen as a temporary reduction of the productive forces, which nevertheless laid the foundation for their massive growth, after the relations of production have been reconstructed on a new footing.[22]

The reconstruction of the relations of production presupposes the 'power of the proletariat', its 'Kommand', in the state machine, in the army as a part of that machine, and in production.

In the process of the struggle for power and in the period of the civil war, during the period of the dictatorship of the proletariat, the curve of the productive forces continues to fall, whilst there is a simultaneous growth in organizational forms. This growth of organizational forms encounters resistance (primarily sabotage) by the 'officers' of industry, i.e. the technical intelligentsia, which does not *wish* to be in a *different* hierarchical system from the one obtaining before. But this resistance is far less dangerous to the new, growing system than was the resistance of the working class to the system of capitalist relations. From the point of view of preserving and developing human society, therefore, socialist relations of production represent the only way out, since they *alone* can create the conditions for a relatively mobile equilibrium in the socio-productive system.

Chapter 4
The General Preconditions for the Building of Communism

In the preceding chapter, we saw how naïve is the concept of a transition of 'the old apparatus' as a whole, directly on to new tracks. An analysis of that part of the transition period which can be defined as the collapse of the capitalist system, brought us to the proposition that the hierarchical, technical and productive system, which is at once an expression of socio-class relations and the relations of production, inevitably disintegrates into its constituent elements. However brief (historically speaking) this intermediate moment of industrial anarchy may prove to be, nevertheless it is a necessary moment in the general chain of events. However, it must be noted here that not *all* the socio-technical links disintegrate, but only those of a hierarchical type. During the decay of the capitalist system and its revolutionary collapse, the links are severed between the working class on the one hand and the technical intelligentsia, the bureaucracy and the bourgeoisie on the other. But the relations of production which express the bonds between worker and worker, engineer and engineer, bourgeois and bourgeois are not severed. Therefore, the general demarcation of the social strata and the break-up of the human, organizational and technical apparatus take place primarily along these lines. Hence, by and large, the nexus *within* the proletariat is not severed and it is this bond which is the basic feature, socialized in the heart of [and by] capitalism.[1]

The new society cannot suddenly appear like a *deus ex machina*. Its component elements develop within the old society and since the issue here is one of economic phenomena, i.e. it touches on the questions of economic structures and relations of production, the elements of the new society must be sought in the relations of production of the old. The question must be put thus: which aspect of the relations of production in a capitalist society can form the basis of the new production structure?

Clearly, the solution to this problem will also apply to the problems of the so-called 'maturity' of capitalist society for its transition through the phase of the dictatorship of the proletariat to a communist society. In the past the question used to be formulated in very general and somewhat primitive terms: the basic criterion of 'maturity', with regard to the 'objective' pre-conditions for the communist social structure, was considered to be the degree of concentration and centralization of capital, the existence of a certain aggregate 'apparatus', the sum total of the relations of production, tightened into one knot by capitalist development. However, such a statement of the issue, as is evident from the preceding analysis, is inadequate. For it is just this centralized apparatus which disintegrates in the process of revolution and, consequently, it cannot serve *in toto* as the basis of the new society.[2]

In the well-known chapter 32 of volume I of *Capital* ('The Historical Tendency of Capitalist Accumulation'), Marx puts forward two basic features: the centralization of the means of production and the socialization of labour, which flourished along with the capitalist mode of production and within it.[3] It is these two features which form the basis of the new mode of production, which develops in the midst of the old.

Let us examine them both. They are part of the 'apparatus' and part of the new organization. Generally speaking, any social system represents an organization of things and people, where 'things' here are not simply objects in the world of nature, but have their own distinctive social existence. A machine is not a machine outside of human society. It becomes a machine only within the system of social labour. From this point of view, society as a system is simultaneously a 'personal and a physical apparatus'.[4]

The physical apparatus is the material and technical foundations of society. It does not enter into the concept of the relations of production, but is related to the productive forces. And in the process of the revolutionary severance of productive relations, this apparatus may come through relatively unscathed. Its disintegration is by no means inevitable. Of course, machines, equipment, factory buildings and so on are damaged in a time of social upheaval, but the fundamental devastation takes place elsewhere. In so far as the destruction of the physical apparatus does take place, it is chiefly as a consequence of the disintegration of the *human* apparatus and as a break in the continuity of the labour process. Hence, the problem lies in the analysis of the second feature, namely, in socialized labour. The human 'apparatus' which embraces the aggregate labour relations, including those social strata which we spoke about earlier, but its *basic* form, the typical and decisive element, is the concentration of the proletariat. The co-operative form of labour, which Marx talks about, is embodied in this decisive feature, the specific relations between workers. It is here that the centre of gravity of the new society lies.

The aggregate labour power of society – a pure capitalist society, the proletariat – is one of the two components of the concept of the productive forces (for the productive forces are merely the sum total of the available means of production and labour power); and labour power, as the old economists repeatedly stressed, is the most important productive force. On the other hand, the relationship between the workers is a fundamental part of the human labour apparatus. So it is here that one ought to look for the basic elements of the new productive structure.

This was Marx's own view of the matter, when he saw in the working class – a class 'disciplined, united and organised by the very mechanism of the capitalist production process' – the *framework* of the future relations of production and at the same time the force which realizes these relations.[5]

This thesis is extremely important. 'The ripening' of communist relations of production within the confines of a capitalist society is that system of collaboration which is embodied in the relations of production between workers, and which at the same time unites the human atoms into a revolutionary class, the proletariat.

The criterion of 'maturity' therefore turns out to be precisely this feature which is, of course, a function of the development of the productive forces, but which is highlighted by social and organizational technology. From this social and organizational viewpoint, the 'maturity' of capitalist society is quite obvious and discourses on this theme which 'refute' that fact are metaphysical nonsense on the part of the apologists of capitalism. The existence of a planned organization within capitalist countries torn by capitalist competition; the existence, in a certain period, of a system of *state capitalism*, is empirical proof of the 'possibility' of building communism. Now, let us digress for a moment from the concrete historical carapace of the production process and look at it solely from the viewpoint of its inherent, abstract, production logic. There can be two, and *only* two eventualities here; either the socialization of labour permits the technical introduction of planned organization into a concrete social structure of whatever type or the process of the socialization of labour is so weak and labour so fragmented (zersplittert, as Marx put it) that the rationalization of the socio-labour process is *technically* quite impossible. In the first instance 'maturity' is present, in the second it is absent. This formulation of the question is *generally* applicable to *any* version of conscious and formal socialization. And it follows from this, that if capitalism has 'matured' enough for *state* capitalism, then it has also 'matured' for the epoch of the building of communism.[6]

The specific problem for the building of communism lies not in the fact that there is no framework of social labour, but in the *new* combination of social strata which have been torn apart and primarily in the inclusion in the new system of the *technical intelligentsia*. But this is a different subject, which we shall examine later.

The gigantic upheaval of the entire capitalist system, which we are evaluating as its collapse, is used by a number of learned and unlearned sycophants of quasi-Marxist tendencies as an argument against socialism.[7] This view is logically based on a complete lack of understanding of the *dialectic* process, which develops through contradictions. The world war and the start of the revolutionary era are a manifestation of precisely that objective 'maturity', which is under discussion. For this conflict of great intensity was the consequence of wide-spread antagonism which continually reproduced and developed within the bosom of the capitalist system. Its tremendous force is a pretty accurate index of the degree of capitalist development and a tragic expression of the sheer incompatibility of further growth of the productive forces in the integument of the capitalist relations of production. This is the same collapse (Zusammenbruch) which was repeatedly forecast by the authors of scientific communism. They proved to be right: the notion of a transition to socialism without a collapse, without a disturbance of the social equilibrium and without a bloody struggle is a pitiful and reformist illusion.[8]

Once the disintegration of the capitalist relations of production is really under way, and once the impossibility of restoring them has been theoretically proven, then the question arises of a solution to the dilemma: the death of civilization or socialism. Basically this question was settled in the foregoing analysis. Indeed, we saw that the epoch of the breaking up of the productive, technical and social strata tends to preserve the unity of the proletariat, which *above all* embodies the material basis of future society. This decisive and fundamental element only partly disintegrates in the course of the revolution. Indeed, it unites, re-educates and organizes itself in an extraordinary way. Empirical proof of this is provided by the Russian revolution, with its relatively weak proletariat, which nevertheless proved to be in truth an inexhaustible reservoir of organized energy.

'The mathematical probability' of socialism is under such conditions transformed into a 'practical certainty'.

But one must completely abandon the idea that the indispensable condition for the maintenance and development of the new system – the progress of the productive forces – a condition which is subjectively the class problem of the proletariat – will begin to take effect as soon as the revolution begins. Socialism has to be built. Available materials and human resources are only the *starting* point for a development which embraces a whole enormous *epoch*.

During the epoch of the disintegration of capitalism, as we saw in the previous chapter, capitalism cannot possibly be saved, because the basic productive force of society, the working class, refuses to fulfil its capitalist and capital-generating function. The basic precondition for the building of socialism is the transformation of this capital-generating function into a *social–labour* function. This is possible only when the proletariat is in control, i.e. under its dictatorship.[9] Only with the transformation of the proletariat from the exploited class into the ruling class does the restoration of the labour process, i.e. social reproduction, become possible. Within this framework the problem facing the proletariat are, by and large, formally, i.e. independent of the *social* content of the process, the same as those facing the bourgeoisie under expanded negative reproduction: the economical use of all resources, their planned utilization and the maximum possible centralization. The exhaustion which was a result of the war and the break in the continuity of the production process during the period of disintegration demands from the viewpoint of social and organizational technology just this transition to socialist relations of production.

One has only to raise the question of how a system of perhaps only relative equilibrium is possible or, rather, how the creation of *conditions* for movement towards such an equilibrium is possible, to understand the categorical imperative for a centralized and formally socialized economy. We saw above that even within the confines of capitalism the curtailment of the productive resources was one of the most important conditions acting as a spur towards a planned, regulated and organized economy. This is where the internal economic logic comes in and it certainly does not disappear but on the contrary makes itself felt even more strongly under the non-capitalist structure of relations of production. The *labour* process cannot continue under the rule of the bourgeoisie. Large-scale production cannot fail to be expropriated and nationalized under the rule of the proletariat. Finally, economic exhaustion is an even stronger incentive to methods of rationalizing the socio-economic process.[10] The aggregate of these conditions demands one solution and one only to the problem: the transformation of capitalism into socialism via the dictatorship of the working class.

We have seen that, what for society as a whole represents the condition for its continued existence, for the proletariat represents an organizational problem to which it must find a practical solution. During this period the proletariat has to *actively build* socialism and at the same time re-educate itself in the process of this construction. This problem can only be solved by specific methods, namely those of organizational work, and these methods have already been prepared by capitalist development.

When the bourgeoisie was overthrowing the feudal lords and the capitalist mode of production – based in its early days on the private economic cell – was blazing itself a trail, the economic process took place almost completely spontaneously; for there was no organized collective, no class subject at work, only scattered, though highly active, 'individuals'. It is small wonder that the slogan of the time was that of *laissez-faire, laissez-passer*. They did not build capitalism, but it was built. The proletariat, as an organized collective subject, is building socialism as an organized system. If the creation of capitalism was spontaneous, the building of communism is to a marked degree a conscious, i.e. organized, process. For it is created by a class which grew up in the midst of capitalism to become that same 'revolutionare Assoziation' of which Marx spoke.

The epoch of communist construction will, therefore, inevitably be an epoch of planned and organized work. The proletariat will solve the social and technical problem of building a new society – a problem which it consciously sets itself and resolves with deliberation. Along with the collapse of capitalism, commodity fetishism and its semi-mystic categories also break down.[11]

> The socialist revolution will promote socialist methods (by no means socialism at a stroke) as a more perfect way (than state capitalism) of averting the collapse of society, preserving the economic base and even expanding it. State capitalism saved the *capitalist* . . . state by active and conscious intervention in the relations of production. Socialist methods will be a continuation of this active process of organisation but only for the sake of saving and developing a *free* society. At first they will only provide a new *economy* of the means of production and consumption which will immediately *save* society; later, they will begin the *restoration* of the productive forces; then they will bring them to a new and higher prosperity. And on the way, stone by stone, and link by link, socialism will be built, both as large-scale, high-powered production and as a system of distinct, simple and free social relations.[12]

What are the phases of the revolutionary process? This question must be answered, for failure to understand the way the various phases change according to established laws accounts for a whole series of ridiculous notions. Herman Beck 'refutes' Marx by asserting that 'social catastrophes (revolutions) do not necessarily have economic causes', as the example of 'anti-militaristic' revolutions has proved, for here 'the change in the relations of power

(Machtverschiebung) which should have come at the end of the chain of events comes at its very beginning'.[13] However, it is not difficult to see that the revolutionary process does not conform to fundamental laws. The historical *prius* is the conflict between the productive forces and the relations of production. This conflict has its class subject expression in 'the rebellion of the proletariat', that is to say, to a certain extent it determines the class will. The stimulus comes from the *economic* sphere, or rather, from the clash between the productive forces and the economic carapace. Then a catastrophically rapid reciprocal influence sets in, from the ideological sphere to the productive forces, and during this process the conditions of equilibrium are created on a *new* basis. This dialectical process passes through the following phases:

1 *The ideological revolution.* Economic conditions demolish the ideology of civil peace. The working class becomes aware of itself as the class which is bound to become master. The ideological system of 'workers' imperialism' is shattered. In its place, we get the ideology of communist revolution, the 'workers' plan' of future action.

2 *The political revolution.* The ideological revolution is converted into action, in civil war and the struggle for political power. Here the political apparatus of the bourgeoisie is destroyed, the whole huge organization of the state machine. It is replaced by a new system, that of the dictatorship of the proletariat, the Soviet Republic.

3 *The economic revolution.* The dictatorship of the proletariat, which is the concentrated power of the working class organized as a state power, acts as a powerful lever of economic upheaval. The capitalist relations of production are smashed. The old economic structure ceases to exist. Surviving links are forcibly cut ('the expropriators are expropriated'). The component elements of the old system are taken up into a new combination and in the long and tortuous process a new model of relations of production emerges. The foundations of socialist society are laid.

4 *The technical revolution.* The relative equilibrium, achieved by the structural reorganization of society, ensures that the productive forces can function properly although initially only on a restricted basis. The next stage is the revolution in technical methods, i.e. the growth of the productive forces, the alteration and speedy improvement of social, rationalized technology.[14]

It stands to reason that when we talk about the stages of revolutionary development it is a question of the centre of gravity of each historical stage, its prevailing characteristics, and the *typical* features of a particular phase. Within these limits, the conformity to laws, which had been inferred deductively, was confirmed in action for the first time in the experience of the Russian proletarian revolution. Failure to understand this change of phase leads to truly monstrous and theoretically vulgar conclusions.[15]

We must now examine the general principles of building communism. It is quite clear that the next epoch must be that of the dictatorship of the proletariat, which will bear a *formal* resemblance to the epoch of the dictatorship of the bourgeoisie, i.e. it will be state capitalism *in reverse, its own dialectical transformation into its own antithesis.*

Let us first examine the very general conditions of equilibrium on the new basis. There is a very tattered physical and technical framework (the centralized means of production, which were partly destroyed by the process of expanded negative reproduction during the imperialist and subsequent civil war, but were also thrown into confusion by the force of the collapse of the human, technical apparatus) but this concerns the productive forces. In the sphere of the relations of production there are the disintegrated links and layers of the technical and social hierarchy. The period of collapse, as we have seen, does not mean that the component elements are destroyed but only that the relations between them are destroyed. The elements as such do partly perish (from the civil war, exhaustion, premature wearing-out, malnutrition, etc.), but this is not the main feature of the period of collapse.

In the same way it can be said that internal group relations are more or less preserved intact (between workers, in the relationships within the class: between the engineers, the technicians, i.e. the members of the 'new middle class', etc.). As we have already shown, to a certain extent these relations actually grow and consolidate amongst the proletariat which, as a class, educates, unites and organizes itself during this period with extraordinary intensity and speed. Hence, the proletariat, as the aggregate of the relations of production, constitute the framework of the whole edifice. But the problem of social and production organization lies in combining the old elements anew. In which way exactly?

There is no problem in seeing that the apex of capitalist society, which was virtually above production and whose production position was expressed in the fact that it was outside production (it includes every possible type of rentier and those who clip share coupons),[16] proves to be unfit for the work of construction; either it perishes or it must be absorbed by the other groups. Ex-bourgeois managers and the technical intelligentsia below are patently essential to the construction period, for they are the social core of organizational and technical-cum-scientific experience. It is quite obvious that both these categories must be accommodated differently. How, and under what conditions is this possible?

Let us first remark that structurally this is the decisive, one could almost say, the most fundamental question. And it is no accident that in the mature period of socialist revolution the problem of 'specialists' plays such an important part. We know that the social relations of the previous model live on in the form of an ideological and psychological deposit in the minds of people of this category. 'Healthy capitalism' looms before them with the obstinacy of an *idée fixe*.

Consequently, the prerequisite for the very possibility of a new social and productive combination must be the disintegration of the relations of the previous model in the minds of this technical intelligentsia.

This process of 'decay' is extremely agonizing and painful. It is accompanied by the partial destruction of the technical intelligentsia which wages a bitter struggle on behalf of the former model of disintegrated and forcibly severed relations. It resists the new model of a combination of social and productive strata, since the dominant position here is occupied by the proletariat. The functional, *technical* role of the intelligentsia had merged with its monopolistic position as a social class group, a position which in the long run could only be monopolistic under the rule of capital. Therefore, resistance by this stratum is inevitable and overcoming this resistance is a fundamental and inherent problem of the construction phase of the revolution. Given the decisive significance of the relations of production within the working class – a class which is constantly re-educating itself and *continuing* the process of the 'Bildung der revolutionaren Assoziation', all the work is shouldered by the working class and its own proletarian intelligentsia, educated in the course of the revolutionary struggle. The new concatenation, i.e. the joint subordination of the technical intelligentsia to the proletariat, is inevitably achieved by the use of force on the part of the proletariat in cases of sabotage by the intelligentsia. The relative stability of the system is achieved only in proportion to the 'decay' in the minds of this social category of the accumulated relations of the model and the slow assimilation of new relations and the model of relations.

What is needed at this point is a theoretical analysis of the aggregate of the new relations of production which are taking shape. For a question of cardinal importance arises here: *how is a different concatenation of human technical and productive elements at all possible, when the very logic of the production process demands an absolutely fixed model of relations?* After all, an engineer or a technician cannot help giving orders to the workers and, consequently, he must stand *over* them. Likewise, a former officer in the Red Army cannot help standing above the army's rank and file. In both cases there is an inner, purely technical and practical logic which must be maintained under whatever system. How is this contradiction resolved?

Here we must direct our attention to a number of circumstances. First of all, under the state power of the proletariat and the proletarian nationalization of production, the process of creation of surplus value as a specific category of bourgeois society disappears. At the same time as it fulfilled its organizational functions in the production process, the technical intelligentsia was *socially* a transmission mechanism for squeezing out surplus value as a specific capitalist category of income. This was bound to be so, since the process of capitalist production is also, and above all, a process of producing surplus value. The technical intelligentsia was, therefore, a tool in the hands of the bourgeoisie and fulfilled its general aims. Its *place* in the social labour hierarchy coincided with its function as an instrument for the squeezing out of surplus value. With the dialectical transformation of the bourgeois dictatorship into the dictatorship of the proletariat, the technical function of the intelligentsia is transformed from a capitalist into a social labour function and the creation of surplus value is converted into the creation (under conditions of expanded reproduction) of surplus product required for the expansion of the reproduction fund.

At the same time, the *basic model* of relations changes, although the intelligentsia maintains the same 'middle' position in the hierarchical set-up. For the supreme state-economic power[17] is the concentrated social might of the proletariat. On the one hand, therefore, the technical intelligentsia stands above large sections of the working class, but on the other hand, *subordinated* to its collective will, which is expressed in the state-economic organization of the proletariat. The transformation of the process of creating surplus value into one of planned satisfaction of social needs, is manifest in a regrouping of the relations of production, despite the formal preservation of the same position in the hierarchical production system. However, the general nature of this hierarchy differs in principle, as it is the dialectical antithesis of the capitalist structure,[18] and leads to the abolition of the hierarchy altogether, by destroying its socio-caste character. Secondly, the *relatively* stable co-existence of the ruling proletariat and the technical intelligentsia occurs *after* the latter actually has fallen out of the production process. It returns in strength only in proportion to the decay in its collective mental attitude to the old accumulated relations. Hence, the intelligentsia enters the new social and technical edifice inwardly regenerated according to all the principles of Heralitus the Dark. Its return is not a repetition of what has gone before, but a dialectical process.[19]

In the third place, in so far as a new network of human systems is being created, then as the whole of the foregoing analysis makes clear, such systems must be founded on the working-class organizations which have matured in the lap of capitalism and in the clamour of class struggles: the soviets, the trade unions, the working-class party in power, factory and works' committees and special economic organizations set up after the seizure of power, with a fairly numerous cadre of organizationally and technically skilled workers. This is the *basic* network of the universal 'revolutionare Assoziation', which has now risen from below to the top, but at the same time this is the environment in which the technical intelligentsia *must* function. Previously the technical intelligentsia and the higher bourgeois management constituted the basic fabric of the highest relations of production and of the systems of economic administration (syndicates, cartels, trusts and organs of state capitalist control). Under the dictatorship of the proletariat, the basic fabric will be made up of various combinations of the workers' organizations which have risen from below plus those recently formed.

Finally – in the fourth place – the technical intelligentsia begins to lose its socio-caste character in this system, as ever new strata arise within the proletariat and gradually take their place alongside the old technical intelligentsia.

Thus the equilibrium of society is established anew. The rule of the proletariat, in conjunction with its self-education and self-discipline, ensures the possibility of the labour process, despite colossal objective difficulties. The structural equilibrium is achieved with a new combination of the social and productive human elements and with the subordination of the intelligentsia to the supreme leadership of the proletarian state.

Let us dwell a while on the question of the structure of the economic and the technical administrative apparatus of the proletarian state power. Under the state capitalist relations of production all the organizations of the bourgeoisie (syndicates, trusts, cartels, etc.) are jointly subordinated to the state power and merge with it. With the destruction of the bourgeois dictatorship and the organization of a proletarian one these administrative apparatuses are also destroyed. Trust organizations and the old society's state control bodies and so on disintegrate. As a rule (and we proved it theoretically in the previous chapter), these apparatuses cannot be taken over intact but this does not mean that they did not play their historical role. For a whole complex series of these sometimes highly refined organizations, whose tentacles embraced all socio-economic life, acted as a screw which intensified and hastened the process of centralizing the means of production and marshalling the proletariat. When these apparatuses disintegrate, their physical and technical framework remains and, looking at it in general terms, just as the proletariat first takes over the centralized means of production, i.e. the physical and technical framework of capitalist production, what is manifest chiefly in a system of machinery and, as Marx said, a 'vascular system' of apparatuses, so here the proletariat takes possession not of the human but of the physical part of the old administrative system (the buildings, bureaux, offices, typewriters and just about the entire stock: books for better guidance and, finally, all kinds of physically symbolic devices such as diagrams, models, etc.).[20] Having taken possession of these, along with the other 'centralized means of production', it builds its own apparatus, whose foundations are the *workers' organizations*.

The working class possesses the following organizations: the soviets of workers' deputies which are transformed from instruments in the power struggle into the instruments of power; the party of the communist revolution, the *spiritus rector* of the workers' movement; the trade unions which are transformed from instruments in the fight against the owners into one of the organs controlling production; the co-operatives which are transformed from instruments in the fight against commercial middle-men into one of the organizations of the general state distribution apparatus; factory and works' committees or similar organizations ('Betriebsrate' in Germany and 'workers committees' and shop stewards committees' in England) which, from being organs in the workers' grass-roots struggle against the owners, become auxiliary branches of general production administration.

The network of these organizations plus completely new ones, specially created on the basis of them, constitutes the organizational backbone of the new apparatus.[21]

In the conditions we face at present, there is above all a dialectical change in the functions of the workers' organizations. Clearly, with the *rearrangement* of the relations of supremacy, this must be the case, since once it has taken the state power into its own hands, the working class must inevitably gain strength and come to the fore as the *organizer of production*.[22]

We must now consider the general principle behind the organizational system of the proletarian apparatus, i.e. the relationship between the different types of proletarian organizations. It is clear, what the working class formally needs is the same method as the bourgeoisie used in the epoch of state capitalism. This method of organization consists in the subordination of all the workers' organizations to the most comprehensive organization, i.e. to the state organization of the working class, the *soviet state of the proletariat*. 'Statification' of the trade unions and the virtual statification of all the mass organizations of the proletariat springs from the inherent logic of the transition process. The smallest units of the workers' apparatus must be changed into the vehicles of a general organizational process, systematically directed and led by the collective intelligence of the working class, which is physically embodied in its highest and all-embracing organization, the state apparatus.[23]

Thus the system of state capitalism is dialectically transformed into its own antithesis, the state structure of workers' socialism.

No new structure can be born before there is an objective need for it. The development and collapse of capitalism led society up a blind alley, and brought to a halt the production process which is the very basis of society's existence. The resumption of the production process was possible only under the rule of the proletariat and that is why its dictatorship is an objective necessity. The stability of the new-born society can only be achieved with the maximum unity, contact and joint action of all the organizing forces. And that is why the general form of an all-workers' apparatus, which we have discussed above, is equally necessary. Out of the bloodstained smoke of war, out of the chaos and debris, the destitution and ruin, there rises the edifice of a new harmonious society.

Chapter 5
Town and Country in the Process of Social Transformation

The foundation of every division of labour that is well developed, and brought about by the exchange of commodities is the separation between town and country. It may be said, that the whole economic history of society is summed up in the movement of this antithesis.[1]

It is necessary to bear this Marxist definition in mind during the transition period more than at any other time. For if, during the 'normal' period of capitalist development, i.e. when a relative proportionality between town and country is obtained as regards the distribution of the socio-productive forces necessary to the equilibrium of the entire system – if, during this period, it was possible to examine the production process in its abstract form as a process of the production of value and surplus value, this no longer suffices now.

The *material and natural* viewpoint is of decisive significance, but along with it, the division of social production into various spheres of 'concrete' labour, primarily into industry and agriculture, also assumes exceptional importance. The growing disproportionality between these branches of the economic system was becoming clear before the war; imperialist attempts to find an economic 'supplement' – i.e. an agrarian basis for the industrial countries – are essentially a manifestation of that same contradic-

108

tion between town and country, of which Marx spoke, but on a world scale.[2] The problem of raw materials – the fundamental problem of the present time – and that of foodstuffs are burning issues. All this compels us to single out the question of town and country as one requiring special analytical attention.

First and foremost, we ought to trace the effect that the process of expanded negative reproduction has had on agriculture.

Let us first consider the process in isolation. It stands to reason that essentially the same phenomena will be observed here as we saw in industry. War diverts an enormous number of productive forces; it transfers workers withdrawing them from productive labour; it takes away agricultural equipment; it deprives agriculture of animal labour power, reduces the number of livestock, decreases the supply of fertilizer and cuts down the area of land fit for cultivation. By extracting manpower, which in agriculture plays a relatively far more significant role than in industry (for the organic composition of 'capital' here is lower), it narrows the basis of production and reproduction. This narrowing of the productive basis is expressed in a decline in the amount of produce. This is the overall picture.

In reality, however, the process of agricultural reproduction is not a separate and isolated process of reproduction. It is part of an overall process which presupposes 'an exchange of substance' between town and country. Consequently, as it concerns the reproduction of the means of production, agricultural production is dependent on the conditions of reproduction in industry (for machines, implements of labour, artificial fertilizers, electricity supply, etc.). Expanded negative reproduction in industry exacerbates a parallel process in agriculture, and vice versa, a reduction in the amount of the means of consumption, which are the elements of reproduction of labour power, for its part aggravates the process of expanded negative reproduction in industry. As an indivisible process, expanded negative reproduction is expressed in the ever-decreasing quantity of the total complex of products made (all means of production and means of consumption).

Paradoxically, this reduction in the productive basis is manifested in a rise in the monetary 'profitability' of agriculture.[3] However, the increase in the price of agricultural products is accompanied by a no lesser (and, as a rule, by an even greater) rise in the prices of industrial products. Nevertheless, during the war, agriculture quickly discharged its debts, accumulated capital in monetary form and stockpiled produce. This contradiction, as Professor Lederer quite rightly observes, can be explained by the fact that the rapidly increased prices of industrial products were a function of such a decrease in their real quantity that agriculture was unable to obtain them. Hence, it follows that the production basis of agriculture was maintained better than that of industry and that agriculture, despite the process of expanded negative reproduction, really has a relatively far greater number of products at its disposal than industry. This is a fairly vital distinction, which is bound to have an effect, too, in the period of the disintegration of the capitalist system.

The most vital distinction, however, is in *the economic structure* of this major branch of production. The peculiarity of this structure lies in the extreme diversity of its economic models, which reflects and expresses the relatively feeble extent of the *socialization* of labour. By and large, we can distinguish the following categories here: the large-scale capitalist farm, based on wage labour, the capitalist peasant farm ('Kulak', 'Grossbauer'), which also uses and relies upon wage labour; the 'working' peasant farm which does not exploit wage labour; and finally, the semi-proletarian's allotment. The various combinations of relations between the human components of these models present an extremely heterogeneous picture. Within the framework of the large-scale capitalist farm, we can observe roughly the same production–social hierarchy as exists in industry; the economic constitution of the *latifundium* is basically the same as that of the factory; at the top is the capitalist owner; then the top general manager; under him a staff of qualified intelligentsia (agronomists, accountants, etc.); further down are the 'white-collar workers'; below them the skilled workers (working with agricultural machinery, on railway sidings and in power stations, etc.) and finally the unskilled labourers. The relationship on a Kulak or Grossbauer's farm is different again, for the production hierarchy is usually confined to two categories: owner and worker. The 'working' farm has no hierarchical ranks and the personnel of the semi-proletarian farm form a lower group in the hierarchical scale than any other economic unit – *latifundium*, factory or plant.

In the preceding chapters we saw that the basic factor determining the possibility of an *immediate* rationalization of production is (in any structure – state capitalist or socialist) socialized labour. Clearly, therefore, with regard to agriculture, even the state-capitalist system had to adopt a somewhat different 'organizational form'. It stands to reason that the bourgeoisie's need to include agriculture in the state-capitalist system was simply enormous. For agriculture – especially at a time of upheaval – is the decisive branch of production; one can live without overcoats, electric light-bulbs or books, but one cannot possibly live without bread. The army may be unshod, but it cannot exist on the bread of St Antony. Hence, the factors working towards a state-capitalist organization were present in force, but at the same time the immediate possibility of rationalizing production was actually very remote.

How did capitalism solve the problem? In two ways: first, by *statification* of certain major production units and second, by *direct control* of the production process through the process of circulation.

The relative 'weakness' of the first method is fairly evident from what we have already said. True, some branches of agricultural production (e.g. the state forests) were already under the command of the capitalist state, but it did not have such strong bases as, for example, the trusts in industry. Therefore, the scope for direct, bourgeois nationalization of *production* was relatively small and usually took various forms of 'communalization' and 'municipalization'. The second method, therefore, acquired greater significance: the control of production through control of the process of circulation or the organization of distribution. The state grain monopoly, rationing agricultural produce, compulsory surrender of produce, fixed prices, the organized allocation of industrial products, etc. – all these, in the final analysis, stimulated development towards the statification of production. In that case we see a less advanced model of development, the first stages of an organization process which, as in industry, had its initial impulse in this process of circulation (corners, rings and syndicates).

In this sphere the state-capitalist system could rely on special syndicate-like agricultural combines, primarily the co-operatives. In fact by controlling the progress of circulation the mechanism of agricultural production as a whole was also brought under control, right down to the small individual farm. The system of 'free trade' in agricultural produce was undermined at its roots. True, the specific conditions of agriculture, the high proportion of small and medium-sized commodity-producing farms created tremendous difficulties even here, as was evident from the 'illegal free' market, and the speculative black market (Schleichhandel, as the Germans call it). However, for a while there was a strong system of state-capitalist organization overall and agriculture became part of the total apparatus, of which organized industry formed the major part.[4]

This gives rise to the following proposition: the collapse of the state-capitalist system which starts with the disintegration of the relations of production in industry, also entails the collapse of this system in respect to agriculture.

The decay of the state-capitalist apparatus is here made manifest in the fact that it is constantly being breached by speculative trade in agricultural produce. The revolutionary severance of relations at first increases the *isolation* of town from country. In the epoch of state capitalism, one can distinguish the following kinds of relations between town and country: 1 that of the credit and monetary, finance capitalist type (chiefly through banking institutions); 2 national and local government organizational apparatuses; 3 the very real process of exchange between town and country which takes place partly through the organized apparatuses and partly without their knowledge. Let us now examine what will inevitably happen to relations between town and country with the conquest of power by the proletariat.

With the conquest of power by the proletariat, relations of the credit and monetary finance-capitalist type are severed completely, irrevocably and for ever. With the seizure of the banks, credit relations are broken and there can be no question of a 'renewal of credit', for the entire fundamental system of traditional relations is violated, all 'confidence' is lost and the proletarian state figures in the bourgeois consciousness as a collective bandit. The national and local government apparatuses likewise disintegrate into their constituent elements along with the disintegration of nearly all the state mechanisms of the old model. The apparatus which expressed the hegemony of industry over agriculture and the town over the country (in the capitalist structure) ceases.

Finally, the extent of the *real* process of exchange, which expresses the unity of the 'national economy', is drastically reduced. After our detailed analysis of the disintegration of capitalist industry, it is not hard to see why this happens. The process of expanded negative reproduction during the imperialist war has already undermined the basis of exchange, by reducing to a minimum the number of products the town could put on the market, i.e. the real product equivalent vital to the country. With the collapse of the capitalist production apparatus, the process of production almost comes to a standstill; people live on old stocks which have survived the war and have been inherited by the proletariat. Money, which in 'normal times' represented a value in itself finally reveals itself as an intermediary symbol, without any independent value. Consequently, for people in command of large quantities of agricultural produce, almost every incentive to deliver it to the town disappears. The social economy disintegrates into two autonomous spheres: the famine-stricken town, and the country, which despite the partial destruction of the productive forces, has a fairly considerable quantity of unmarketable 'surplus' produce. The disintegration of the entire socio-production system reaches its climax. This phase in the 'economic history of society' is evinced in the isolation of the two chief subdivisions of social labour – a circumstance which renders the continued existence of society impossible.

But before passing on to analyse the terms of the *new* equilibrium we must first consider the basic forms which the collapse of capitalism assumes *within* the 'countryside' itself.

What is immediately striking in this situation is the fact that, given the relative stability of the country and the existence of a considerable amount of produce, the process of disintegration of relations within agricultural production is bound to proceed much more slowly. Moreover, since there is such a diversity of economic structures, with which large-scale capitalist industry is unacquainted, the very form of the transformation process and all its phases will be different in the countryside to that which we have analysed in the previous chapters.

Let us first take the large-scale capitalist farms. Here the process of severing relations most resembles that which takes place in industry. With some modifications, however. In the first place, it is accomplished more slowly than in the town. This happens because in agriculture, where there is on-the-spot production of the means of consumption, under-consumption by the working class does not have such an immediate effect. The transition to a system of partial payment in kind actually ensures the reproduction of labour power and consequently the incentive to severe relations between the human components of the system is considerably less. Second, the proletariat itself is by no means as 'disciplined' by the mechanism of the capitalist production process. Its personnel (semi-peasant elements), work methods (the seasonal character of labour, much greater physical dispersal of labour, etc.) all this impedes its 'ideological revolution' and the drawing up of a 'workers' revolutionary plan'. These factors, however, only delay the general process of development, they do not negate it. The influence of the town and the organizations of the industrial proletariat provides an external impetus which reinforces an independent process, and ultimately a severance of the relations of production along the same lines as in industry is inevitable.[5]

But the severance of the rural relations of production also takes place in other areas as a result of the specific structural peculiarities of rural economics. We saw above that part of the human mechanism (the semi-proletarian owners of allotments) is involved as the lowest strata in the capitalist hierarchy; the other elements (the middle peasants, the working peasantry) are not only competitors of the large-scale farm in the market but are often objects of exploitation in a covert form of extraordinarily complex and diverse relations (rent, usury, dependence on land banks, etc.). What we have here is a group of low and low-to-middle elements in the labour hierarchy, which has no place in a purely capitalist set-up and does not represent socialized labour, but is, so to speak, an appendage. Nevertheless, its importance is quite considerable, when we examine the social system in its entirety.

The nature of production relations, where the lowest links of the system include a huge quantity of independent farms, also determines the pattern of disintegration of these relations, which is expressed here in a struggle between the farms, i.e. in a struggle between the working peasantry and the semi-proletarians on the one hand, and the major peasants and semi-landowners on the other. The actual composition of the contending elements may be extremely diverse, depending on the significance of the various farming models (for these are extremely fluid categories, with many nuances). Taken by itself, in isolation from the rest of the economic system this severance of relations is also fraught with the prospect of a return to more primitive forms, for the active force here is just this scattered labour of the small owners and not the socialized labour of the proletariat. But in the present historical context, it is a constituent part of the general process of collapse of the capitalist system.[6] This then is the agrarian-peasant revolution and, the less highly developed the capitalist relations are, the greater is its significance. The struggle can be, and usually is, accompanied by tremendous waste of resources and the breaking-up of the physical production base (partially by dividing up large estates, implements, live-stock, etc.),[7] i.e. by a *further* reduction in the productive forces.

Now the question arises as to how a new equilibrium is possible, an equilibrium *within* agriculture itself and also one *between* town and country. It is a decisive question for the fate of mankind, for it is a most important and highly complicated one.[8]

We have already seen that the general model of the *new* equilibrium is bound to be the model which prevailed under state capitalism turned inside out (its dialectical opposite).

Let us first consider the process within agriculture.

The severance of the relationships between the various human elements of the large-scale capitalist farm must give way to the organization of these elements in a new combination. Essentially the problem here is similar to that of industry. However, it is complicated by two factors: first, by the partial destruction of the large-scale capitalist farm as a large-scale farm; and second, by the inevitable struggle for the land on the part of the peasantry. It is clear that the magnitude of concessions fluctuates abruptly according to the ratio of the peasantry and its distribution throughout the various categories. The second factor creates a far greater number of intra-organizational conflicts and the process of self-education of the proletariat takes place more slowly.

As for the equilibrium in the remaining sphere of agricultural production, it tends to establish itself on the basis of an equalizing redistribution as the starting point for development. Clearly, such a situation, taken independently of the development in the towns, would be bound to trigger off a new 'American-style' cycle. This possibility, however, no longer arises with the abolition of a commodity economy in the town and with socialist organization in industry. Hence, the dictatorship of the proletariat is inevitably accompanied either by a hidden, or by a more or less open, struggle between the proletariat's tendency towards organization and the tendency of the peasantry towards commodity anarchy. Now, in what ways can the organizing influence of the proletarian town make itself felt? And how can a new equilibrium *between* town and country be achieved?

It is obvious that only the real process of 'exchanges of substances' between town and country can serve as a firm and stable basis for the influence of the town to be decisive. The resumption of the process of production in industry, the rebirth of industry in its socialist version is, thus, an essential condition for the more or less rapid involvement of the country in the organization process.

But since the rebirth of industry is itself dependent on the flow of vital resources into towns, the absolute necessity for this influx at *any* price is quite clear. This minimal 'equilibrium' can be achieved only, 1 at the expense of part of the resources left in the towns, and 2 by the use of force on the part of the proletarian state. This state coercion (the removal of grain surpluses, tax in kind or some other form) is economically funded: in the first place, directly, since the peasantry itself has an interest in the growth of industry, which supplies it with agricultural machines, implements, artificial fertilizers and electric power, etc; in the second place, indirectly, since the state power of the proletariat is the best means of protection against the restoration of the economic pressure of the large-scale landowner, banker and capitalist state, etc. Consequently, state coercion here is not 'brute force' of the Dühring type, inasmuch as it is a factor in the mainstream of general economic development.[9] Since the industrial proletariat relies on formally socialized large-scale agriculture (statified by the proletariat), it directly organizes the *production* process. The shortage of agricultural equipment may induce some agricultural owners to farm a production combine (agricultural commune, associations and cartels), but for most of the *small* producers, their involvement in the organizational apparatus is primarily made possible through the *sphere of circulation*. Hence, nominally in the same way as under the system of state capitalism.[10] The national and local government (in theory it is impossible to differentiate between the two) organs of distribution and state procurement are the chief apparatus of the new system of equilibrium.

There is a problem here with those peasant organizations which, even in the period of capitalist development, had served to unite scattered producers in just such a process of circulation, i.e. in *agricultural co-operatives*. After all, it became clear from an analysis of the disintegration of the relations of the capitalist system in

agriculture that in this process of disintegration small-scale production remained relatively stable. True, the peasant co-operatives
had a tendency to turn into farming syndicates, by the capitalist,
landowning upper strata. To this extent then the apparatus of the
co-operative system inevitably proved to be damaged. It is therefore clear that some forms of co-operation will inevitably break up
– such is the lot of the credit co-operative system. At the same
time, however, without a doubt the stability of the peasant farm
must also be evident in the relative stability of the peasant co-
operative system. What will become of it? Will it disintegrate as the
syndicate and the trust inevitably do, or not? Before answering this
question it is necessary to analyse more precisely another fundamental problem: the struggle between the proletariat and the
peasantry who are the class vehicles of various agricultural models.
'The fundamental forces and the fundamental forms of social
economy (are) capitalism, small-scale commodity production and
communism. . . . The fundamental forces (are) the bourgeoisie, the
petty bourgeoisie (particularly the peasantry) and the proletariat.'[11]

> The peasant farm continues to exist as small-scale commodity
> production. Here we have an extremely broad base of capitalism
> with very deep and very strong roots. Capitalism is preserved
> on this base and is restored to life again in a very fierce struggle
> with communism. The forms of this struggle – bag-trading
> and speculation directed against state grain procurements and
> other products too – are generally opposed to the state
> distribution of produce.[12]

A fight for or against the commodity market, as a covert struggle
for models of production – such is the economic climate in the
relationship between town and country – a circumstance which
generally arises *after* the seizure of power by the proletariat. There
is a profound difference here from what happens in the town. In
the towns, the main struggle for the economic model comes to an
end with the victory of the proletariat; in the country it only comes
to an end as far as victory over large-scale capitalism is concerned
but at the same time it is resurrected in other forms as a struggle
bewteen the state planning of a proletariat which embodies socialized labour and the commodity anarchy, the speculative licence of
a peasantry which embodies scattered property and the anarchic
element of the market. But since a simple commodity economy is

merely the embryo of a capitalist economy, the struggle between the tendencies described above is essentially a continuation of the struggle between communism and capitalism.

However, there resides two 'souls' within the bosom of the peasant himself and the poorer he is, the greater will be the significance of the proletarian tendency, so the struggle is also complicated by the internal struggle within the peasantry itself.

How is this circumstance reflected in the fate of the peasant co-operative apparatus? Clearly, the case is somewhat different here from that of industry. The co-operative apparatus may atrophy (with the continuing collapse of the exchange relations between town and country), it may be destroyed (with the preponderance of kulaks in the country and the aggravated struggle between them and the proletariat), or it may be absorbed into a mainly socialist organization of distribution and gradually be reconstructed (with a resumption of the real process of product exchange and the decisive *economic* influence of the towns). Hence, in theory a complete disintegration of the apparatus is not necessarily bound to happen. Thus the new equilibrium arises on a prolonged struggle and that is why its establishment is slow and painful. The process will be accelerated as reproduction in industry is restored and as the proletariat sets about the most profound task – the *technical* revolution, which completely alters the conservative forms of the economy and is a powerful incentive to socialization of agricultural production. But this topic belongs to the next chapter.

Chapter 6
The Productive Forces, the Costs of the Revolution and the Technical Revolution

We have already touched upon the question of the productive forces and the costs of the revolution in general in chapter 3. Now we must investigate the question in detail, since everything depends on this appraisal. For, the productive forces of society, their level and their *movement* determine, in the final analysis, a whole complex of social phenomena. The stability of any structural equilibrium, i.e. equilibrium between the various human social groups, the human elements of a social system, rests on a certain equilibrium *between society and the external environment* – an equilibrium whose character is determined by the level attained in the development of the social and material productive forces.

But first let us consider the question: what are the productive forces? In *The Poverty of Philosophy*, Marx wrote:

Thus it is slapping history in the face to want to begin by the the division of labour in general, in order to get subsequently to a specific instrument of production, machinery. Machinery is no more an economic category than a bullock that drags the plough. Machinery is merely a *productive force* (my emphasis N.I.B.). The modern workshop, which depends on the application of machinery, is a social production relation, an *economic* category. (My emphasis N.I.B., i.e. the social relations of production.)[1]

By productive forces, Marx evidently means here the material and personal elements of production and, as a corollary of this, the category of the productive forces is a technical and not an economic one. On the other hand, we find that Marx also gives another definition of the productive forces: in *Capital*, vols I and II, he frequently uses the term 'productive forces' with the same meaning as the expression 'the productivity of social labour'.[2] However, whilst calling the productive forces the productivity of social labour, Marx himself repeatedly points out that labour power is the basic productive force of society.

That may well be, but it is clear that even if one can work with a vague concept in the first stages of an analysis, subsequently the inexactitude of that concept will make itself felt.

First of all, what does the concept mean? When one talks about productive forces one means thereby the extent of man's power over nature, the degree of mastery over nature. And this is just what ultimately determines the level of development attained. It is from this point of view that we need to examine, overall, the question of how Marx's definitions relate to each other. Rodbertus proposes a strict differentiation between the two ideas in his work *Zur Beleuchtung der sozialen Frage* when he writes:

The productive force must be strictly distinguished from productivity. Productivity means the activity or beneficial effect of the productive force. If 20 workers are employed instead of 10, or if, instead of one machine of a certain degree of efficiency, two such machines are installed, then the productive force is doubled; if 10 workers produce as much as 20 have done hitherto, or if one machine costing no less than another is twice as efficient by comparison, then productivity is doubled. Labour is here the definitive yardstick. Greater sums of labour represent a greater productive force; a larger quantity of products from the same sum of labour represents an increase in productivity.[3]

From the way the issue is formulated here the reason for the 'vagueness' of the concept of the productive forces is plain; the fact of the matter is that this is a *border-line* concept, which is the dividing line between technology and economics. The concept of the productivity of social labour is important in *economic terms*. The material equivalent of this productivity of social labour, i.e. the available aggregate of the means of production and labour power, is important in *technical* terms. We can therefore speak of the productive forces and the productivity of social labour as two sides of the same mathematical quantity $\dfrac{M}{a+b}$, where M is the entire number of products expressed in any units of utility (be it power quantities or whatever, it does not matter here) and a and b are units of social labour, where a represents units of dead labour and b of living labour. If we examine this formula from a 'material' point of view, we have 1 a large number of heterogeneous products; 2 a large number of heterogeneous means of production and 3 a large number of heterogeneous labour skills. These three quantities are wholly dependent on each other, but the primary elements are the means of production. The means of production break down into the instruments of labour and other means of production (raw materials, auxiliary substances, etc.). These two in their turn are organically linked to one another. The concrete means of production, generally speaking, presupposes an equivalent amount of qualitatively determined labour power, for the production process has its own technical logic and at any given moment the material and personal elements of production are linked together according to a fixed pattern and in a fixed proportion. But on the other hand, the means of production themselves in their material definition break down into two mutually determining parts. From this standpoint we can take as the fundamental point for analysis the active part of the means of production, namely the instruments of labour, the *technical* system of society. This, as Marx says, is what 'forms the real criterion for the progress of the productive forces'.

Thus, when we talk of the growth and regression of the productive forces of society, we mean thereby the rise and fall of the social productivity of labour; when we talk about the distribution and redistribution of the productive forces, we are talking about the distribution and redistribution of the means of production and labour power. Furthermore, when we talk about the physical destruction of the productive forces, we are similarly talking about the destruction of the means of production and labour power. If we need a sociological definition of the productive forces, we can take the *technical* system of society, the active, variable 'factor' of social development.

However, this mutual relationship between the part of the formula $\frac{M}{a+b}$, where a and b stand for all the available means of production and labour power, presupposes a 'normal' course of social reproduction, i.e. a state of fluid, mobile equilibrium. The technically fixed proportionality of these quantities (and hence also the possibility of substituting one quantity for another) disappears when the social equilibrium is disturbed. The productivity of social labour will, as before, be expressed by the formula $\frac{M}{a+b}$ but a will not now stand for *all* the available means of production, nor b for *all* the available (i.e. utilizable) labour power; instead the correlation between a and b, which under normal conditions is a technically determined given quantity, *ceases* to be such.

The dynamics of the productive forces are bound up with the dynamics of production, i.e. with the process of reproduction. The material and human components of the productive forces (the totality of the means of production and labour power) are reproduced *in natura* in this process, so as to become the active factors of the process. Therefore, with regard to reproduction the formula $\frac{M}{a+b}$ must be considered from the angles of a and b, i.e. the social and human elements of the process of reproduction. In this case a and b are not isolated complexes but quantities, *organically* connected in the labour process. Only in so far as they enter into the labour process are they direct items of the productive forces.

The development of the productive forces is by no means a smoothly rising curve. On the contrary, it must be clear by now, *a priori*, that in an antagonistic society, a society based on productive and social anarchy, there *cannot* be an uninterrupted development of the productive forces, for in such a society the laws of equilibrium are and can only be realized by means of continual or recurrent disruptions of the equilibrium. Consequently, the starting point for the restoration of the equilibrium must be its disruption, the function of which in the present case is to restore the balance, but at the same time even more deeply contradictory basis. And since every violation of the equilibrium is inevitably bound up with a decline in the productive forces, it goes without saying, that in an antagonistic society, the development of the productive forces is made possible *only by means of their periodic destruction*.

This becomes strikingly apparent in capitalist *crises*. 'World market crises must be considered as a real expression and *forcible levelling out* (my emphasis N.I.B.) of all the contradictions of bourgeois economics.'[4] This 'forcible levelling out' of the contradictions, i.e. the creation of conditions for a new equilibrium, is accompanied by the destruction of the productive forces. The new equilibrium reproduces the old contradictions on an expanded basis and so on. Hence, from this point of view the process of capitalist reproduction is not only one of expanded reproduction of the capitalist relations of production; *it is at the same time a process of expanded reproduction of capitalist contradictions.*[5] A new equilibrium is established each time by means of 'a mass destruction of the productive forces' and, moreover, on an ever-increasing scale. In *Theories of Surplus Value*, Marx gives an excellent analysis of the chief forms of this destruction and from two points of view: from the real material ('natural') viewpoint and from the fetishistic capitalist ('value') viewpoint.

When speaking of the *destruction of capital* through crises, one must distinguish between two factors.

In so far as the reproduction process is checked and the labour process is restricted or in some instances is completely stopped, *real* capital is destroyed. Machinery which is not used is not capital. Labour which is not exploited is equivalent to lost production. Raw material which lies unused is not capital. Buildings (also newly built machinery) which are either unused or remain unfinished, commodities which rot in warehouses – all this is destruction of capital. All this means that the process of reproduction is checked and that existing means of production are not really used as means of production, are not put into operation. Thus their use-value and their exchange-value go to the devil.

Secondly, however, the *destruction of capital* through crises means the depreciation of *values*. . . . This is the ruinous effect of the fall in the prices of commodities. It does not cause the destruction of any use-values. What one loses, the other gains. . . . As regards the fall in the purely nominal capital, State bonds, shares, etc. – in so far as it does not lead to the bankruptcy of the state or of the share company, or to the complete stoppage of reproduction through undermining the credit of the industrial capitalist who hold such securities – it amounts only to the transfer of wealth from one hand to another.[6]

But because 'generally' the process of reproduction is destroyed in the latter instance as well, the destruction of capital in its material form takes place here too. On the other hand, the *centralization* of capital which is precipitated by the crises creates a 'higher form' of progression and the further development of the productive forces is bought at the cost of their *temporary and partial destruction*, i.e. at the cost of *lowering their level*.

Essentially the same phenomenon can be observed in an analysis of *capitalist competition*, which has its foundation in the scattered nature of social production. If there were a judiciously controlled system, then labour would be allocated to the separate branches and enterprises in the necessary proportions. In capitalist society no such conscious control mechanism exists, therefore the law of equilibrium – the law of value – functions as a natural law, 'like the law of gravity, when your house collapses about your ears'. But just because it is a blind law of social anarchy, it can only be accomplished by means of *continual violations*. And here the violation of the equilibrium is the *sine qua non* for the establishment of a new equilibrium, which is followed by another violation and so on. The mechanism behind these oscillations, i.e. behind the constant violations of the equilibrium by means of which the latter is continually achieved, is the mechanism of competition. Hence it follows that the development of the productive forces in a capitalist society is bought at the cost of their continual wastage.

This waste ('the costs of competition') is the necessary condition for the advancement of the entire capitalist system. For every new link in the chain of mobile equilibrium reproduces that equilibrium in a higher form, based on a process of centralization.

It is necessary to examine war, too, from this point of view, since it is merely one of the methods of competition at a certain stage of development, i.e. the method of *combined competition between capitalist trusts*. Consequently, the costs of war in themselves are merely the costs of the centralization process. From this standpoint of the capitalist system as a whole, they play a positive role, so long as they do not result in the collapse of the system itself.

At a general level, both crises and competition can be examined from three angles: with regard to the links in the reproduction process when a drop in the productive forces takes place, to the reproduction of the present system of production when a temporary drop in the productive forces is itself the condition for their subsequent progress, and to the collapse of the old system and the social transformation, when its contradictions blow up the old system sky high and the costs of the collapse become the costs of the revolution.

The costs of the revolution can, in their turn, be considered either sub-specie of those same cycles of reproduction which involve destruction of the material productive forces, or sub-specie of a transition to a new and more productive social structure, which eliminates the contradiction between the development of the productive forces and their structural 'bondage'. It goes without saying that the transition to a new structure, which is a new 'form of development' of the productive forces, is inconceivable without a temporary reduction of the productive forces. And the experience of all revolutions, which have played a colossal, positive role with regard to just this development of the productive forces, shows that it was bought at this cost of their, sometimes, colossal destruction and plunder. It could not be otherwise, since it is a question of revolution.[7] For in a revolution the 'integument' of the relations of production, i.e. of the human labour apparatus, is burst open (wird gesprengt) which means, and can only mean, a violation of the process of reproduction and, therefore, the destruction of the productive forces.

If in the case – and it undoubtedly is so – then, *a priori*, it must be clear that the *proletarian* revolution is inevitably accompanied by an extremely profound decline in the productive forces, for no other revolution knows such a profound and far-reaching *breaking* of the old relations and their reconstruction on a new footing. Yet, nevertheless, with regard to the development of the productive forces, the proletarian revolution is an objective necessity, occasioned by the fact that the economic integument had become incompatible with the productive forces. *World-wide* productive forces cannot be reconciled with the nation-state structure of society and the contradiction is 'resolved' by war. War itself becomes incompatible with the existence of the fundamental productive force – the working class – and the contradiction can only be resolved – really resolved – by revolution.[8]

The working class alone, the fundamental productive force of society,[9] can *save* this society and stimulate further development. But it can do this only at the cost of the inevitable sacrifices caused by the resistance of the bursting capitalist 'integument', which is personified in the *capitalist bourgeoisie*.[10]

The magnitude of the costs of the proletarian revolution depends on the depth of the communist upheaval and on the fundamental change in the production structure. In bourgeois revolutions no such fundamental change took place, for private property as the legal expression of a fixed model of relations of production was also the basis of pre-capitalist relations. It was in accordance with this that the social equilibrium after the revolution was achieved, in the economic sphere, merely by some amendments to what had existed previously and in the political sphere, by a transfer of power from one type of *owner* to another. Hence, it is clear, that there is not and cannot be such a disintegration here as is inevitable with a fundamental and radical breaking up of the old relations, which is the inevitable law of a proletarian revolution.[11]

All the *real* costs of a revolution come down to the *curtailment of the process of reproduction* and to the reduction of the productive forces. They can be broken down into several headings, according to the *form* they take:

1 The physical destruction of the elements of production. This concerns the destruction of the means of production (factories, machines, railways, apparatuses, live-stock, etc.); the destruction of people – workers etc. – in the process of the civil war and the class war between proletarian and bourgeois states; the destruction of machines and other means of production and their damage from ill-treatment, sabotage, failure to replace certain parts in time, etc.; the destruction of the technical intelligentsia (during the civil

war and from the general repercussions of the devastation, etc.).

Clearly, it is a question of the destruction of the material elements of production on the one hand and of its human elements on the other.

2 The de-skilling of the elements of production. Mention should be made of the wearing out of machines and the means of production in general; the (physical) exhaustion of the working class; the de-skilling of the technical intelligentsia; moreover to the use of 'surrogates' in the means of production and 'labour power' (a higher percentage of women and non-proletarian elements in the proletariat etc.).

3 The disintegration of the relations between the elements of production. This refers to the disintegration, analysed in detail above, of the hierarchical labour system of capitalist society, the social schism and the loss of equilibrium, all of which entails the temporary paralysis of the production process. It also concerns the disintegration of the relations between town and country, relations between states and so on. In the course of this disintegration not only do the *human* parts of the over-all labour apparatus drop out of real production, but so do the material and physical ones: when machines, their 'network' and whole factories stand idle, they are, to all intents and purposes, wasted. Here the productive forces are not physically destroyed, but they change to being *potential* productive forces. They exist *in natura*, but they exist outside the process of social production.

The disintegration of the relations between the elements of production is the most important cause of the drop in the level of the productive forces in the transition period. It is bound up with and really inseparable from the structural reorganization of society, it is an *inevitable* consequence and must therefore stand at the centre of any theoretical analysis. Other costs of the reconstruction proper must also be reckoned in here; for example, the initial *inability* of the working class to 'shoulder' the elements of production, the 'mistakes' of the construction period and so on, i.e. all the energy which goes into the reorganization of the social labour apparatus, with all the *faux frais* of that process.

4 The redistribution of the productive forces in the direction of non-productive consumption. Here we must mention above all servicing the needs of a civil war and class socialist war. With the development of the revolutionary process into a *world* revolutionary

process, civil war is transformed into a class war which is fought on the proletarian side by the regular 'red army'. Obviously, with regard to the immediate cycles of reproduction, the costs of this war will give rise to the same economic exhaustion as do the costs of any other war. It *can* be fought because a process of structural *organization* is taking place on a new basis, but the decline in the productive forces, in conjunction with the process of expanded negative reproduction, goes on for as long as the war continues. This war not only demands material resources, it also takes away the best personnel, worker-administrators and organizers.

It is not hard to see, that in all the events enumerated above, it comes down to curtailment, interruptions, stoppages and sometimes even paralysis of the process of reproduction, with a corresponding decline in the productive forces, to 'deny' which is just as stupid as to 'deny' the very process of revolution. The problem is to clarify the functional significance of this decline. The difference here between the short-sighted ideologists of the bourgeoisie and the ideologists of the proletariat lies not in the fact that one group 'confirms' these facts, whilst the other denies them, but in the fact that the bourgeois ideologists examine these phenomena in statistical terms, whilst the only correct (and therefore meaningful) method lies in examining the temporary decline in the productive forces from the viewpoint of the transformation process, i.e. not just with regard to the *next* cycle of social reproduction but from the broad perspective of the large historical scale.

It stands to reason, that since the process of reduction of the productive forces is expressed in the direct destruction of the elements of production, then the greater the reduction in the productive forces was during the civil war, the more painful the process is. The decline in the productive forces from this latter cause is bound up with their 'revolutionary' decline; the war and the revolution as an explosion of the capitalist system merge in the process of social transformation.[12]

From the foregoing analysis, it follows that there can be no halt to the decline in the productive forces before a new social structure and a new socio-productive equilibrium are established. It is the necessary condition for the resumption of the process of reproduction. Only after the reconstruction of the human labour apparatus – a reconstruction which sweeps away all obstacles to the development of the productive forces and tears asunder the 'integument', which changed from being 'forms of development' into 'shackles on development' – only after this is the last phase of the revolution possible, the *technical* revolution, a revolution not in the relations between people but in the relations between the human collective and the outside world.

At first we shall have to go through a period of 'primary socialist accumulation'.[13] What was the nature of production of *capitalist* primary accumulation? It lay in the fact that the political power of the bourgeoisie mobilized large numbers of the population by robbing them, turning them into proletarians and creating from them the fundamental productive force of capitalist society. *The production of the proletariat* – that is the 'nature' of the period of primary accumulation.

> In the history of primitive accumulation, all revolutions are epoch-making that act as levers for the capitalist class in the course of formation; but, above all, those moments when great masses of men are suddenly and forcibly torn from their means of subsistence, and hurled as free and 'unattached' proletarians on the labour market.[14]

By pillage, class violence and robbery, *capital* thus mobilized the productive forces, making them the starting point for further development.

But socialism, too, as it arises from the midst of the debris, must inevitably begin with the mobilization of the living productive forces. This mobilization of labour is a fundamental aspect of a socialist primary accumulation, which is the dialectical opposite of capitalist accumulation. Its class nature lies not in creating the preconditions for a process of exploitation, but in economic rebirth with the *abolition* of exploitation, not in coercion by a handful of capitalists, but in the self-organization of the working masses.

We saw above that the process of disintegration of the capitalist system is accompanied not only by the destruction or de-skilling of living labour power, but also by a simple dropping out of the labour process. It is quite clear, therefore, that when the proletariat sets about restoring the process of reproduction, it must begin with the stabilization of those armed forces which had dropped out of the production process. But it cannot confine itself to this. In the first stages of development, when the proletariat inherits a material, machine and technical framework which has suffered cruelly, living labour power acquires a special significance. So the transition to a system of *universal labour service*, i.e. by pushing the vast *non-proletarian* masses, above all the peasantry, into the labour process of the proletarian state, is an imperative necessity.[15] The creation of a living, mass productive force, which operates collectively, is the starting point for further work. Initially, the most important areas of labour are transport and the procurement of fuel, raw materials and food-stuffs.[16] From this, an *ascending* line of development begins, with a concomitant of a high-powered technical development. The abolition of private ownership of the means of production, the abolition of patent rights and commercial secrets, a unified plan, etc. make the transition to electric power possible. If, under capitalism, private ownership of land, with all its natural resources (waterfalls, rivers, peat deposits, etc.) and the monopoly of capitalist cliques were a terrible obstacle to the development of the productive forces, and even in the most powerful capitalist countries, the application of electrical energy and the construction of new power stations, etc. came up against the limits set by private ownership,[17] then under the rule of the proletariat, the period of 'primary socialist accumulation' will be followed by a real technical upheaval, a revolution in socio-productive technology. 'The steam age is the age of the bourgeoisie. The age of electricity is the age of socialism' – this is perfectly true of the technological characteristics of the initial stages of evolving socialism.[18] The electrification of industry, the construction of huge power stations and the creation of a mighty transport network will also radically overturn the relationship between town and country. It will not only promote the transformation of small, scattered owners into socialized workers, it will rationalize and radically transform the whole process of agricultural production. It will replace primitive, almost barbaric, implements with the last word in technology and thereby destroy the basic imbalance of capitalist production, the imbalance between the development of industry and the development of agriculture, which was caused by the existence of ground rent and private ownership of land, and which even before the war had led to an enormous increase in the prices of agricultural produce.[19] The antagonism between town and country will gradually disappear and with it the specific 'idiocy of country life'. The productive forces of human society will be distributed between the various spheres according to the most appropriate natural conditions (proximity to sources of fuel and raw materials, etc.). The question of the 'Standard der Industrie' will be resolved with no regard to the existence of capitalist barriers and the development of the productive forces will take gigantic steps forward on a smooth and confident course.

Chapter 7
The General Organizational Forms of the Transition Period

1 *State capitalism*
2 *The system of socialist dictatorship*
3 *Socialization*
4 *Nationalization*
5 *Municipalization*
6 *Other forms of socialization*

It is a 'principle' of bourgeois political economy to abstract from the *historical and social forms* of the production process, and it therefore considers relations of supremacy, exploitation and the class character of a given social structure, etc. 'unimportant'. It is not surprising that such 'high-mindedness' makes a 'principle' of an incredible theoretical confusion, which is not without its practical advantages for the bourgeoisie. This confusion reached its peak during the war and in the immediate post-war period. It manifested itself above all in a complete failure to distinguish between the system of state capitalism and that of the socialist dictatorship of the proletariat.

Werner Sombart, in the preface to *Gundlagen und Kritik des Sozialismus*,[1] defines socialism thus: 'socialism is practical social rationalism with an anti-chremastic tendency' ('Sozialismus ist praktische Sozialrationalistik mit anti-chrematistischer Tendez'). This 'definition', if one may call it such, has deep literary roots, for an ancient tradition exists which has acquired the strength of a prejudice, a tradition which puts the slave-owning 'communism', the Prussian Junker 'state socialism' of Rodbertus, the finance state capitalism of the war era and Marx's communism all in the same bracket, on the sufficient grounds that all these forms reveal 'social rationalism with an anti-chremastic tendency'. It is clear, however, that such an attitude is no better than those barbarously crude, but at the same time naïve and cunning definitions which during the war were applied to imperialism, as a non-historical and sometimes even universal, biological function.[2]

This confusion is logically connected with the fact that here the class character of the state, which appears under the pseudonym of the 'aggregate', the 'whole', 'the social totality' and other fine phrases, is hidden, as is the specific character of the relations of production. These latter are considered only with respect to the fact that the anarchy in production and the monetary system connected with it are being destroyed. But, since they can use this formula to approach all and every kind of economic structure based on natural economic and at the same time systematically controlled relations, *whatever class or non-class characteristic these relations may have*, clearly the formula is useless precisely because it is too general and embraces social structures which are directly *opposed* in their class characteristics.

If we now pass on to state capitalism, we shall see that it is a quite specific and purely historical category, despite the fact that it possesses both a 'social rationalism' and an 'anti-chrematistic tendency', for it is also one of the forms – the most absolute form – of *capitalism*. The fundamental relation of production in the capitalist system is the relation between the capitalist who owns the means of production and the worker who sells him his labour power. In an examination of the state capitalist structure, one cannot preposterously discard this fundamental class attribute. With respect to the correlation of the social forces, state capitalism represents the *exponential* (raised to a power) authority of the bourgeoisie, where the rule of capital reaches the peak of its strength, a truly enormous magnitude.[3] In other words, *state capitalism is the rationalization of the production process on the basis of antagonistic social relations under the rule of capital which is expressed in the dictatorship of the bourgeoisie.*

Since state capitalism is the coalescence of the bourgeois state with the capitalist trusts it is obvious that there can be no question of any 'state capitalism' whatsoever under the dictatorship of the proletariat, which rules out such a possibility on principle.[4] Reasoning 'in general', one could argue the possibility of a new form where the proletarian state at the very start of its life controls the activities of the capitalist trusts, *before* 'expropriating the expropriators', 'judiciously preparing' for this expropriation so as to keep all the 'apparatuses' intact. If such a system were possible, it would not be state capitalism, for this latter presupposes a capitalist state. It would be, not a higher expression of the capitalist order, but some intermediary stage in the development of the revolution. Such a form is impossible, however, for the assumption rests on the illusion – true, an extremely wide-spread one – that the proletariat can supposedly 'take possession' of all the capitalist apparatuses without affecting their capitalist virginity, and the messrs capitalists submit with pleasure to all the commands of proletarian power. Here, therefore, a state of equilibrium is being posited in conditions which preclude any equilibrium.[5]

The system of socialist dictatorship, which could be called state socialism if this term had not been corrupted by common usage, is the dialectical negative, the antithesis of state capitalism. Here the *model* of the relations of production is radically changed and the sovereignty of capital in production is abolished, for the basis of the foundations of the capitalist system – the relations of property – is changed. Here, too, there is 'social rationalism with an anti-chremastic tendency', but these features exist on the basis of a completely different correlation of the classes, which radically changes the entire character of the production process. In the system of state capitalism, the economic subject is the *capitalist* state, *the collective capitalist*. Under the proletarian dictatorship, the economic subject is the *proletarian* state, the collectively organized working class, 'the proletariat, organized as a state power'. Under state capitalism, the production process is that of the production of surplus value, which falls into the hands of the capitalist class, for the purpose of transforming this value into surplus product. Under the dictatorship of the proletariat, the production process is a means for the planned satisfaction of social needs. The system of state capitalism is the most absolute of all forms of exploitation of the masses by a handful of oligarchs. The system of proletarian dictatorship makes any exploitation whatso-ever altogether inconceivable, for it transforms collective-capitalist property and its private-capitalist form into collective-*proletarian* 'property'. Hence, despite their formal similarity, they are dia-metrically counterposed in content.[6] This contraposition also determines a contraposition in all the functions of the systems under consideration, even if they are formally similar. So, universal labour service under state capitalism means the enslavement of the working class; whilst under the dictatorship of the proletariat it is merely the self-organization of labour by the masses; the mobilization of industry in the first case means strengthening the power of the bourgeoisie and the consolidation of the capitalist regime, whereas in the second case, it means the strengthening of socialism.

In the state-capitalist structure, all forms of state coercion are a weight which ensures, extends and deepens the process of exploitation, while state coercion under the dictatorship of the proletariat is a method of building communist society. In short, the *functional* contraposition of formally similar phenomena is wholly predetermined by the functional contraposition of the system of organization, by their contraposed *class* characteristics.[7]

Communism is not the form of the transition period, but its *consummation*. It is a classless, state-less structure, harmoniously constructed in all its parts. Only there, for the first time, does an absolutely united and organized 'whole' emerge. As it evolves, the dictatorship of the proletariat 'ripens' into communism, and dies off along with the state organization of society. The transition from capitalism to socialism is accomplished by the concentrated might of the proletariat – the lever of the proletarian dictatorship. The system of measures by which this transition is accomplished is usually designated 'socialization'.[8] It is clear from the foregoing that this term is not altogether accurate. If one talks about socialization, meaning by this that the labour process as a whole satisfies social needs, i.e. the needs of the whole of society as a system, then such socialization did exist even within the limits of capitalism. This is what Marx meant when he talked of 'socialized labour'. Rodbertus, too, maintained the same thing when he advanced his thesis that the essence of society is communism. Clearly, however, this is not the point in this case. Here it is a question of such measures as would create a new model of relations of production, on the basis of a *radical change* in the relations of property. In other words, the socializing process must also include the 'expropriation of the expropriators'. Hence, by socialization is meant the transfer of the means of production into the hands of society. However, on this point, too, some inaccuracy of terminology comes to light. For in the transition epoch between state capitalism and communism, the conscious economic subject is not 'the whole of society', but the *organized working class*, the proletariat. None the less, since we are examining the entire process as a whole, from the forced expropriation right up to the dying off of the proletarian dictatorship, which is also a *process*, the disparity between the proletariat and the sum total of all socialized workers gets smaller and smaller and finally disappears altogether.

By the same token, the term 'socialization' is also justified,[9] if by socialization we mean the transfer of the means of production into the hands of the organized proletariat as the ruling class. Then the question arises as to the concrete form of that transfer. In essence we have already discussed this in previous chapters. Here we need only distinguish one from another concepts which are constantly being confused by the opponents of the communist revolutionary upheaval.

Undoubtedly, since the economic subject of the transition period is the working class – constituting the state power – the basic form of socialization of production will be its statification or nationalization.[10] However, it is quite obvious that statification (nationalization) 'in general' conceals within itself a quite different, material class content, depending upon the class characteristics of the state in question. If, unlike the representatives of bourgeois science, one does not regard the state apparatus as an organization of neutral and mystical virtues, then one must also recognize that all the functions of the state have a class character.

Hence, it follows that one must make a strict distinction between *bourgeois* nationalization and *proletarian* nationalization. Bourgeois nationalization leads to a system of state capitalism. Proletarian nationalization leads to the state structure of socialism. In just the same way as the proletarian dictatorship is the negative, the antipode of bourgeois dictatorship, proletarian nationalization is the negative, the complete opposite of bourgeois nationalization.

The same thing must be said about the various forms of 'municipalization' and 'communalization', etc. It is a major theoretical error to *contrast* these concepts with that of statification. For the system of so-called 'local government' in *any class* society (hence, any society where there is a state) is merely a component part of the local apparatus of the state organization of the ruling class.[11] The specific class character of state power imbues the local organs of this power with the same specific class character. Therefore, just as strict a distinction must be drawn between proletarian municipalization and bourgeois municipalization as between the heterogeneous 'nationalizations'.

It goes without saying, that in addition to these basic forms, where the proletariat as a whole takes direct possession of the production process, there is also a series of *lower* forms of this same process, especially with regard to the countryside. Here the relationship with the proletarian state is less close, but it does exist all the same. For the dictatorship of the proletariat is the means for overturning the old order and building the new. In the final analysis, the process of socialization in *all* its forms is thus a function of the proletarian state.

Chapter 8
The Systems of Production Control under the Dictatorship of the Proletariat

1 The class character of the state and methods of control
2 Workers' control of industry in the period of the destruction of the capitalist system
3 Workers' control of industry in the critical periods ('militarization')
4 Management and management training in the various phases of the transformation process
5 The probable course of development

Under the rule of capital, production is production of surplus value, production for the sake of profit. Production under the rule of the proletariat is production for the satisfaction of social needs. The different functional significance of the entire production process is shown by the difference in the *relations* of property and in the *class* character of state power.[1] It is a grave theoretical error to think that a certain class is bound by one form of control which is immutable in its details. Any social class may find itself in a variety of circumstances to which the methods and forms of control must be adapted. These forms are determined by the norms of technical expediency, whereby *different* forms have the same class content, given certain relations of property and a certain class character of state power.

The practice of the bourgeoisie will serve as the best example of this. In the era of imperialism, the bourgeoisie went over from the forms of 'broad democracy' to a restriction of the rights of parliament, to a system of 'small cabinets' and the reinforcement of the role of the president, etc. But was this restriction of the 'rights of parliament' and the 'crisis of parliamentarianism' a restriction of the rights of the bourgeoisie and a crisis in its rule? Not a bit of it.

On the contrary, these phenomena signified the *reinforcement* of bourgeois supremacy, the centralization and militarization of its power, which in the imperialist era was a categorical necessity from the bourgeoisie's point of view.

When Spencer supposed that the 'industrial state' must be anti-militarist by nature, because militarism is the specific character-istic of a feudal regime, he was gravely mistaken, for he trans-formed the features of one *phase* of capitalist development into a universal form. World competition brought all development under the banner of war and forced the bourgeoisie to change the form of its supremacy. But only vulgar minds can see this as the robbery of the rights of the bourgeoisie in favour of some non-existent quantity. It is quite wrong to contrapose even the so-called 'personal regime' to class supremacy. On the contrary in a certain set of circumstances the supremacy of a class may be expressed most appropriately in just such a personal regime. One example of this is the rule of the landowners, which manifested itself in an autocracy. Another is the bourgeois dictatorship in the epoch of civil wars, where it finds its most perfect formula (i.e. one fitted to the conditions of the moment) in the dictatorship of the 'honest sword'. Subject to the technical advisability, change in the form may also take place in the area of industrial control.

Given that these theses are, on the whole, correct, then they also hold true for the epoch of the dictatorship of the proletariat.

Hence, it is plain that the different systems of industrial control in the process of social transformation should be considered in the light of the *specific* phases of development. It is only by examining them thus that one can understand the necessary changes of form, the inevitable variations in the various systems of control within the limits of the fixed class 'nature' of this particular system.

The initial phase of development is a period of decomposition and severance of the capitalist relations of production and a period, too, where the proletariat takes possession of strategic centres of the economic structure. Generally speaking, this period begins before the 'transition' of political power to the proletariat, because there is no sharp dividing line delimiting the stages of the revolu-tion (ideological, political, economic and technical) and one period overlaps with another. The struggle for the socialization of pro-duction, i.e. for the workers' factory, proceeds from below and runs parallel to the rising tide of revolution. It is evinced in the fact that organizations, like the revolutionary 'factory and works' commit-tees (e.g. in Russia), 'factory councils' ('Betriebsate' in Germany), and other analogous representatives and broadly collective organs, united in the course of the working-class struggle, cut into the old system like a wedge and finally split it apart. This phase of develop-ment must be analysed first.

In the period under consideration, society is in a major state of instability. The relationship between the social forces is such that no equilibrium whatsoever is possible on the old foundations. The capitalist bourgeoisie and the technical intelligentsia, who as a general rule go along with the bourgeoisie during this period, have no special interest in putting production to rights. Their attention is focused on preventing the victory of the working class. The factories and plants are increasingly left 'without an owner'. The organizations of the proletariat, enumerated above, represent the first attempt to install a new 'owner'-working class. Is this system of broad collective leadership by factory councils the best *tech-nically* speaking? Of course not. But that is not its function. In the period under discussion the issue is one of the *first step* towards establishing a new equilibrium, *without which* any construction whatsoever of actually more perfect forms is inconceivable. Even in 'normal' capitalist times, bourgeois organizers of production considered one of the major problems of management to be that of the relationship between the organs of the capitalist and those of the workers.[2] In this case the problem is quite insoluble. It is solely a matter of groping towards a *new* system of equilibrium. Hence, at this particular stage of development it is quite impossible to establish 'perfect technical control' as the immediate task. The solution to this problem presupposes a certain stability in the elements of production, not only in the material elements, but also in the human ones. But in the period under examination, such a condition does not and cannot exist. Nevertheless, even here one can in a certain sense talk of a step forward.

Now, we saw earlier that human and technical labour relations are at the same time social relations. Therefore, by comparison with the absolute disarray of the economic apparatus, where there is no organizing principle in an enterprise, 'the seizure of power' in a factory by workers' cells represents a gain even with regard to the logic of 'pure production'. It is immeasurably more important from the point of view of its role in the overall historical process.

For only thus can the working class be brought into the production process as the organizing principle. In point of fact, the *urgent* task economically here is: to consolidate the working class as the *ruling* class in every aspect of economic life. Technically, such a system is far from perfect, accompanied, as it inevitably is, by the broadest collective leadership, the principle of absolute electivity (where electivity is a *political* concept and not one of technical length of service), frequent removability and, as a result of broad collective leadership, the decentralization and fragmentation of responsibility.[3] But this is the only way the working class strengthens its positions in economic life; by creating cells to control the apparatus, cells which quickly establish contact among themselves and merge with the working-class organizations which have already ripened in the 'lap of capitalism', and thus form the new fabric of the proletarian economic apparatus. The decay of the old, and a rough draft of the new – this is what the model of the administration of production represents.

It would not be out of place here to draw an analogy with the process which takes place in the army. Instead of the very strict imperialist subordination and discipline, the principle of wide electivity is introduced; numerous committees in all units of the army apparatus are created; army matters become the subject of the broadest discussion and debates; 'the old authority' in the army is finally discredited and undermined; new organs and through them new classes becomes the real centres of power. What are the objective implications of this process? The first and most important is the *demoralization and destruction of the old imperialist army*. The second is the *education and training* of the active organizing forces of the future proletarian army, an education purchased at the cost of destroying the old. Nobody will begin to contend that the regimental committees make the army efficient. But their objective task, after all, is not to maintain the fighting efficiency of the old army but is, on the contrary, to demoralize it and train the forces for a *different* apparatus.

However, despite the similarity of the process in both cases there is, nevertheless, one major difference. In production greater *continuity* in the whole process is preserved. This happens because the *framework* of the future production apparatus already existed within the capitalist system, chiefly in the form of the trade unions. There were no corresponding military organization, nor could there be. Therefore, in the military sphere development proceeds in leaps and bounds and the whole process is expressed in stronger, coarser, if you like, more revolutionary terms.

The model of production militarized by the proletariat differs sharply from the case under investigation. The 'military' category of any organization comes on the scene when the existing system is in a critical position. In war, there is the constant threat of destruction, both of the individual parts of the fighting machine (the army) and of the 'whole'. Therefore, what is required here by the very terms of the organization's existence is an unquestioning execution, speed of decision, unity of will and therefore a minimum of discussion and talking, a minimum of boards and a maximum of individual management. On the other hand, since the components of this organization are not united internally and do not implement all decisions themselves, the army has to depend on the system of repressions, which reach their peak in just this sphere and are at their most pronounced here.

This latter element must be particularly strong when the army recruits from elements, which *themselves* have no personal interest in war, when the war is waged *against* their interests. Such is an imperialist war. But, under the rule of the proletariat, too, the element of coercion and repression has a major role, which is greater, the higher is the percentage of purely non-proletarian elements on the one hand and unconscious or half-conscious elements within the proletariat itself on the other.[4] In this case, the 'militarization'[5] of the population – above all in the army – is a method of *self-organization of the working class and organization of the peasantry*.

So long as the workers' dictatorship and its classical paradigm the soviet state system is in a critical situation, quite clearly it must assume the character of a proletarian *military* dictatorship. This means that the practical apparatuses of control contract, broad-based committees give way to narrow ones and all the available working-class organizers and administrators are distributed in the most economical way.

This phenomenon – in an intensified form – necessarily occurs with the danger of economic catastrophe. This danger has been brought about by economic exhaustion during the time of the imperialist and civil wars. Hence the burden of the proletariat's tasks is transferred to the sphere of economic construction, where the basic fabric of the economic apparatuses is *already* saturated with worker-administrators and where the workers' organizations have already become the foundation and pivot of these apparatuses, then of necessity curtailing collective management, even leading in some cases (in individual plants and factories) to the introduction of individual control [i.e. one-man management]. This latter situation is neither a diminution of the rights of the class nor a diminution of the role of its organizations. It is a contracted, condensed *form* of workers' control of industry, a form adapted to the conditions of rapid work and a 'military' tempo. Technically, this form is much better, for its significance lies not in destroying the old, or in merely safeguarding the supremacy of the new relations or in educating the masses; the centre of gravity here lies in the construction of a practical apparatus and in a smooth, accurate work flow. The revolution solves this problem *after* the foundation has been laid for the proletarian administrative apparatus in general.

In this case attention no longer needs to be focused on the problem of consolidating the class position of the proletariat – basically this question has been solved. Here the difficulty is not to change the principle behind the relations of production, but to try to find the form of management which will secure maximum efficiency. The principle of broad electivity from below (usually by the workers according to factory) is replaced by the principle of careful *selection* in the light of the technical and administrative length of service, competence and steadfastness of the candidates. At the head of workers' management boards are the individuals in charge – workers or specialist engineers – but they are elected and appointed by the economic organs of the *proletarian* dictatorship; the workers' organizations, too, propose and nominate them. In such a system no engineer can fulfil any other function than the one required of him by the proletariat.

This model of workers' control of industry is possible and advisable only under certain conditions; first of all, it presupposes the stability of an established soviet order, and a certain social equilibrium already achieved on a new basis. Such a system would be impossible and inadvisable in the first phase of the revolution, the phase of destruction of the old relations and the seizure of the productive areas. This cannot be too strongly emphasized.[6]

One more question must be raised here, in connection with those already discussed, namely that of the relationship between the methods of *management* and the methods of management *training*. One of the most important tasks of the soviet system overall lies in involving the vast masses themselves directly in administration. The same applies to the economic organizations of the state apparatus. In the first period the functions of training *merge* with the functions of management itself. It cannot be otherwise. The bourgeois organizers of production, the technical intelligentsia, are at that time opposed to the proletariat and though the workers do not yet have the administrative experience, everything falls on their shoulders. In such a state of affairs, the progressive workers manage as they learn and learn as they manage. There is *no other* alternative, in the first stage of the construction of socialism. But a broadly based system of collective management is actually highly suited to the fulfilment of these aims. It is not so much management as *a school* of management. However, it is quite obvious that one should not make a virtue of necessity. In subsequent phases of development, as the positions of the working class, as the ruling class, have been consolidated, and as a firm framework for competent industrial management is created, based on the existing stratum of elected worker-administrators; and as the technical intelligentsia, on the other hand, returns like a prodigal son to the production process – so the functions of management are separated from the functions of management training. This training is no longer bought at the cost of mistakes in management itself.

The masses, in ever-increasing numbers, start to take an interest in and learn industrial management, in special institutions, by special ways and means, and much more systematically than was possible in the previous phase.[7]

What is the probable course of subsequent development on the road to communism? Since the acuteness of the economic crisis (the crisis of exhaustion) will pass and ever-increasing human resources able and competent in management, will accumulate, there will be no need for the harsh military style of management. For all its undoubted advantages there are also some major defects arising from this type of compulsory discipline. It is a categorical imperative in conditions where we must act decisively and quickly; in that case its defects are outweighed by its merits. However, once it has fulfilled its purpose, it is replaced by a new phase, that of an 'improved' system of management, which is by no means a simple repetition of a stage which has already passed, but a synthesis of the two previous stages. Then, to use the language of Hegel, the first phases represent the thesis, the second the antithesis and the third their synthesis into some higher unity. Development, of course, does not stop here. With the dying off of the state power and all compulsory standardization of human relations, communist mankind will create the highest model of 'control over *things*', where the very problem of collective or individual management, in any form or combination will disappear, for the people of the future will do what the dry computations of statistical calculation demand. Control over *people* will disappear forever.

Chapter 9
The Economic Categories of Capitalism in the Transition Period[1]

In an analysis of the economics of the transition period, one must not only deal with 'pure' forms and categories. This analysis is therefore difficult, because there are no stable quantities here. If knowledge in its present state is generally concerned with fluid 'processes' and not with fixed metaphysical 'essences', it is in the transition period, for reasons which are obvious, that the categories of being are replaced by categories of 'becoming'. Fluidity, mutability and motion – these features are peculiar to the transition period, to a much greater extent than to relations which have evolved 'normally' within a stable production system. Therefore we are faced with the question: are those methodological procedures and 'categories of abstract thought', which Marx used with regard to capitalist society, of any use or not? Will they serve now in an epoch when capitalism is breaking up and a new social foundation is being laid?

Indeed, 'in the analysis of economic forms, moreover, neither microscopes nor chemical reagents are of use. The force of abstraction must replace both.'[2] By studying the capitalist form of society and using this power of abstraction, Marx created a whole system of concepts and tools for being cognizant with living economic reality. These concepts have been vital to the scientific mastery of the economic processes, not just in the hands of a genius, but in the hands of all subsequent researchers – not apologists and sycophants, but truly scientific researchers – into the phenomena of economic life. Scientific mastery of the economic process implies an understanding of its development, an understanding of the origin, evolution and disappearance of every phenomenon and an understanding of it as part of the whole – with this kind of scientific understanding the concepts coined by Marx functioned 'smoothly'. The corner-stones of the entire edifice of theoretical, political economy, i.e. of the theory of economics in their capitalist form, the basic concepts of the entire system, were the concepts: *commodity, value and price.*

But the knell of capitalist property has sounded. The expropriators are being expropriated. Capitalist production with the inevitability of a natural process has arrived at the negation of itself. The communist revolution is shaking the whole economic system to its deepest foundations, blasphemously smashing up the 'eternal' temple of capitalism. A process of gigantic economic improvements and grandiose changes is under way, a process of reconstruction of the entire system of relations of production. The old is interwoven with the new, the new battles with the old and now gets the better of it, now retreats helplessly. We must cognitively master this complex process, and in this, we are time and again forced to fall back on the powers of abstraction.[3]

In the first serious attempt to really scientifically master that highly restless specific state which we call the economy of the transition period, we come up against the fact that the *old concepts* of theoretical economy instantly refuse to be of any use. We come up against a curious contradiction. The old categories of political economy continue to take the form of practical *generalizations* about a *continuously changing*, living, economic reality. At the same time, these categories do not enable one to penetrate beneath the 'surface of phenomena', i.e. to shake off vulgar thinking and to understand the process and development of *economic life as a whole.* But this is understandable. By their very nature these elementary relations, which in ideological terms are represented by the categories of commodity, price, wages, profit, etc., simultaneously exist and do not exist. It is as if they are non-existent. They drag out a strange kind of illusory real, and really illusory existence, like the old Slav notion of the souls of the dead or heathen gods in the pious Christian religion. Therefore, the old, tested tools of Marxist thought, coined by Marx on the basis of the very real existence of the appropriate relations of production, begin to misfire. But in everyday practical life, they continue to be uncritically regarded as a means for a true understanding of the phenomena of economic life.[4]

To make use of these categories for theoretical analysis now presupposes a complete understanding of their restricted historical nature, an understanding of the limits of their significance and an understanding of the conditions, meaning and limits of their applicability to economic relations which are jumping over to fundamentally different rails. We are, therefore, faced in the first place, with analysing the starting points, the 'methodology' of economic theory and with elucidating the role of its fundamental concepts; and in the second place, with tracing the modifications and limitations to them which arise out of the system of a transitional economy.

One can distinguish three characteristic features of Marxist economic methodology: the objective-social point of view, the material-productive approach and, finally, the dialectical-historical approach to the question. The objective-social viewpoint affirms the primacy of society over the individual economic subject – man. He is considered not as an 'atom' or an isolated Robinson Crusoe, but as a small part of the social system. 'Production by isolated individuals outside of society . . . is as great an absurdity as the idea of the development of language without individuals living together and talking to one another.'[5] The material-production approach affirms the primacy of production over consumption and over the whole of economic life in general. The first (the objective-social) viewpoint is, as the mathematicians say, essential, but it by no means suffices to characterize the whole method. Society exists as a certain stable system. What are the material conditions for this system's existence? 'Every child knows that if a country ceased to work, I will not say for a year, but for a few weeks, it would die.'[6] Society depends for its existence on its production, which has a 'socially determined character'. Society itself is regarded first and foremost as 'a productive organism' and the economy as 'the production process'. The dynamics of production determine the dynamics of needs. Production as the fundamental condition of society's existence represents the *given* element.[7]

The dialectical-historical method examines society in its specifically historical forms and the general laws of social development in their concrete manifestation as the laws of a certain social structure, which are restricted in their effect to the historical limits of that structure.[8] Therefore, economic categories, too, are the 'theoretical expression of historical relations of production, corresponding to a particular stage of development in material production.[9] On no account are they eternal, as bourgeois scholarship maintains, which immortalizes them because it immortalizes the capitalist mode of production.[10]

Besides these basic features of the Marxist method, we should note one more methodological approach which can conditionally be called the *postulate of equilibrium*. In view of its particular importance, on the one hand, and the misunderstanding of it in the usual accounts of the Marxist doctrine on the other, we ought to dwell at some length on this approach.

In his theoretical grasp of the capitalist system of relations of production, Marx proceeds *from the fact of its existence*. Since this system exists, it means that – whether well or badly – social needs are satisfied, at least to the extent that people not only do not die off, but indeed live, act and multiply. In a society with a social division of labour – and a commodity capitalist society presupposes this – there must be a definite *equilibrium* of the whole system. Coal, iron, machines, cottons, linens, bread, sugar, boots, etc. are produced in the necessary amounts, Living human labour, using the necessary quantities of the means of production, is correspondingly expended in the necessary quantities for the production of all this. There may well be all sorts of deviations and fluctuations here; the whole system expands and becomes complicated, develops and is continuously in motion and oscillating but, taken as a whole, it is in a state of equilibrium.[11]

To find the law of this equilibrium is the basic problem of theoretical economics and theoretical economics as a scientific system is the result of an examination of the entire capitalist system *in its state of equilibrium*.

Every child knows, too, that the mass of products corresponding to the different needs require different quantitatively determined masses of the total labour of society. That this necessity of distributing social labour in definite proportions cannot be done away with by the *particular form* of social production, but can only change the *form it assumes*, is self-evident. No natural laws can be done away with. What can change, in changing historical circumstances, is the *form* in which these laws operate. And the form in which this proportional division of labour operates, in a state of society where the interconnection of social labour is manifested in the *private exchange* of the individual products, is precisely the exchange value of these products.[12]

Here the whole approach to the solution of a fundamental problem – that of *value* – is concisely and clearly indicated.

If we look at the entire structure of 'capital' from this point of view, we shall see that the analysis begins with a firm and stable system of equilibrium. Gradually, complicating factors are introduced, the system starts to oscillate, and become mobile. These oscillations, however, still conform to laws and, despite the most severe violations of the equilibrium (crises), the system as a whole remains; through the violations of the equilibrium, a new equilibrium is established, so to speak, of a higher order. Only after the laws of equilibrium have been understood is it then possible to go on and raise the question of the oscillations of the system. The crises themselves are regarded not as a suspension of the equilibrium, but as a violation of it, in view of which it is considered necessary to find the law of that motion after one has understood not only how the equilibrium is upset, but also how it is subsequently restored. A crisis does not overstep the limits of the *oscillation* of the system. By the end of the investigation, this *system* moves and oscillates, but through all the movements and oscillations, the equilibrium is restored time and again. The law of value is *the law of equilibrium in a simple commodity system of production.* The law of the *costs* of production [plus the average rate of profit] is the law of equilibrium in a transformed commodity system, i.e. the capitalist system. The law of market price is the law of oscillation in this system. The law of competition is the law of the continual restoration of the upset equilibrium. The law of crises is the law of the inevitable periodic disturbance of the equilibrium of the system and its restoration.

Marx always posed the question thus: equilibrium exists, how is it possible? The equilibrium is upset – how is it restored? This is the *postulate of equilibrium*; it is an examination of the entire system in a *typical* case, where the question of the possibility of equilibrium *not* being restored and the system being destroyed *does not arise*.[13]

The examination of the social and, moreover, irrational and blind system from the viewpoint of its equilibrium, has nothing in common, of course, with *harmonia praestabilitata*, for it proceeds from the *fact* that this system exists and that it develops. The latter presupposes the form of this equilibrium to be a mobile and not a static one.

These are the fundamentals of the methodology of theoretical economics. We must now pass on to the question of the 'significance' of these viewpoints with respect to the period of the breakdown of capitalism and the period of the rule of the proletariat.

The social-objective approach remains obligatory and does not require any qualification. Indeed, in the process of social transformation, the economic subject, in his motives and his actions, is dependent on the social environment, even whilst he remains an individual commodity producer. The task is to analyse the reconstruction of the *social*. Here: 1 the joint collective and conscious economic subject is growing – the proletarian state with all its jointly subordinate organs; 2 so long as the anarchic commodity system remains, so does the irrational blind 'fate' of the market, i.e. once again, the social anarchic elements which increasingly come under the controlling influence of the crystallized, socially conscious centre; 3 finally, in so far as components of the disintegration of social relations do exist (e.g. the formation of isolated natural-economic cells), on the one hand, they 'are limited' in their actions by the economic environment (their internal reorganization itself is a function of social advances) and on the other hand, they are increasingly drawn into the construction work by being continually subjected to the systematic influence of the state economic organization of the proletariat (compulsory labour service, all sorts of duties in kind, etc.). In this way, even when individual elements do drop out of the socio-production process, they still find themselves in a permanent sphere of influence and are themselves in a permanent sphere of influence and are themselves considered from the standpoint of the *social* system of production; at the point of their maximum isolation, they are theoretically interesting as an object of social attraction, as a potential constituent part of the new social system.

However, despite the fact that the objective-social method is still valid, it does acquire a *different logical tone*. In an analysis of the social structure of the capitalist commodity model, all economic regularity expresses itself in conforming to *anarchic* laws, 'blind' force, since the entire socio-production process is *irrational*. In an analysis of the structure of the transition period, the case is somewhat different, because here the *rationalization* of the socio-economic process increases exponentially.

The material-production approach on the whole also remains obligatory. However, it does undergo substantial changes and restrictions. In the first place, the process of production is not an *a priori* given quantity. To be more precise: whereas in 'normal' periods of social development, the process of social reproduction is taken for granted and the continuous renewal of the elements of production in the course of that production is assumed during the transition period, with the shaking up of the entire socio-labour apparatus, the process of reproduction is called into question. Therefore, the problem here reads not '*how* is production possible?' but 'is production *possible*?' The same thing with regard to the productive forces can be expressed in the following way: if, in normal times, the development of the productive forces was the latent [or underlying] premise of all theoretical judgments, now the question must also be raised both of the possibility of their being stationary and also of the possibility of their catastrophic decline.

In the second place, a very significant reduction and in places a stoppage in the production process may ensue. So long as society does not become extinct, this is compensated for in other ways: 1 by a more economic distribution of what is left over from previous production cycles – here the process of consumption is divorced from the process of production and becomes incommensurate with it; 2 by compulsorily extracting the fruits of agricultural production from the countryside (the difference here from the 'normal' situation being that this extraction is partly funded by direct economic methods; hence, only one half of the 'national economy' takes part in the cycle of reproduction); 3 by unproductive methods of obtaining products (military plunder, central warehouse changing hands, etc.).

In the third place, so long as the process of production is divorced from the process of consumption, even where the free market remains, consumption motives appear on the surface of events.

The dialectical-historical approach is not only free from limitations, but on the contrary thrusts itself to the fore. The component forms of the new relations and their interlacing with the old, sometimes in extraordinarily odd combinations – all this makes the relations of production of the transition period a system *sui generis*. Furthermore, it is quite clear that the dialectical-historical viewpoint, which advances the principle of the constant changeability of forms and the principles of knowledge of the *process*, must inevitably be emphasized in an analysis of an era when faults in the social strata of a straight geological type occur with unprecedented speed. The relativity of the categories of political economics becomes as clear as daylight.

The postulate of equilibrium is invalid. Equilibrium must be taken as the condition which a system should reach (if it is to exist), but may in fact fail to reach. There is no proportionality, either between production and consumption or between the various branches of production (and we might add nor between the human elements of the system). Therefore it is fundamentally wrong to carry over into the transition period the categories, concepts and laws which sufficed for the state of equilibrium. To this one can retort that, since society has not perished there is an equilibrium; however, such reasoning would be correct if the period of time under consideration was extremely protracted. Without equilibrium society cannot survive for long and dies. But this same social system can exist in an 'abnormal' state for some time, i.e. minus a state of equilibrium. In this case, a *relative* equilibrium is purchased (in so far as there is no extra-production compensating factor, which is also impossible in the long run) at the cost of the partial *destruction of that very system*.

Thus, the general characteristic of the changes and variations in the research method may be expressed in the following manner: in an analysis of the transition period, a whole series of methodological simplifications are inadmissible, which are quite appropriate and permissible in conditions of a stable production system. Marx's formulation of the question went like this: how is the existence of a given form of economy possible and what are the laws of its origin, development and disappearance?

The formulation of the question, as amended for the transition period, reads: what are the material conditions for the existence of society at the present moment, how long can it continue to exist under present conditions; how is production possible; is the establishment of equilibrium possible; what will be the result of its establishment and what would be the result of a negative solution to this question; what is the change in the relations of production in *both* cases and what are the laws of motion in *both* cases, and so on.

Now we must pass on to some basic concepts of political economy in order to ascertain the extent of their usefulness to the period under discussion. For 'ideas and categories are no more eternal than the relations they express. They are historical and transitory products.'[14]

The limits to the applicability of these categories will become instantly clear if we define the basic conditions of existence for the real relationships which correspond to them (i.e. to these categories).

Commodity. This category presupposes first and foremost the *social* division of labour or its fragmentation and, following from this, the absence of any *conscious* control mechanism over the economic processes. The social division of labour becomes apparent in the difference of the use value of commodities; the universal labour relationship between the parts of the system which has no conscious control mechanism is expressed in their value. For any product or simply any thing to become a commodity, a condition of stable social relations is not essential as, for example, with so-called 'chance' transactions. Often social relations are here established for the first time (overseas merchants on rare expeditions, rare colonial commodities, 'Raubhandel', etc.).[15] In these cases, however, commodity cannot be a *universal* form. There is no commodity production here nor a commodity economy as a form of social structure; there does not even need to be a unified society (e.g. early colonial exchange). Commodity can be a universal category, only in so far as there is a constant and not a chance social relationship on the *anarchic basis of production*. Consequently, as the *irrationality* of the production process disappears, i.e. as a *conscious* social control mechanism is introduced, in the place of the anarchic element, so commodity is *transformed into product* and loses its commodity character.

Value emerges when we have true *commodity production*. Here, a *constant* and not a chance model of anarchic relations via exchange is obligatory. A state of *equilibrium* is also necessary. The law of value is merely the law of equilibrium of an anarchic commodity system. From this point of view it is clear, for example, that the exchange of ivory for beads (where, as Marx said, the exchange is really a fraud) is not a value exchange. Not every exchange is a *commodity* exchange (when boys exchange pens; or when the proletarian state practises *product-exchange* between town and country). On the other hand, not every commodity exchange is a *value* exchange (e.g. exchange on the 'free market' with its 'absurd' prices is not a value exchange although it is a commodity exchange). Consequently, *value, as a category* of the capitalist commodity system in its equilibrium, is *least* useful of all during the transition period, where commodity production to a considerable extent disappears and there is no equilibrium.

Price, generally speaking, is the expression of a value relation. But not always. In the first instance, we can distinguish the following variants: 1 value coincides with price according to magnitude (the static equilibrium of a simple commodity system); 2 value does not coincide according to magnitude (the typical case); 3 price represents a derived magnitude particular to a commodity, which in itself has no value (e.g. the price of land as capitalist rents). One must distinguish from the cases the *imaginary* form where price *does not rest* on a value correlation. Here price is absolutely divorced from value. Consequently, in the transition epoch, the case of the imaginary form inevitably comes close to the *typical case*.

This phenomenon, in its turn, is also bound up with the collapse of the *monetary* system. Money represents the material social ligament, the knot which ties up the whole highly developed *commodity* system of production. It is clear that during the transition period, in the process of abolishing the commodity system as such, a process of 'self-negation' of money takes place. It is manifested in the first place in the so-called devaluation of money and in the second place, in the fact that the distribution of paper money is divorced from the distribution of products, and vice versa.

Money ceases to be the universal equivalent and becomes a conventional – and moreover extremely imperfect – symbol of the circulation of products.

Wages become an imaginary value without content. Since the working class is the ruling class, *wage labour* disappears, and since there is no wage labour, *there are no wages either*, as the price at which labour power is sold to the *capitalist*. Only the external husk of wages is preserved – the monetary form, which is also heading for self-destruction along with the monetary system. Under the dictatorship of the proletariat, the 'workers' receive a *socio-labour ration* and not wages.

Similarly, the category of *profit* also disappears, as well as the *category of surplus value*, inasmuch as we are talking about new production cycles. However, to the extent that the 'free market' still exists, there is speculation etc.; speculative profit does exist, but its laws of motion are defined differently from those in the normal capitalist system. Here the seller is in a monopoly position which makes products in their mass from other spheres adhere to him.

Generally speaking, one of the main trends in the transition period is the break-up of the commodity integument. With the growing socio-natural system of economic relations, the corresponding ideological categories also burst, and once this is so, the theory of the economic process is confronted with the need for a transition to natural economic thinking, i.e. to the consideration of both society and its parts as systems of fundamental elements in their natural form.

Chapter 10
'Non-Economic' Coercion in the Transition Period

In theoretical political economy, i.e. in the science which studies the way a capitalist commodity society conforms to blind laws, 'pure' economic categories predominate.

In actual history, it is notorious that conquest, enslavement, robbery, murder, briefly force, play the great part. In the tender annals of Political Economy, the idyllic reigns from time immemorial. 'Right and labour' were from all time the sole means of enrichment, the present year of course always excepted.[1]

There is no doubt that throughout history the role of violence and coercion has been extremely great. This is the soil on which theories could thrive which see violence as the alpha and omega of history.[2] On the other hand, a number of contrary theories rest on the denial of violence, theories which simply refuse to recognize empirical phenomena, a series of facts obstinately demanding an explanation. Marxism cannot 'think away' what is in reality a major historical factor. The robbery of the common land in England and the period of primary accumulation, the mass forced labour of the slaves in ancient Egypt, colonial wars, the 'great mutinies' and the 'glorious revolutions', imperialism, the communist revolution of the proletariat, the labour armies in the Soviet Republic – aren't all these ill-assorted phenomena connected with the question of coercion? Of course they are. The vulgar investigator would set his mind at rest by putting them all in the one category. The advocate of the dialectical method must analyse these forms in their historical context, in their relationship with the whole, their specific features and their functional significance, which is sometimes quite the opposite in substance.

Social violence and coercion (and we are only concerned with this) has a twofold relationship with economics: first it is a function of economics and second, it, in its turn, influences economic life. In this latter role, its influence may take one of two directions; it either takes the line of the objectively developing economic relations – in which case it satisfies a pressing social need, *accelerates* economic development and appears as its progressive form, or else it conflicts with this development – in which case, it *retards* development, acts as 'fetters' on it and, as a general rule, must yield to another form of coercion with, if one may express it thus, a different mathematical symbol.[3]

The role of violence becomes particularly prominent during 'critical epochs', 'wars and revolutions are the driving forces of history', and both these 'driving forces' are forms of violence – violence, moreover, at its harshest. On the transition from feudalism to capitalism, Marx wrote:

> These methods depend in part on brute force (auf brutalster Gewalt) e.g. the colonial system. But they all employ the power of the State (Staatmacht) the concentrated and organised force of society, to hasten . . . the process of transformation of the feudal mode of production into the capitalist mode and to shorten the transition (die Uebergange). Force is the midwife of every old society pregnant with a new one. It is itself an economic power (oekonomische Potenz).[4]

In the transition epoch, when one production structure is giving way to another, the midwife is revolutionary violence. This revolutionary violence must destroy the fetters on the development of society, i.e. the old forms of 'concentrated violence' which have become a counter-revolutionary factor, the old state and the old model of the relations of production. On the other hand, revolutionary violence must actively assist in the formation of new relations of production, after it has created a new form of 'concentrated violence', the state of the new class, which acts as a means of economic upheaval by changing the economic structure of society.[5] Hence, on the one hand, violence plays a destructive role and on the other, it is a force for cohesion, organization and construction. The greater the magnitude of this 'non-economic' force which in fact *is* an 'oekonomische Potenz', the smaller the 'costs' of the transition period will be (other things being equal, of course), the shorter this transition period will be, the more quickly social equilibrium will be established on a new basis and the more rapidly the curve of the productive forces will begin to rise. This force is not some super-economic mystical quantity, it is the power of a class accomplishing a revolution, its social might.

Clearly, therefore, its magnitude depends, first and foremost, on the extent to which that class is organized. And a revolutionary class is most highly organized when it constitutes the state power. That is why state power is 'concentrated and organized social violence'; and that is why *revolutionary* state power is the most powerful means of economic upheaval.

In the era of transition from capitalism to communism by the revolutionary class, the creator of the new society is the proletariat. Its state power, its dictatorship, the soviet state is the main factor in the destruction of the old economic relations and the creation of the new. 'Strictly speaking, political power is the organized use of force by one class in order to keep another class in subjection.'[6] In so far as this political power, as 'concentrated violence' against the bourgeoisie, is itself an *economic* force, it is the force which severs the capitalist relations of production, by putting the proletariat in charge of the material and physical framework of production and gradually introducing the *non-proletarian* human elements of production into a system of new socio-production relations. On the other hand, this same 'concentrated violence' is partly turned inward, where it is a factor in the *self-organization* and compulsory *self-discipline* of the workers. Thus we must analyse both aspects of coercion: in relation to the non-proletarian strata and in relation to the proletariat itself and the social groups closely connected with it.

The ruling proletariat, in the first phase of its supremacy, is up against 1 the parasitic strata (former landowners, investors of every sort and bourgeois entrepreneurs who had little to do with the production process), trade capitalists, speculators, stockbrokers, bankers; 2 the non-productive administrative aristocracy recruited from these same strata (the prominent bureaucrats of the capitalist state, the generals, the bishops, etc.); 3 bourgeois owner-organizers and managers (the managers of trusts and syndicates, the 'doers' of the industrial world, the most important engineers, inventors directly connected with the capitalist world, etc.); 4 the skilled bureaucracy – civil, military and ecclesiastical; 5 the technical intelligentsia and the intelligentsia in general (engineers, technicians, agronomists, live-stock experts, doctors and professors, lawyers, journalists, most of the teaching profession, etc.); 6 the officers; 7 the large-scale prosperous peasantry; 8 the middle and also in part the petty urban bourgeoisie; 9 the clergy, including the unqualified members.

All these strata, classes and groups inevitably carry on an active struggle against the proletariat under the political hegemony of the representatives of finance capital and under the military hegemony of the generals. These attacks must be repulsed and the enemy thrown into disorder. Other methods of struggle on their part (sabotage) must be crushed. Only 'concentrated violence' can do all this. As the proletariat triumphs in this struggle and its forces increasingly rally round the basic crystallization point of socio-revolutionary energy – the dictatorship of the proletariat – an accelerated process of decay in the old mentality ensues among the economically useful and non-parasitic groups in the enemy camp. These elements must be taken into account, gathered together, given a new place and introduced into the new labour framework; and only for the organization of the proletarian state using coercion can do this. It hastens the process of absorption of those human elements which are also useful in the new system; above all the technical intelligentsia. It stands to reason that these forces cannot possibly be used in any planned, socially expedient way, without compulsory pressure. For remnants of the old mentality still linger in the minds of these human categories, with their partly individualistic and partly anti-proletarian psychology, and they interpret a plan of social expediency as the grossest violation of the rights 'of the free individual'. Therefore, external state coercion is absolutely essential here. Only in the course of development, with the constant re-education of these strata as they lose their class structure and are transformed simply into socialized workers, does the element of coercion gradually decrease. Obviously, the higher a given group stood in the capitalist hierarchy the more difficult and the more painful the process of psychological re-education is; those social groups whose existence was most closely connected with the specific forms and methods of capitalist production succumb to the social processing with the greatest difficulty of all. The immediate struggle with them, in the first phase of the revolution, organizing them into conditions where they can perform socially useful work without being able to harm the cause of the communist construction, the expedient accommodation of these forces, a correct *policy* in relation to them which changes according to their psychological make-up – all this presupposes, in the final analysis, the 'sanction' of 'concentrated violence', guarding over the communist society *im Werden* (in embryo).

Coercion, however, is not confined to the former ruling classes and groups closely connected with them. In the transition period – in other forms – it is also carried over to the workers themselves and to the ruling class itself. We must investigate this side of the matter in great detail.

In the transition period analysis must not be limited to the premise of the complete homogeneity of a class. In the study of the abstract laws of the capitalist mechanism, there was no point in dwelling on the molecular movements within the classes and the differentiation among these 'real aggregates'; they were accepted as being a certain integral quantity, more or less homogeneous. To transfer this view, which was quite correct within the framework of an abstract, theoretical analysis of 'pure capitalism', to an analysis of the transition period with its extremely fluid forms and its, so to speak, fundamental dynamics would be a gross methodological error. Not only inter-class mechanics, but also intra-class mechanics have to be taken into consideration. Both the correlations of social forces and the relationships within the classes are extremely mobile values, whose mobility becomes particularly great in 'critical epochs'.[7]

In exerting an influence on nature, man changes his own nature, said Marx. But the same thing also happens in the course of social struggle, and this is what the process of revolutionary *education* of the proletariat is. If one examines this process from the viewpoint of the intra-class strata, one can designate it a process of continual rapprochement to the vanguard of the working class by its middle and lower strata. There is also a transformation of the 'class in itself' into a 'class for itself'. The attitude to 'the people' of a repentant gentleman is one of idealization of every member of the 'lower classes' in concrete terms. The proletarian–Marxist attitude operates with real values.

The proletariat comes to power as a class. But this does not signify the cohesive nature of the class where every one of its members represents some ideal mean. The proletarian vanguard actively leads the others behind it. It is a conscious, organizing quantity operating along well-thought-out lines. It carries along with it the sympathetic middle which is instinctively 'in sympathy' with the upheaval, but cannot clearly formulate aims and accurately outline ways. In the course of development *there is no* dividing line between the vanguard and this very extensive stratum. On the contrary, new forces are continually being drawn into the advanced stratum. This is the process of internal cohesion that makes a class of a class. Behind the middle layer of sympathizers is a stratum of those who are indifferent and then the so-called self-seekers. The process of education, however, touches even them; the proletarian vanguard grows and expands numerically as it absorbs the ever-growing strata of the class, which more and more becomes a 'class for itself'.

If we approach this question from a slightly different angle, then we discover roughly the following groups: a nucleus of the industrial proletariat, the typical working class, which has severed its links with the countryside and is permanently engaged in industry; the workers' aristocracy, sometimes extremely closely bound up with the interests of capital (especially the skilled workers of America, Germany and England; printers in almost all countries, etc.); seasonal workers who periodically enter and leave the industrial sphere; workers encumbered with private property (houses, sometimes land, etc.); workers with connections with the countryside, sometimes running a household on the land too; those who became workers during the war, without having completed their capitalist schooling and who are sometimes recruited from the municipal petty-bourgeoisie, the artisans and tradesmen, etc.; workers specially selected on a socio-political basis by the capitalist states (e.g. certain sections of the railwaymen); agricultural workers, outright farm labourers and semi-farm labourers, etc. Thus we get a pretty motley picture of the 'way of life' of the various categories of the working class and, therefore, of their social consciousness too. Clearly, among all these groups there are some which have been completely corrupted by capitalism, whose motives are of the narrowest, egotistical and 'self-centred'. But even comparatively broad sections of the working class bear the stamp of the capitalist commodity world. Hence, *compulsory discipline* is absolutely inevitable, and the less voluntary internal discipline is, i.e. the less revolutionized a given section or group of the proletariat is, the more strongly its compulsory nature will be felt. Even the proletarian vanguard which is united in the party of the revolution, the communist party, establishes such *compulsory self-discipline* within its own ranks. It is little felt by many component parts of its vanguard, since it coincides with their inner motivations; but nevertheless it does exist.[8] However, it is *not* established by *another* force, but expresses the collective will of all, binding on everyone.

It stands to reason that this element of compulsion, which is the self-coercion of the working class, increases from its crystallized centre towards the much more amorphous and scattered periphery. It is the *conscious cohesive force* of a fraction of the working class which for certain categories subjectively represents an external pressure but which, for the whole of the working class, objectively represents its *accelerated self-organization*.

In *communist* society there will be absolute freedom of the 'individual', spontaneous activity without coercion and no external standardization of the relations between people. In *capitalist* society, there was no spontaneous activity at all for the working class, only *coercion* on the *hostile class*. In the transition period, working-class spontaneity of action exists side by side with compulsion, set up by the working class as a class for itself and for all its parts. The contradiction here between compulsion and spontaneous independent action is an expression of the contradictory nature of the transition period itself, where the proletariat has *already* left the confines of capitalist compulsion, but has not *yet* become a worker communist society.

One of the main forms of compulsion of the new model, operating within the working class itself, is the abolition of the so-called 'freedom of labour'. 'Freedom of labour' in capitalist society was one of the many myths of that society, since in reality the monopolization of the means of production by the capitalists *forced* the workers to sell their labour power. This is what that 'freedom' amounted to: in the first place, to the relative possibility of *choosing* your own master (moving from one factory to another), the possibility of being 'fired' and getting 'the sack'; in the second place, this 'freedom' implied *competition between the workers themselves*. In this latter meaning, 'the freedom of labour' was already partly overcome *by the workers' organizations* in the capitalist period, when the trade unions partly abolished competition between the workers by uniting them and making them stronger in their struggle against the capitalist class. The trade unions demanded that only union members should be allowed into a factory; they boycotted (i.e. used violence against) the strike-breakers – that living embodiment of the bourgeois 'freedom of labour', etc.

Under the proletarian dictatorship, the question of an 'owner' no longer arises, since the 'expropriators have been expropriated'. On the other hand, the remaining disorganization, lack of solidarity, individualism, parochial narrow-mindedness and the defects of capitalist society are apparent in the form of the failure to understand general proletarian tasks, which are expressed most forcibly in the tasks and demands of the soviet dictatorship, the workers' state. Since these tasks must be accomplished whatever the cost, obviously from the proletariat's point of view, the abolition of the so-called 'freedom of labour' is essentially *in the name* of the real and not mythical freedom of the working class. For this freedom of labour cannot be reconciled with a correctly organized, 'planned' economy and distribution of the labour force. Hence, a regime of compulsory labour service and state distribution of workers under the dictatorship of the proletariat already shows a comparatively high degree of organization throughout the entire apparatus and the stability of the proletarian power in general.[9]

Under the capitalist regime, compulsion was defended in the name of 'the interests of all', whilst in reality it was a case of the interests of the capitalist groups. Under the dictatorship of the proletariat, *for the first time*, compulsion is an instrument of the majority in the interest of that majority.

The proletariat, as a class, is the only class which is, on the whole, devoid of ownership prejudices, but it is compelled to operate cheek by jowl with a sometimes very numerous peasantry. If the upper peasantry (the kulaks) are actively fighting against the measures of the proletarian dictatorship, then the 'concentrated violence' of the proletariat has to repulse the kulak 'Vendee', more or less convincingly. But the masses in the middle, and in part even the poor peasantry, constantly waver, vacillate, prompted now by hatred of capitalist-landowner exploitation, a hatred which drives them to communism, now by the attitudes of an owner (and consequently, in times of famine, by the attitudes of a speculator too) which drive them to embrace reaction. This latter is expressed in resistance to the state grain monopoly, in the yearning for free trade, which is speculation, and for speculation, which is free trade, in resistance to the system of compulsory labour service and in general to any form of state control over economic anarchy. These stimuli are especially emphasized when the exhausted towns cannot at first supply any equivalent for the grain and labour service going 'into the common pool'. Here, therefore, coercion is an absolute categorical imperative.

Thus with regard to the former *bourgeois groups*, coercion on the part of the proletarian dictatorship is coercion on the part of an alien class, waging a class struggle against the objects of its compulsion; with regard to the non-kulak *peasant* mass, coercion on the part of the proletariat is a class struggle only in so far as the peasantry is an owner and speculator; in so far as the peasant is a worker, an opponent of capitalism, and not an exploiter, coercion represents his unity and labour organization, his education and involvement in the building of communism.

Finally, with respect to the proletariat itself, coercion is a method of organization, established by the working class itself, i.e. a method of compulsory, accelerated *self-organization*.

From a wider point of view, i.e. on a longer historical perspective, proletarian coercion in all its forms, from executions to labour service, is, however paradoxical this may sound, a method of creating communist mankind from the human material of the capitalist epoch. Indeed, the epoch of the dictatorship of the proletariat is, at the same time, the epoch of the *deformation* of the classes. Capitalism was accompanied by the progressive social *fragmentation* of society: it demoralized the peasantry, destroyed 'the middle estate' and brought class contradictions to a head. At first an expression of the gaping schism in the capitalist world, the dictatorship of the proletariat, after the establishment of a certain equilibrium, *begins to gather mankind together again.*

The former bourgeoisie, stricken, defeated, impoverished and trained to physical labour, is being spiritually remade and re-educated. Part of it perishes in the civil war, but the part which survives already constitutes a different social category. The intelligentsia likewise. The peasantry, much more steadfast in the general current than the others, is still being drawn into the mainstream and re-educated, slowly but surely. The proletariat is likewise 'changing its own nature'. Thus specific class features are erased and the classes begin to disintegrate as classes, by taking the proletariat as the standard. The period of the de-formation of the classes is under way. The dictatorship of the proletariat is the means for this de-formation. As concentrated violence, it ultimately does away with all violence whatsoever. As the highest expression of the class, it does away with all classes. As the regime of a class organized as a state power, it will prepare the downfall of every state. In its struggle for its own existence, it destroys its own existence. In a classless, stateless communist society where, in place of external discipline, there will be the simple inclination to work on the part of the normal social being, external norms of human behaviour will become meaningless. Coercion, in any form whatsoever, will disappear once and for all.

Chapter II
The World Revolutionary Process and the World System of Communism

Before the war, the world economic system was in a state of mobile equilibrium. The process of exchange between countries, the international movement of capital (the export and import of capital) and the international movement of labour power bound the separate parts of this system firmly together with the strong ties of the 'normal' processes which are vitally necessary to the very existence of the world economy and its component elements. The laws of the capitalist commodity system, which in pure theory were analysed in their abstract form as the laws of an abstract, 'pure' capitalist society and which were concretely realized in the epoch of industrial capitalism within the limits of nationally delimited territories, became, above all, the spontaneous laws of an anarchic *world* system. World prices and, hence, universal social labour, as their control mechanism in the last resort; world competition, the world market, the tendency towards a universal average rate of profit, the gravitation of interest rates towards a single, but again universal mean; parity of wages and their gravitation to one world-wide level, which propelled labour power from one country to another; world industrial crises and so on and so forth – these were all a manifestation of the basic *fact*, contained in the state of mobile equilibrium, but developed in the contradictions of the system of *world* capitalism.

This universal cohesion and the interdependency of the individual capitalist states – the fact that they were all component parts of a *common* system – inevitably entailed the *world* nature of war. Just as crises assumed the character of *world* crises, on account of the chain-like connection between the parts of the world economy, war too was bound to assume the character of a colossal world slaughter. A crisis spreads and rolls like a wave, because a disturbance of the equilibrium in one part of the system is inevitably carried, as if by telegraph wire, to all its parts. In the conditions of a world economy war, as a loss of equilibrium in one part, unavoidably turns into a gigantic shock to the *entire* system, into a world war. The breakdown in the relations of the world economy meant that it fell to pieces and the process of expanded negative reproduction, which ran parallel in the warring countries in these conditions of breakdown, ultimately led to the collapse of the entire system.

With which links was this collapse bound to begin? It stands to reason that it was bound to begin with those links which were the weakest *in terms of capitalist organization.*[1]

Indeed, we have already seen in chapter 3 of this work that the stability of particular capitalist systems within the world economy, when war became a concrete fact, was explained by the internal reorganization of the relations of production, which led to the form of state capitalism. On the whole, therefore, one can say that the stability of these systems was directly proportionate to the level of state capitalist organization. Without it, capitalism could not even have survived the term which history allotted it. This stability, linked to the form of state capitalism, developed along both production and socio-class lines. However, the state capitalist form of national economy was itself only possible with a certain 'maturity' of capitalist relations in general. All other things being equal, the higher the development of the productive forces, the finance-capitalist organization and the concatenation of monopolistic relations of the new capitalism, the more absolute the state capitalist form was. The more backward and agrarian a given country, the less developed its productive forces and the weaker the finance-capitalist organization of the economy was, the less absolute it was. But with regard to both the economic and social structure and the technical-production structure, the systems with the most highly developed technology, required by the imperialist war, were bound to prove the most stable in a mighty conflict. This *technology* had a decisive military significance. Perfection of the *organizational form* partly made up for the process of expanded negative reproduction. The *concentration* of the social might of the bourgeoisie into a state power united with the economic organizations of capital created a tremendous resistance opposing the workers' movement. Therefore, the collapse of the world capitalist system began with the weakest national economic systems, with the least highly developed state–capitalist organizations.[2]

The question of the chronological order of proletarian revolutions should not be confused with that of the height [level of development or maturity] of the model of a particular revolution, which is determined by the importance of the system of production relations, which are embodied in the proletariat. The greater it is relative to the concentrated proletariat, the higher is the model of the communist revolution and the harder it is to triumph, but the easier it is to build.[3]

The preconditions for the organization of communism are, as we have seen, concentrated means of production and socialized labour. In the world capitalist system, these preconditions are most closely expressed in the 'Great Powers' of capital, where the power of the bourgeoisie is strongest. On the other hand, precisely because we are faced with an *anarchistic* world system, whose component parts occupy a particular position in the world economy, the opportunity was created for these 'great' imperialist systems to exploit the colonies. And from this arose yet another possibility, that of a temporary 'community of interests' between the imperialist 'fatherland' and the working class. This 'Interessengemeinschaft', in its turn, severely hampered the course of the revolution, which was based on the severance of any community between the bourgeoisie and the proletariat. Nevertheless, inasmuch as the revolution is already an established fact, it takes its highest form of all in just those countries where the working class constitutes the highest possible percentage of the whole population and where the means of production are the most heavily concentrated, because these two factors provide, first, the material and physical framework for the

169

new society and, second, its fundamental relation of production. From this point of view it is easy to understand why the revolution of the proletariat took place first of all in Russia. Here, the organization of the state machine was very weak and the forms of state capitalism had only just begun to show. The technological weakness of a mainly agrarian country caused an unprecedented military defeat. The state apparatus turned out to be so unstable that it could be toppled comparatively easily by the proletariat in the major urban centres. On the other hand, however, after the victory of the proletariat, the causes of the ease of that victory were dialectically transformed into the causes of supreme difficulties. The economic backwardness of the country, the enormous field of fragmented, scattered labour of small property-owners as opposed to truly socialized labour – this was all a tremendous obstacle to the organization of a planned socio-economic system. The revolution was also an easy victory because the proletariat in its striving for communism was backed up by the peasantry, which was opposed to the landowners. But that same peasantry is proving to be the greatest obstacle in the period of the construction of communist relations of production.

In contrast, the revolution in Germany has been a much more painful process. The capitalist state puts up much more stubborn resistance; the proletariat represents the sole revolutionary force; victory is won with much greater difficulty. But the model of the revolution here is higher, despite the fact that the revolution comes later.[4]

Thus, if we examine the revolutionary process on a world scale, we can advance the following general proposition: the world revolutionary process begins with the partial systems of the world economy which are at the lowest level, where the victory of the proletariat is easier but the crystallization of the new relations harder; the speed with which the revolution advances is inversely proportional to the maturity of the capitalist relations and the height of the model of the revolution.

Bringing the imperialist war to an end cannot stop the disintegration of the capitalist system, its collapse and the communist revolution of the proletariat. The decline in the productive forces continues even after the conclusion of peace. The imperialists hoped to organize a world economy, by methods which deny a world economy. The victors hoped to get out of their difficulties by dint of ruthless exploitation, which ultimately destroys the very possibility of this exploitation. But the spirit of world competition plays a spiteful trick on them by forcing them to fight each other. Thus, history gives evidence to imperialism of its fatal *a posteriori* quality, which suddenly appears before the 'victors' in all its horrific nakedness.[5]

The economic isolation and the disintegration of relations during the war, and the consequences of this after the war, aggravate the process of destruction of the productive forces and precipitate the collapse of the capitalist system, link by link; the revolutionary conquest of power by the proletariat and the upheaval in the mode of production, if only in one country, greatly intensifies the process of destruction of the old ideology and 'revolutionizes' the working class in other countries, the sub-soil for which has been prepared by all that has gone before.

In the first soviet republic, the world proletariat has its own organizations, possessing a maximum of social and material power. Therefore, in the midst of the disintegrating system of a world capitalist economy, they inevitably represent new points of crystallization, centres of attraction for proletarian energy and the most important factor in the further decomposition of the capitalist system. The devastation proceeds in leaps and bounds throughout the capitalist world, despite efforts to breathe new life into it. The productive forces diminish; the relations of production decompose and tear apart. There is no economic equilibrium between the production spheres, and the loss of equilibrium assumes increasingly severe forms. There is no socio-class equilibrium either and the situation heads for a decisive conflict. The political organization, or rather the state of the bourgeoisie suffers a crisis, for world imperialism proves incapable of pursuing an absolutely united policy, which is homogeneous in all its parts. The capitalist army becomes demoralized. Inasmuch as the world production anarchy and its outward expression, world competition, dictates its blind will to the bourgeois state organizations, the entire process increasingly assumes the spontaneous nature of a collapse. The anarchic element of capitalist relations on the basis of their destruction creates a characteristic state of uncertainty, which betokens the approaching end. And in the midst of this unravelling world fabric, the *growing* organizations of the new model appear, offering a fundamental opportunity for *development*, since here alone is the restoration of social equilibrium possible: organizations which derive additional power from the very decay of the capitalist system; the states of the proletariat with a new system of economic relations, which strengthens as the disintegrating, old, capitalist groups weaken.

The capitalist system in the area of industrial capitalism was the embodiment of the spontaneous process, for relations here were completely unregulated; the unconscious 'market' took the place of a conscious, control mechanism. The state-capitalist form of society, which did nothing to organize world relations, replaced unconscious processes with the conscious regulation of economic relations by putting the class plan of the bourgeoisie in the place of conformity to the blind laws of a commodity society. The epoch of the collapse of state-capitalist organizations once again un-leashes this anarchy, which differs from the commodity anarchy of the past in the direction it takes; the anarchy in the former case was the means of capitalist concentration and centralization, of the *growth* of capitalist society and finally of its organizations; in the present case the anarchy is the mechanism whereby the organized system falls apart. But again, in the midst of this spontaneous process of disintegration, the process of organization and rational-ization of economic life can only take place in the proletarian states, but this time on a fundamentally different basis. The decomposi-tion and disintegration of the old system and the organization of the new – these are the *basic* and most common laws to which the transition period conforms. Therefore, whatever deviations there may be, the resultant force follows the course of socialism. The relationship between the states of the proletariat and those of the bourgeoisie is most clearly seen in their military conflicts, in the class war where the old armies are demoralized because the entire course of development makes social equilibrium on a capitalist basis impossible.

The disintegration of relations between the imperialist states and their numerous colonies is a major factor in the decomposition of the capitalist system. The so-called 'nation state' was a pure myth even in the pre-war period. What really existed in practice were the subjects of colonial policy, the imperialist states representing complex systems with a strong nucleus and a subordinate peri-phery, and the subjects of this colonial policy with varying shades and degrees of subordination. It is in the formation of these enormous bodies that organized 'non-economic' violence, which, as Marx said, is in fact an economic force, plays a colossal role. 'Machtpolitik' (power politics), 'Armée und Flotte' and other charms of imperialism were the means of organizing the imperialist state system.

State cohesion, resting ultimately on armed force, had a decisive significance. Hence, as the state power of capital decays, the decay of the imperialist systems must also ensue, colonies break away, the 'Great Powers' split up and independent 'nation states' separate off. From the point of view of the struggle of the social forces, this may be expressed in a series of colonial uprisings, national uprisings, small national wars, etc. Of course, the colonial uprisings and national revolutions (Ireland, India, China etc.) would have absolutely no *direct* bearing on the unfolding proletarian revolutions; their *local* and immediate significance does not lie in the establishment of a proletarian dictatorship at all; as a general rule, the proletariat does not play a leading political role here, because it is extremely weak. But nevertheless, as a component part, these colonial uprisings and national revolutions do enter into the great, world revolutionary process, which shifts the entire axis of the world economy. For what we have here are factors in the general disintegration of the capitalist relations of production, a disintegration which facilitates the victory of the proletarian revolution and the dictatorship of the working class.

The dictatorship of the proletariat cannot triumph if the proletariat in different countries are isolated from each other. Therefore, during the course of the struggle an adhesion, a bond, a cohesive union between all the emerging, proletarian soviet republics is inevitable. Even for the bourgeoisie during the transition period its world union is an objective necessity: it needs it economically, for only thus can it hope to overcome the crisis and it needs it politically, for only thus can it put up a resistance to the proletariat. Hence, the efforts to create the 'League of Nations'. However, the disintegration of the capitalist system, which has already set in, its colossal disorganization and the large number of newly emerging conflicts have greatly reinforced decentralization tendencies and therefore the bourgeoisie is in a state of collapse. The anarchistic element of disintegration outgrows the organizational intelligence of the bourgeoisie.

For the proletariat, economic and political unity is a matter of life or death, and since its partial victories (its dictatorships) represent a triumph over the disintegration, this gives rise to the objective need for the unification of the proletarian state systems. With the regeneration of the economic and political fabric of the world economy and the shift of the centre of gravity to the proletarian states and their alliances, the entire picture of the world economy is altered. Former colonies and backward agrarian countries, where there is no dictatorship of the proletariat, nevertheless enter into economic relations with the industrial, socialist republics. Little by little they are drawn into a socialist system, roughly along the same lines as peasant agriculture is induced to participate within the individual socialist states.

Thus the world dictatorship of the proletariat gradually gains in strength. As it grows, the resistance of the bourgeoisie weakens and, towards the end, any remaining bourgeois complexes will in all probability surrender with all their organizations in *corpore*.[6]

But the world dictatorship of the proletariat is already in fact the beginning of the negation of proletarian dictatorship altogether. The state power of the working class inevitably increases as the resistance of the capitalist groups grows. Since the unfolding process of capitalist collapse and communist revolution is an entire historical period, a whole era, which also includes a number of ruthless class wars, not to mention civil wars, it is quite understandable that the state cannot die off under such conditions. But as soon as the decisive world victory of the proletariat is assured, the growth curve of proletarian state power will start to fall steeply, since the major and fundamental tasks of state power as such, the task of suppressing the bourgeoisie, will be finished. Externally enforced standardizations will begin to die off: the first to go will be the army and navy as the sharpest instruments of external coercion; then the system of punitive and repressive organs: then the forced nature of labour etc. The productive forces, distributed not according to national divisions, but according to the principle of economic advisability, develop at an unprecedented rate. Gigantic reservoirs of energy, which were previously spent on the class struggle, wars, militarism, overcoming crises, competition, etc., now turn to productive labour. The de-formation of the classes, the industrial training and education of new generations and the rationalization of the entire production process accelerates the growth of the productive forces even further. Distribution ceases to be a compulsory equivalent distribution 'according to one's work'. The socialism of the proletariat dictatorship and of the subsequent period develops into a world system of communist society.[7] For the first time in the history of mankind, a system is established which is harmoniously constructed in all its parts: it is ignorant of both production and social anarchy. It abolishes the struggle of man with man for ever and unites the whole of mankind into a single body which quickly takes possession of the incalculable riches of nature.

The proletariat, which actively builds the future of mankind and has a clear vision of this future, can say in the words of the great champion of knowledge: *Novarum rerum mihi nascitur ordo.* Let the blind refuse to see this new order, its advent is inescapable and inevitable.

Part III

Diagrammatic Tables relating to *The Economics of the Transition Period*

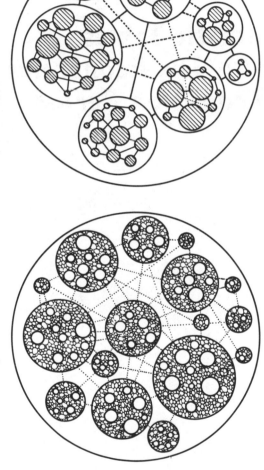

A World Economy in the epoch of industrial capitalism

1 The very small circles and dots stand for the separate enterprises within unorganized 'national' economics.

2 The dotted lines stand for the relations between the latter which mainly take the form of exchange relations.

B World Economy in the epoch of finance capitalism

1 The very small circles are the banks, trusts and syndicates, connected to each other in an organized manner, forming a state capitalist trust.

2 The dotted lines stand for the less stable links between state capitalist trusts; the solid lines for the stable links, chiefly through profit sharing and financing.

The system of State Capitalism

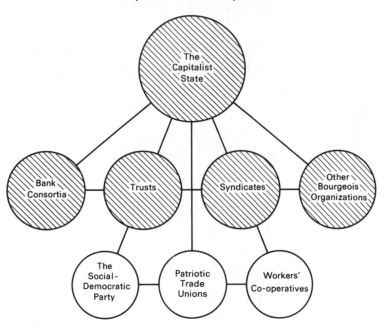

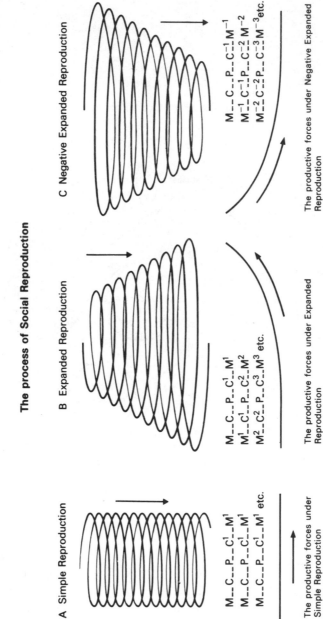

The process of Social Reproduction

A Simple Reproduction

B Expanded Reproduction

C Negative Expanded Reproduction

$M\_\_C\_\_P\_\_C^1\_\_M^1$
$M\_\_C\_\_P\_\_C^1\_\_M^1$
$M\_\_C\_\_P\_\_C^1\_\_M^1$ etc.

$M\_\_C\_\_P\_\_C^1\_\_M^1$
$M^1\_\_C^1\_\_P\_\_C^2\_\_M^2$
$M^2\_\_C^2\_\_P\_\_C^3\_\_M^3$ etc.

$M\_\_C\_\_P\_\_C^{-1}\_\_M^{-1}$
$M^{-1}\_\_C^{-1}\_\_P\_\_C^{-2}\_\_M^{-2}$
$M^{-2}\_\_C^{-2}\_\_P\_\_C^{-3}\_\_M^{-3}$ etc.

The productive forces under Simple Reproduction

The productive forces under Expanded Reproduction

The productive forces under Negative Expanded Reproduction

For simplicity we have left out of consideration non-productive consumption, with the exception of group 'A'

State Capitalism and the System of the Dictatorship of the Proletariat

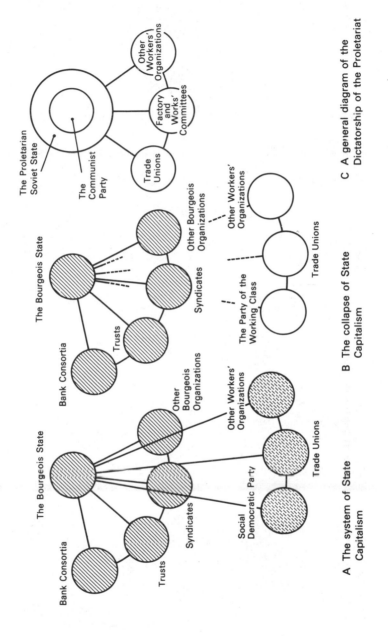

A The system of State Capitalism

B The collapse of State Capitalism

C A general diagram of the Dictatorship of the Proletariat

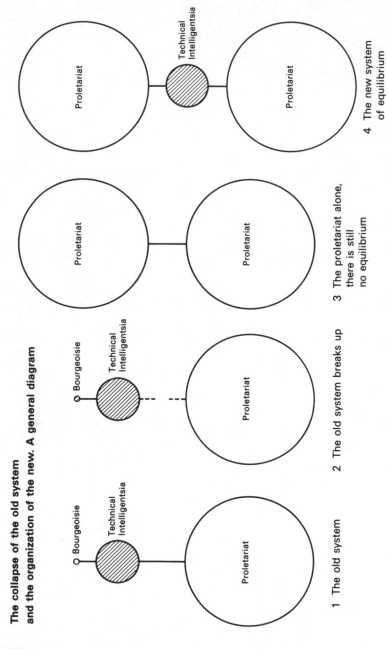

The collapse of the old system
and the organization of the new. A general diagram

Bourgeoisie
Technical Intelligentsia
Proletariat

1 The old system

Bourgeoisie
Technical Intelligentsia
Proletariat

2 The old system breaks up

Proletariat
Proletariat

3 The proletariat alone,
there is still
no equilibrium

Proletariat
Technical Intelligentsia
Proletariat

4 The new system
of equilibrium

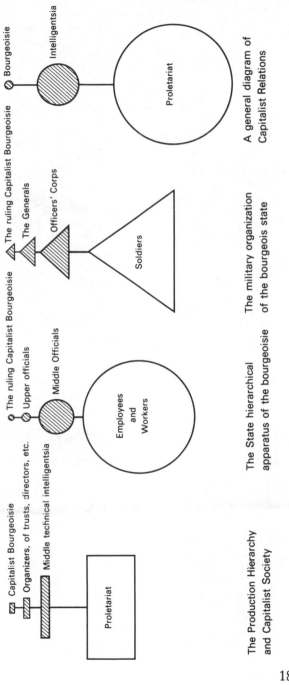

The relations of the Capitalist Hierarchy

Bourgeoisie
Intelligentsia
Proletariat
A general diagram of Capitalist Relations

The ruling Capitalist Bourgeoisie
The Generals
Officers' Corps
Soldiers
The military organization of the bourgeois state

The ruling Capitalist Bourgeoisie
Upper officials
Middle Officials
Employees and Workers
The State hierarchical apparatus of the bourgeoisie

Capitalist Bourgeoisie
Organizers, of trusts, directors, etc.
Middle technical intelligentsia
Proletariat
The Production Hierarchy and Capitalist Society

Town and Country in the process of transformation

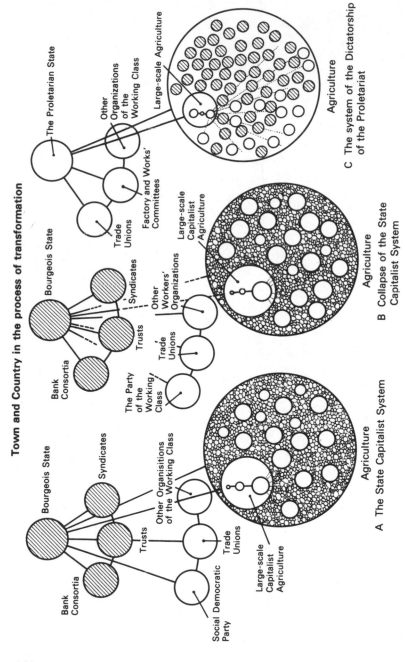

A The State Capitalist System

B Collapse of the State Capitalist System

C The system of the Dictatorship of the Proletariat

Editor's Appendices

Appendix I
Bukharin's Theory of Expanded Negative Reproduction

I

As was seen in chapter 3, Bukharin discussed the effects of war production upon an economy, that is to say an abstract notional economy. However, this abstract economy was based upon, in part, his observations of the effects of the First World War and the Russian civil war. He pointed to the illusory growth of the gross national product, measured in monetary terms, to which a war economy gave rise. He argued that such an illusory growth could in fact obscure an actual decline in output in real terms. Although it will be fairly easily understood that war destroys large amounts of material means of production and means of consumption, Bukharin went further in his analysis of this process and examined its effects upon valorization and the accumulation of capital. In so doing he introduced the concept which he termed 'expanded negative reproduction'. This process is partially illustrated by Figure 3.

Here, I want to draw out some of the implications, and use Marx's schema of reproduction to illustrate Bukharin's theorem in a different manner.[1]

In developing his concept Bukharin was directly challenging the 'truly monstrous theoretical constructions that drew the conclusions about the *beneficial* (!) influence of war on "national economic" life. . . .' By implication he was also challenging the view of Rosa Luxemburg (and all who have since followed her on this point) in her assumption that armaments were a field for the accumulation and valorization of capital.[2]

Although he was primarily concerned with a war situation – he was writing in the midst of a destructive civil war – in which there was not only a direct diversion of a large part of the gross national product to means of destruction but also the direct destruction of the forces of production, Bukharin's formulation can also be applied in an analysis of modern 'peace time' capitalism. The phrase usually applied to cover this latter situation is 'the permanent arms economy'.[3] It is not the purpose of this note to explore all the ramifications of the debate on the role of the so-called arms economy in modern capitalism, rather I want to attempt to elucidate Bukharin's idea in relation to the main question, i.e. state expenditure.

I begin this examination with an algebraic model, then later I use a simple numerical model. There are slight variations in the methods adopted, since each one has its own particular logic. There may be some objections to my assumption that Department III, when introduced into the schema of reproduction, is non-productive of surplus value. However, I feel that an examination of the numerical model will be sufficient to allay doubts on this point. To develop, in depth, arguments as to whether particular activities are or are not productive of surplus value in the capitalist mode of production would take us too far afield from the main purpose of this note.

Let us begin by examining this question algebraically. We have a two-department schema of reproduction, where Department I produces means of production and Department II produces means of consumption. This is a closed model, with no external trade and with only two classes, capitalists and workers.

Dept. I $\quad c1 + v1 + s1 = y1 = w1$
Dept. II $\quad c2 + v2 + s2 = y2 = w2$

Here, c = constant capital, v = variable capital and s = surplus value created during the production process, c + v = capital inputs for any given production period. I assume all constant capital and variable capital is turned over once per production period. I also assume y = value of the product and, given that I assume that one hour's socially necessary labour time equals, or is embodied in, one unit of value and one unit of value is embodied in one unit of material production, y = w, where w denotes material product. Therefore, $y1 + y2 = Y$ and $w1 + w2 = W$, therefore $Y = W$.

Let us first look at a schema of simple reproduction, i.e. where no accumulation takes place, and all surplus value is consumed unproductively. In this case we have:

Dept. I $c1 + v1 + s1 = y1 = w1$, therefore the value of $y1$ is embodied in $w1$ units of means of production.

Dept. II $c2 + v2 + s2 = y2 = w2$ and the value $y2$ is embodied in means of consumption.

Within this framework exchanges between the two departments are relatively uncomplicated. In Department I we have $w1$ units of means of production, this means that for production to continue at the existing level $c1$ must be reconstituted in the material form of a certain number of units of $w1$, therefore we have $w1 - c1 = c2$ material form or $y1 - c1 = c2$ value form. This tells us that Department II *may* have the quantity $w1 - c1$ for it to also continue production at the existing level.

In Department II we have $w2$ units of means of consumption. From this must be deducted $v2 + s2$, therefore $w2 - (v2 + s2) = c2$ material form and the same applies to the value form. This $c2$ in the value form is that which Department II must advance for the next production cycle. However, the material form of $c2$ is at the moment means of consumption. Let us therefore examine all the demands for the material form made upon both departments. We have:

$c1 + c2 = c1 + v1 + s1$, and $v1 + s1 + v2 + s2 = c2 + v2 + s2$. And this will also be true for the value form. These equations may reduce to a single one, by removing all the terms which appear on both sides of them, namely $c2 = (v1 + s1)$. We can look at this equation in the following manner:

$$c1 + \boxed{v1 + s1}$$
$$\boxed{c2} + v2 + s2$$

The quantities in the boxes must be in equilibrium for our equation to hold.

Now let us examine expanded reproduction, i.e. where the accumulation of capital takes place. We start with the same basic schema:

PP1 (Production Period 1)
$c1 + v1 + s1 = y1 = w1$
$c2 + v2 + s2 = y2 = w2$
and $y1 + y2 = Y$, $w1 + w2 = W$ and $Y = W$

Here I have introduced the notation PP1, this tells us that this is production period one, and for further cycles we shall have PP2, PP3, etc. Where accumulation takes place surplus value is divided into three basic parts, sc = capital accumulated in the form of constant capital sv = capital accumulated as variable capital and sk = surplus value consumed unproductively by the capitalists. So, for expanded reproduction we have:

$$\overbrace{c1+v1+sc1+sv1+sk1}^{s1}=y1=w1$$
$$\underbrace{c2+v2+sc2+sv2+sk2}_{s2}=y1=w1$$

Since sk represents the unproductively consumed part of the surplus value only sc and sv represents *potential* capital. The balance of supply and demand for PP1 will be:

Supply PP1		Demand, including inputs for PP2
w1@y1	=	c1 + sc1 + c2 + sc2
w2@y2	=	v1 + sv1 + v2 + sv2 + sk1 + sk2

In this situation $v1+sv1+sk1>c2$, and equilibrium will only hold if we have $v1+sv1+sk1=c2+sc2$. Starting the second production period we have:

Dept. I $(c1+sc1)+(v1+sv1)+s1^*=y1^*=w1^*$
Dept. II $(c2+sc2)+(v2+sv2)+s2^*=y2^*=w2^*$

Alternatively we can put it as:

Dept. I $(c1+\varDelta c1)+(v1+\varDelta v1)+s1^*=y1^*=w1^*$
Dept. II $(c2+\varDelta c2)+(v2+\varDelta v2)+s2^*=y2^*=w2^*$

Assuming all increments are positive, we have $s1^*>s1$ and $s2^*>s2$. But none of the value form of $s1^*$ or $s2^*$ falls upon PP1 as demand. Moreover, the material form and value form of sk1 and sk2 fall out of the production process. The material form of v1, sv1, v2 and sv2 also falls out of the productive process since they are consumed by the workers. However, the value form of v1, sv1, v2 and sv2 reappear as money capital in the hands of the capitalists for the replacement and expansion of variable capital, i.e. to buy labour power.

Let us now examine what will happen when a third department

is created, for the production of armaments. We start with PP1 again, only we shall call it PP1' to distinguish it from our previous PP1.

Dept. I $\quad$ $c1' + v1' =$ capital input
Dept. II $\quad$ $c2' + v2' =$ capital input

and at the end of the production period we have:

Dept. I $\quad$ $c1' + v1' + s1' = y1' = w1'$
Dept. II $\quad$ $c2' + v2' + s2' = y2' = w2'$

If we now allocate the surplus value in both departments into four parts, the fourth part being an allocation of surplus value for arms production, this I designate su, we have:

$$\text{Dept. I} \quad c1' + v1' + \overbrace{sc1' + sv1' + sk1' + su1'}^{s1'} = y1' = w1'$$
$$\text{Dept. II} \quad c2' + v2' + \underbrace{sc2' + sv2' + sk2' + su2'}_{s2'} = y2' = w2'$$

Looking at supply and demand we have:

Supply PP1'		Demand, including inputs for PP2'
w1' @ y1'	$=$	$c1' + sc1' + c2' + sc2' + uc3'$
w2' @ y2'	$=$	$v1' + sv1' + v2' + sv2' + sk1' + sk2' + uv3'$

and starting PP2'

Dept. I $\quad$ $(c1' + sc1') + (v1' + sv1')$
Dept. II $\quad$ $(c2' + sc2') + (v2' + sv2')$
Dept. III $\quad$ $c3' \quad\quad + v3'$

It would be a mistake to divide the sum of $su1' + su2'$ into $c3'$, $v3'$ and $s3'$. To do so would introduce a fundamental disequilibrium into the schema. There has to be a correlation between the value form and the material form for the schema to be in equilibrium. Looking at the constant capital of w1 @ y1 of PP1, which must serve as input for PP2, this also holds for PP1' and PP2'. Given our assumptions we can say that c1 of PP1 = c1' of PP1', but sc1 $\neq$ sc1'. And given that we have introduced the quantity c3', sc > sc' in Departments I and II, again on the assumption that w1 = w1'. However, it must be the case that the sum of all workers and capitalists consumption must equal w2 = y2 for there to be equilibrium.

It follows from this that the demand made upon Department I must be $c1 + sc1 + c2 + sc2 = w1 = y1$ without arms production; and with arms production this demand must be $c1' + sc1' + c2' + sc2' + c3' = w1' = y1'$. To take the sum of the value form of $c3'$ and $v3'$ and divide it so that either of them represents a different material from $su1'$ and $su2'$ will throw the whole schema into disequilibrium, unless there are corresponding adjustments made in all the other terms of the equations. If one merely examines the *value* form of the schema without correlating it with the material form, one can be led astray.[4]

Let us look at PP2' again; we left it with only capital input. I assume that since Department III is non-reproductive its 'capital' is in reality revenue drawn from the surplus value of Departments I and II. Therefore we have:

PP2'
Dept. I	$c1' + v1' + s1' = y1' = w1'$
Dept. II	$c2' + v2' + s2' = y2' = w2'$
Dept. III	$c3' + v3' \qquad = w3' \neq y3'$

But

Dept. I	$c1' + v1' + sc1' + sv1' + sk1'^{\circ} + su1' = w1' \neq y1'$
Dept. II	$c2' + v2' + sc2' + sv2' + sk1'^{\circ} + su2' = w2' \neq y2'$
Dept. III	$c3' + v3' + sk3'^{\circ} \qquad\qquad\qquad = w3' = y3'$

And

$$w1' + w2' + w3' = W', \quad y1' + y2' + y3' = Y'$$

How does this come about? This is because I have introduced sk'° which is a modified form of sk'. Here the sum of $sk1'$ and $sk2'$ has been divided between the three departments and is apportioned according to the 'capital' invested in each one. Although the material form of the production of each department is the same, the value form in monetary terms *is* changed. We have:

Supply PP2'	Demand, including inputs into PP3'
$w1'$	$c1' + sc1' + c2' + sc2' + c3'$
$w2'$	$v1' + sv1' + v2' + sv2' + v3' + sk1'^{\circ} + sk2'^{\circ} + sk3'^{\circ}$
$w3'$	$su1' + su2' + sk3'^{\circ}$

There may appear to be a discrepancy between the totals in the above schema, however, this arises because of the nature of the arms production department. We can see, for example, that $c1'$ and $sc1'$ are produced in PP2' and used as inputs for PP3'. But with Department III the $w3'$ of PP2' was produced in PP1' in the forms of means of production and means of consumption, and then transformed into armaments in PP2'. The material and value forms of the arms are *not* recirculated and thus end their life in the final commodity form once they are purchased by the state.

II

Here we arrive at Bukharin's proposition of expanded negative reproduction. I have, up to now, assumed that $sc1'$, $sc2'$, $sv1'$ and $sv2'$ have all been positive increments, i.e. the total of $sk' + su' < s1' + s2'$. However, it may well be, that if su' grows at a much faster rate than the total social production, we may have $- \Delta sc1'$ etc. This would indicate that the change in c will be negative and not positive as we have previously assumed. Let us assume that $su1' + su2'$ grows at this increased rate and examine what will happen in PP4'.

PP4'
Dept. I $c1' + v1' + s1' = y1' = w1'$
Dept. II $c2' + v2' - s2' = y2' = w2'$
Dept. III $c3' + v3' \qquad = w3' \neq y3'$
But, $w1' + w2' + w3' = W'$, $y1' + y2' + y3' = Y'$

And for reproduction we have:

Dept. I $c1' - \Delta c1' + v1' - \Delta v1' + sk1'^\circ + su1'$
Dept. II $c2' - \Delta c2' + v2' - \Delta v2' + sk2'^\circ + su2'$
Dept. III $c3' + \Delta c3' + v3' + \Delta v3' + sk3'^\circ$

and:

$$(c1' - \Delta c1') + (c2' - \Delta c2') + (c3' + \Delta c3') = c1' + v1' + s1'$$
$$(v1' - \Delta v1') + (v2' - \Delta v2') + (v3' + \Delta v3') + sk1'^\circ + sk2'^\circ + sk3'^\circ = c2' + v2' + s2'$$
$$(c3' + \Delta c3') + (v3' + \Delta v3') + sk'^\circ = su1' + su2' + sk3'^\circ$$

From the above we can, therefore, say that given the primacy accorded arms production, PP5' will be as follows:

Dept. I $\quad (c1' - \Delta c1') + (v1' - \Delta v1') + s1' = y1' = w1'$

Dept. II $\quad (c2' - \Delta c2') + (v2' - \Delta v2') + s2' = y2' = w2'$

Dept. III $\quad (c3' + \Delta c3') + (v3' + \Delta v3') \qquad = w3' \neq y3'$

And in this case, PP5′ s1′ <PP4′ s1′, PP5′ s2′ <PP4′ s2′, and PP5′ W′ <PP4′ W′ and PP5′ Y′ <PP4′ Y′.

III

Let us now look at a simple numerical model. Here we can separate the personal consumption of the capitalists from their collective consumption. Let us assume that – with a two department schema – of the sk in both departments 20 per cent is personal consumption and the other 80 per cent is collective consumption. Most Marxist writers tend to assume that sk is *only* personal consumption, however, I feel that this is incorrect. Since in our present model sk represents *all* the unproductively consumed surplus-value, it must represent both personal and collective consumption. Now, by collective consumption I mean those expenditures by the state which are necessary to provide the *general conditions* of capitalist production, valorization and accumulation. Therefore these items of collective consumption, while *necessary*, are unproductive of surplus value. Armaments and armies fall into this category. Let us examine a two-department schema, as follows:

PP1

Dept. I $\quad 440c + 110v + 110s = 660$

Dept. II $\quad 160c + 40v + 40s = 240$

$$\overline{600c + 150v + 150s = 900}$$

Assuming that accumulation takes place at the rate of 10 per cent per production period, we have:

Dept. I $\quad 44sc1 + 11sv1 + 11sk1 + 44sk*1 = 110s1$

Dept. II $\quad 16sc2 + 4sv2 + 4sk2 + 16sk*2 = 40s2$

Here sk represents personal consumption of the capitalists and sk* represents the collective consumption by them. As constructed the schema can move forward from cycle to cycle accumulating 10 per cent in each production period.

However, to make the numerical model more closely resemble

our algebraic one, we can put the sk* into a separate department, i.e. into a third one. In this respect we follow Marx's use of a third department – or a sub-department of II – for luxury goods which are wholly consumed by the capitalists.

PP1

Dept. I $440c + 110v + 110s = 660$
Dept. II $120c + 30v + 30s = 180$
Dept. III $40c + 10v + 10s = 60$

$$600c + 150v + 150s = 900$$

So, we have the same total social product, the same total surplus value and the same amount of labour power being used. For accumulation we would have:

Dept. I $44sc1 + 11sv1 + 11sk1 + 44sk*1 = 110s1$
Dept. II $12sc2 + 3sv2 - 3sk2 + 12sk*2 = 30s2$
Dept. III $4sc3 + 1sv3 + 1sk3 + 4sk*3 = 10s3$

$$60sc + 15sv + 15sk + 60sk* = 150 = \Sigma s \text{ of PP1}$$

Again the schema can move forward adding 10 per cent per production cycle to capital in all departments.

What we need to know is, to what extent can Department III really be considered to be productive of surplus value? Let us allow that there is a real product, a material one and that the workers in Department III do provide surplus labour. Also, as we can see, the capitalists in Department III do indeed obtain the average rate of profit of 20 per cent.

We know that Departments I and II produce means of production and means of consumption, therefore let us examine them in detail and see what their relationship is to Department III.

The workers in Department II produce a total of 180, of which 30 represents surplus product/value. Let us examine the apportionment of both total and surplus value in Department II. First, there is the necessary consumption for the workers in Departments I and II, which maintains production at the existing level, i.e. $v1 + v2 = 140$. Second, there is the product/value which goes to maintain *extra* workers in these departments if production is to expand, i.e. $sv1 + sv2 = 14$. Next, there is the capitalists consumption, necessary but unproductive consumption in Departments I and II, i.e. $sk1$ and $sk2 = 14$. The total of these items is 168, if this is deducted from the total product of Department II we have $180 - 168 = 12$. This residue of twelve is equal to the sum of $v3 + sv3 + sk3$, and this is also equal to sk*2.

From Department I, where the workers produce 660 total product/value we have, first, the necessary productive consumption to maintain production at the existing level, i.e. $c1 + c2 = 560$. Second, there is the necessary productive consumption to expand production, i.e. $sc1 + sc2 = 56$. Therefore, we have $c1 + sc1 + sc2 = 616$. Total product $660 - 616 = 44$, and this is equal to $c3 + sc3$ and in turn this is equal to sk*, i.e. 44.

The result of this examination shows that it is quite possible for Departments I and II to actually *decrease* their respective production by 6.6 per cent and, providing Department III was abolished at the same time, they would still be able to maintain accumulation at 10 per cent. In terms of total social capital, of accumulation and reproduction Department III *has no direct economic function*. On the other hand, if all the resources that go to Department III were to be used for accumulation in Departments I and II, accumulation could proceed at a rate of 18 per cent. Therefore, when looked at from the point of view of the aggregate capitalist Department III does not produce surplus value, on the contrary it consumes it, and is not productive in the Marxist sense. This examination fully accords with Marx's view that 'although all surplus-value takes the form of surplus product, surplus product as such does not represent surplus value'.[5] Marx considered 'the production of surplus-value is the chief end and aim of capitalist production'.[6] And, given this overwhelming consideration, 'surplus-value is convertible into capital solely because the surplus-product, whose value it is, already comprises the material elements of new capital'.[7] It follows from this, that 'it is characteristic of all unproductive labourers that they are at my command . . . only to the extent as I exploit productive labourers . . . however, my power to employ productive labourers by no means grows in the same proportion as I employ unproductive labourers, but on the contrary diminishes in the same proportion'.[8]

IV

If we examine the numerical model in terms of gross and net income the above points can be further clarified. If we call sk* 'tax', and set it at the rate of 6.666666 per cent, we shall be able to proceed to a numerical demonstration of Bukharin's basic proposition.[9]

Let us start with PP1 again, of our three-department schema:

Dept. I $440c + 110v + 110s = 660$
Dept. II $120c + 30v + 30s = 180$
Dept. III $40c + 10v + 10s = 60$
$$\overline{600c + 150v + 150s = 900}$$

Department I has a 'gross' income of 660, from which is deducted 'tax' at the above rate. This is 44. Department II has a 'gross' income of 180 minus 'tax' of 12 and Department III has a 'gross' income of 60 minus 'tax' of 4. So we can calculate the net 'income' for each department.

Dept. I $660 - 44 = 616$ 'net income'
Dept. II $180 - 12 = 168$ 'net income'
Dept. III $60 - 4 = 56$ 'net income'

On our assumption that each department accumulates 10 per cent per production period, the above 'net income' may be laid out as follows:

Dept. I $484c + 121v + 11sk = 616$
Dept. II $132c + 33v + 3sk = 168$
Dept. III $44c + 11v + 1sk = 56$

And supply and demand will equilibrate in the following manner:

Supply PP1		Demand, including input into PP2	
Dept. I	160	$c1 + sc1$	484
		$c2 + sc2$	132
		$c3 + sc3$	44
			660
Dept. II	180	$v1 + sv1$	121
		$v2 + sv2$	33
		$v3 + sv3$	11
		$sk1$	11
		$sk2$	3
		$sk3$	1
			180

Dept. III   60   state expenditure 60 = total tax

PP2

Dept. I $484c + 121v + 121s = 726$
Dept. II $132c + 33v + 33s = 198$
Dept. III $44c + 11v + 11s = 66$

$660 + 165 + 165 = 990$

Assuming that 'taxes' remain constant and all other conditions remain the same, we would have for the next production period:

PP3

Dept. I $532.4c + 133.1v + 133.1s = 798.6$
Dept. II $145.2c + 36.3v + 36.3s = 217.8$
Dept. III $48.4c + 12.1v + 12.1s = 72.6$

$726 + 181.5 + 181.5 = 1089$

Let us now assume that the total 'tax' is increased to 12.121212 per cent, we then have:

	Gross	Net
Dept. I	$798.6 - 96.8$ 'tax'	$= 701.8$
Dept. II	$217.8 - 26.4$ 'tax'	$= 191.4$
Dept. III	$72.6 - 8.8$ 'tax'	$= 63.8$

Accumulation and consumption will now take the following form:

Dept. I $550.792c + 137.698v + 13.31sk$
Dept. II $151.008c + 37.752v + 2.64sk$
Dept. III $50.072c + 12.518v + 1.21sk$

In addition, there will arise extra demand for input into Department III which will account for the increased 'taxation'. This will be

$46.728\Delta c3 + 11.682\Delta v3 + 0.99\Delta sk3$

Supply PP3		Demand, including input into PP4	
Dept. I	798.6	$c1 + sc1$	$= 550.792$
		$c2 + sc2$	$= 151.008$
		$c3 + sc3$	$= 50.072$
		$\Delta c3$	$= 46.728$
			798.6

Dept. II   217.8

$$
\begin{aligned}
v1 + sv1 &= 137.698 \\
v2 + sv2 &= 37.752 \\
v3 + sv3 &= 12.518 \\
\varDelta v3 &= 11.682 \\
sk1 &= 13.31 \\
sk2 &= 2.64 \\
sk3 + \varDelta sk3 &= 2.2 \\
\hline
&\ \ 217.8
\end{aligned}
$$

Dept. III   72.6   'tax' expenditure upon arms 72.6

It will be noted that state expenditure upon armaments is less than the total 'taxation'. However, if the expenditure upon arms is added to $\varDelta c3 + \varDelta v3 + \varDelta sk$ it will be found to be 132, i.e. the total 'tax' for PP3. The reason for this is, as stated earlier, the product of Department III is determined by what are inputs from a previous period. This means that the difference between 'taxes' and arms production will be accounted for in the *following* production period. The temporal factor in periodization becomes quite crucial in understanding the mechanism of the reproduction schemas. It will be noted that Departments I and II have not been able to accumulate 10 per cent in PP3, because of the increased 'taxation'.

Let us look at PP4, and assume a further increase in total 'taxation' of the order of 50 per cent, i.e. to 17.574692 per cent.

PP4   Gross
Dept. I $550.792c + 137.698v + 137.698s = 826.188$
Dept. II $151.008c + 37.752v + 37.752s = 226.512$
Dept. III $96.8c + 24.2v + 24.2s = 145.2$

And after 'taxation'

             Gross   Net
Dept. I $826.188 - 145.2 = 680.988$
Dept. II $226.512 - 39.6 = 186.912$
Dept. III $145.2 - 13.2 = 132$

Comparing the net of PP4 with that of PP3 we can see that only Department III has a positive increment. For accumulation and consumption we will have the following:

Dept. I $534.1424c + 133.5356v + 13.31sk$
Dept. II $146.8456c + 36.7114v + 3.355sk$
Dept. III $103.84c + 25.96v + 2.2sk$

And, again, there will be additional increments to Department III because of the increased 'taxation', i.e. $41.36\Delta c3 + 10.34\Delta v3 + 1.1\Delta sk$, this will give us the following supply and demand pattern:

Supply PP4		Demand, including input into PP5	
Dept. I	826.188	c1	534.1424
		c2	146.8456
		c3 + sc3	103.84
		Δc3	41.36
			826.188
Dept. II	226.512	v1	133.5356
		v2	36.7114
		v3 + sv3	25.96
		Δv3	10.34
		sk1	13.31
		sk2	3.355
		sk3 + Δsk3	3.3
			226.512
Dept. III	145.2	'tax' expenditure on arms 145.2	

PP5
Dept. I $534.1424c + 133.5356v + 133.5356s = 801.2136$
Dept. II $146.8456c + 36.7114v + 36.7114s = 220.2684$
Dept. III $145.2c + 36.3v + 36.3s = 217.8$

Here we can see the illusory growth that Bukharin writes about, total social product in PP4 was 1197.9 and in PP5 it was 1239.282. However, when we examine the reproductive departments, i.e. I and II, we find that in PP4 their total product was 1052.7 but in PP5 had been reduced to 1021.482. If armament production was maintained at the level of PP5, not only would the output of Departments I and II continue to decline, but the total social product would *also* decline.

PP5	Gross	Net
Dept. I	$801.2136 - 145.2$ 'tax' $= 656.0136$	

Dept. II   220.2684 −   39.6 'tax' = 180.6684
Dept. III   217.8   −   13.2 'tax' = 204.6

And PP6 gross would be the following:

Dept. I   771.83007
Dept. II   212.76125
Dept. III   217.8

Here, total social product is 1202.3913, as against PP5's 1239.282, and total reproductive production has declined from 1021.482 in PP5 to 984.59132 in PP6. Thus we can see the process of expanded negative reproduction becoming visible, as Bukharin predicted.

However, a note of caution should be entered here, the schemas are highly abstract and are not intended to illustrate any particular economy nor to illustrate the precise mechanism for the redistribution of the surplus value that occurs in our examples in the 'money' form. These examples in fact ignore state paper money, the main form of capitalist money today, and therefore do not attempt to show the mechanisms for the averaging of the rate of profit etc. since all our examples assumed an organic composition of capital the same in all departments. These were all simplifying assumptions, and as such must be borne in mind.

Nevertheless, the crises that overtook the capitalist world in the 1970s have exposed the contradiction inherent in the large increases in state expenditure since, say, 1945. Given a decline in the rate of profit there emerges a contradiction between the general conditions of capital accumulation and valorization and the particular ones. Bukharin's theorem, whilst being primarily directed at the question of armaments – and their value-consuming role – helps to focus one's attention upon the whole question of state expenditures and their role under mega-monopoly capital.

Appendix II
On Lenin's Remarks on *The Economics of the Transition Period*

When the factional struggle between the Right Opposition and the Stalinist faction began in earnest in 1929 there appeared in *Lenin's Sbornik* vol. XI notes which Lenin had made in the margins of his copy of Bukharin's 1920 text. These were obviously not considered opinions, but rather the spontaneous reactions of a reader as he worked his way through the text. The reason for the appearance of these rough notes only in 1929 was all too clear: Lenin had interspersed his jottings with some critical remarks regarding some of the formulations of Bukharin. Their publication was obviously designed to further the campaign against Bukharin and to try to discredit him as a collaborator of Lenin.

However, despite the criticisms that Lenin made, two points should be kept in mind. First, those notes were never intended for publication in their original form, if at all, and as such cannot be accepted as the considered opinion of Lenin on Bukharin's book. Second, we do have Lenin's final comment at the end of his copy 'To sum: a spoonful of tar in a barrel of honey.' Of course, most people remember this old adage since it is said that the spoonful of tar will spoil the barrel of honey. But, in this case, it would be as well to remember that Lenin thought that Bukharin had actually produced a 'barrel of honey'.

To have attempted to reproduce Lenin's comments in this book would have detracted from the text and distracted the reader, and because of this would have served no useful purpose. Moreover, I feel that Bukharin's text should stand in its own right, since Lenin cannot be used as an authority to legitimize or discredit it. The critical reader will use his own judgment as to the merits or otherwise of Bukharin's text.

Notes and References

Editor's Introduction

1 See Cohen, *Bukharin and the Bolshevik Revolution*, for an account of this dispute, in chapter 1.
2 See introduction by Max Shachtman to Trotsky's *Terrorism and Communism*, pp. v–vi.
3 See Heitman, *Nikolai I. Bukharin: A Bibliography*.
4 Parvus was one of the few, in his work *Der Staat, die Industrie und der Sozialismus*. Also Bebel in *The Society of the Future*.
5 Rosmer, *Lenin's Moscow*, p. 43.
6 It is pertinent to clarify Bukharin's 'right-wing' position of the 1920s. The farcical trial of 1938 which condemned him for 'counter-revolutionary' activity has clouded his previous stature. To apply the term right-wing to him in the 1920s is in no way to impute any more than that he was on the right of the *Bolshevik Party*. This was hardly a dishonourable position for a communist, since Lenin had at times been in the same position, e.g. the Brest–Litovsk controversy.
7 For details see Nove, *An Economic History of the USSR*; Dobb, *Soviet Economic Development Since 1917*; Trotsky, *1905*.
8 See Nove, op. cit.; also Carr, *The Bolshevik Revolution 1917–1923*, vol. 2.
9 For Lenin's attitude see Carr, op. cit.
10 See Cohen, op. cit., chapter 3; also Daniels, *The Conscience of the Revolution*, chapter 3. Both works have fairly detailed accounts of Bukharin's activities in this period. For the details of Left-Communist proposals see the *Theses of the Left Communists (1918)*.
11 Carr, op. cit., pp. 176–7. See also *First Decrees of Soviet Power*.
12 Carr, op. cit., p. 129.
13 Ibid., p. 144.
14 Serge, *Memoirs of a Revolutionary 1901–1941*, p. 117.
15 Lenin in *Severnaia Kommuna*, no. 58, March 1919, quoted by Medvedev, *Let History Judge*, p. 45.

16 For examinations of the role and scope of multinational corporations see e.g. Barratt-Brown, *From Labourism to Socialism*; Mandel, *Late Capitalism*.

17 For an analysis of this experience see Holland, *The Socialist Challenge*, particularly chapter 5.

18 It is true that in many advanced capitalist countries there are a number of 'free' public services. But, as Ernest Mandel points out, 'It is only the commodity-*form* of wages that have been given up; the *content*, poor and measured out with miserly care, is still the same' (*Marxist Economic Theory*, p. 658).

19 For a full and rounded exposition of Bukharin's theory of equilibrium see his *Historical Materialism*. This work was first published in 1921 and was printed in numerous editions and languages during the rest of the 1920s.

20 See Wollenburg, *The Red Army*.

21 Bukharin returned to this theme of state capitalism (see Luxemburg and Bukharin), e.g. *Imperialism and the Accumulation of Capital* and 'Organised Mismanagement in Modern Society'.

22 See Mandel, *Marxist Economic Theory*, chapter 10, for some evidence of this process at work in the Japanese economy during the Second World War.

23 Davies, *White Eagle–Red Star*, p. 142.

24 Carr, op. cit., p. 197.

25 Deutscher, *The Prophet Unarmed*, p. 4.

26 See appendix I for an exposition of Bukharin's theory.

27 For an account of the economic processes and effects see Boorstein, *The Economic Transformation of Cuba*.

28 Marx, *Critique of the Gotha Programme*, p. 11.

29 Ibid., p. 28.

30 See Bebel, op. cit., ch. 1. Bebel quotes researches to show that the existing means and forces of production could afford a high standard of living with greatly reduced hours of work. This is based upon material published in *1886*.

31 Trotsky, *The Revolution Betrayed*, p. 49.

Part I   The Theory of the Dictatorship of the Proletariat

1 From a collection of articles *The October Revolution and the Dictatorship of the Proletariat*.

2 Gumplovicz, *Geschichte der Staatstheorien*, p. 8.

3 See, for example, Loening, 'Der Staat'; Wygodzynsky, 'Staat und Wirtschaft'; or, among recent books, Jerusalem, *Der Krieg im Lichte der Gesellschaftslehre*, p. 61.

4 Engels, *The Origin of the Family, Private Property and the State*, p. 137. 'The state is the organisation of the propertied classes against the classes without property' (ibid., p. 138).

5 Oppenheimer, 'Staat und Gesellschaft', p. 117; see also by him *Der Staat*. For Oppenheimer's views on the development of politics and economics see his *Theorie der Reinen und Politischen Oekonomie*.

6 'Staat und Gesellschaft', p. 115; *Der Staat*, p. 9.

7 See Schmoller, 'Das Wesen der Arbeitsteilung und der sozialen Klassenbildung', p. 72. Schmoller criticizes Gumplovicz, but goes too far in the direction of 'mitigating' the real historical picture; see also his 'Die Tatsachen der Arbeitsteilung'. There are also general theoretical observations in Durkheim's, *De la Division du travail social*.

8 For this see Mayers, *The History of Great American Fortunes*.

9 Engels, *The Origin of the Family*, p. 135. That the origin of theories *à la* Oppenheimer has a social origin, which we mentioned above, is also revealed by the 'system' of practical demands made by Oppenheimer and his 'liberal' socialism which, in actual fact, means a return to a simple commodity economy with 'fair' buying and selling of labour.

10 At the same time, Mr Renner, one of the most conspicuous representatives of so-called 'Austro-Marxism', who in his outwardly brilliant articles in *Kampf* beat all the records, I think, for the falsification of Marxist teaching, substantiated the slogan of 'self-defence' by the fact that capital, according to Marx, is the relation between two equally *necessary* poles of society – the workers and the capitalists. Renner only forgets the trifling fact that it never occurred to Marx to perpetuate these relations, even in a version still bound by the limits of a given state.

11 Marx, *Kritische Randglossen*, vol. II, p. 50.

12 Engels, 'Dell' Autorità', p. 32; the German translation from the Italian by D. Ryazanov.

13 Adolph Wagner in 'Staat in Nationaloekonomischen', for example, writes that a socialist 'state' has all the attributes of a state 'to the highest power', for the class coating of the contemporary state is merely the product of 'excesses' and 'abuses'. All this nonsense is analogous to the theoretical constructions of contemporary bourgeois economists (Bohm-Bawerk, Clark and Co.); capital, in their opinion, is not the relation of the state, but simply the means of production; 'abuses' (usury, for example) are non-existent, in future society there will be both capital and profit and so on.

14 Gumplovicz, op. cit., p. 373.

15 See e.g. Jellinek, *Allgemeine Staatslehre*, pp. 89, 194, 195ff. He makes the curious declaration that 'Machttheorie' inspires 'madness and horror' for 'it paves the way to permanent revolution' (p. 196), and 'the practical consequences of the power theory lie not in the foundation but in the destruction of the state' (p. 195).

16 Kautsky, *Die Diktatur des Proletariats*, p. 60. [The English translation of Kautsky's pamphlet has rendered the sentence Bukharin quotes as 'They remembered opportunely the expression "dictatorship of the proletariat", which Marx used in a letter written in 1875', p. 140, 1964 edition.]

17 See the articles appearing during the war in *Sotsial-Demokrata*, *Kommunist*, and *Sbornik Sotsial-Demokrata*. A reprint can be found in the Petersburg Soviet edition: Zinoviev and Lenin, *Against the Stream*.

18 For an analysis of the structure of world capitalism see our work, *Imperialism and World Economy*.

19 This was openly said in his time by Mr Taft, a first-class American imperialist and, at the same time, one of the founders of the pacifist league. By 'peace' he meant primarily *civil* peace and therefore he is prepared to drown the disturbers thereof, i.e. the workers, in blood.

20 Kautsky, op. cit., p. 18.

21 Engels, 'Dell' Autorità'. We quote the Russian translation from the wonderful pamphlet by comrade Lenin, *The State and Revolution*. In view of the unusually careful selection of quotations from Marx and Engels in this pamphlet we consider it unnecessary to repeat them here and refer the reader to the work of Vladimir Illich.

22 *Thesen über die sozialistische Revolution und die Aufgaben des Proletariat wahrend seiner Diktatur in Russland*, Verlag Freie Jugend, Zurich. Polish, Finnish and other translations have also appeared.

23 Kautsky, op. cit., p. 15.

24 Kautsky's craving for social peace is so strong that he 'explains' the civil war between the Bolsheviks and the right-wing S.R.s not as a difference in classes and groups but as a difference in 'tactical methods'. All Russian 'socialists', according to him, 'want the same things.' This is reminiscent of the arguments of the old liberals, who assured us that they too were striving for the 'happiness of mankind', only by different means.

25 This need for the suppression of the exploiters was not only clear to Marx and Engels. Plekhanov once said that we shall take away universal suffrage if the revolution so demands. He also supported mass terror and opposed any freedom for the overthrown class under certain conditions. See his pamphlet on *A Century of Great Revolution*. It would be advisable for every comrade to be familiar with it.

26 See above.
27 This absolutely vital aspect of the matter is brilliantly set out in Lenin's *The State and Revolution.*
28 Of course, it is not worth refuting every piece of high-sounding nonsense of a factual nature that is to be found in such abundance in the works of Kautsky; he has been strongly influenced by Menshevik slanders.
29 Lenin, *Can the Bolsheviks Retain State Power?*
30 Kautsky, who does not understand a thing, writes about the dreadful 'apathy of the masses' as an inevitable consequence of the soviet dictatorship. But it has long been known that *ignorantia non est argumentum.*

Part II The Economics of the Transition Period

Chapter 1 The Structure of World Capitalism

1 Marx, *Capital*, vol. I, p. 75.
2 Dietzel develops these same ideas in a much less scientific, though in a more ingenious, fashion in *Theoretische Sozialoekonomie.* See also Struve's *Economy and Price.*
3 von Tyszka, *Das weltwirtschaftliche Problem der modernen Industriestaaten.*
4 Harms, *Volkswirtschaft und Weltwirtschaft.*
5 Kobatsch, *La Politique économique internationale.*
6 Diehl, 'Privatwirtschaftslehre, Volkswirtschaftslehre, Weltschaftslehre'. Harms, 'Volkwirtschaft und Weltwirtschaft' and 'Antikritischer Darlengungen'.
7 This term was introduced by the author of the present work, N. I. Bukharin, *Imperialism and World Economy.*
8 The question of the division of labour has been comparatively little elaborated, but concerning the diverse nature of the works there is complete unanimity. Cf., Petty, 'Political Arithmetic', pp. 260ff. Also Petty's 'Another Essay on Political Arithmetic', pp. 473ff. Smith, 'The Separation of Different Trades and Employments from One to Another', *The Wealth of Nations*, book 1, chapter 1. Marx, *Capital*, vol. I. For the latest writings see Schmoller, 'Die Tatsachen der Arbeitsteilung' and 'Das Wesen der Arbeitsteilung und der sozialen Klassenbildung'; Durkheim, *De la Division du travail social* (the only work of its kind specifically devoted to the question); Clark,

The Distribution of Wealth; Fischer, *Elementary Principles of Economics*; Oppenheimer, *Theorie der Reinen und Politischen Oekonomie* (he thinks he is being original by introducing a division of labour between worker and machine! pp. 115ff.). The classification of Lexis in *Allgemeine Volkswirtschaftslehre* are curious.

9 See Marx, *Capital*, vol. III, part I.

10 See our work on this: *Imperialism and World Economy*.

Chapter 2 Economics, State Power and War

1 *The Moral and Political Works of Thomas Hobbes*, 'Non est potestas super terram quae comparetur ei'.

2 Marx attached the greatest economic significance to war. See his Introduction to *A Contribution to the Critique of Political Economy*. A completely distorted picture is given by Sombart in his booklet *Krieg und Kapitalismus*. A critique of it can be found in Kautsky's 'Krieg und Kapitalismus'.

3 Engels, *The Origin of the Family, Private Property and the State*, p. 138. 'Politics is nothing more than a method of persistence, an instrument of maintaining the extension of property' (Loria, *Les Bases économiques de la constitution sociale*, p. 362).

4 Quoted from Gumplovicz, *Geschichte der Staatstheorien*, p. 8. See also Loening, 'Der Staat'; Wygodzynsky, 'Staat und Wirtschaft'; Jerusalem, *Der Krieg im Lichte der Gesellschaftslehre*, p. 61.

5 For those who are acquainted with the literature devoted to questions of population in connection with the outcry about 'the degeneration of the nation', it is obvious that the whole series of measures to forestall 'degeneracy' is directly caused by the desire to have a suitable quantity of high quality cannon fodder.

6 Cf. Dellbruck, *Regierung und Volkswille*, p. 133: 'Where does the real power lie ultimately? In arms. The key question for the internal character of the state is, therefore, always the one of who owns the army.' Also see the naïve prophecies of Spencer in his *Man Versus the State*.

7 Social Democrats have completely misinterpreted this point of view. At the beginning of the war, the author of this present work was seriously advancing it in a number of newspaper and magazine articles: in the Dutch *De Tribune* (the article 'De Nieuwe Lyfeigensckap', 25 November 1916); in the organ of the Norwegian Left *Klassenkampen*; in the Bremen magazine *Arbeiterpolitik*; and finally in the magazine *Jugendinternationale* (Switzerland), as well as in polemical articles in the Russian newspaper *Noviy Mir*. From classical Marxist works see Engels, *The Origin of the Family, Private*

Property and the State, and his *Anti-Dühring* and 'Dell' Autorità'; Marx, *Kritische Randglossen*, p. 50, and 'A Critique of Hegel's Philosophy of Right'. The reader will find an excellent treatment of the question, with a selection of appropriate quotations from Marx and Engels, in comrade Lenin's pamphlet *The State and Revolution*. Like the Social Democrats, the bourgeois professors too have failed to understand Marx's communist teaching. Thus, Wagner, for example, says that the socialist state has all the attributes 'to the highest power', for the class character of the modern state is merely the product of 'abuses'.

8 Oppenheimer, 'Staat und Gesellschaft' and *Der Staat*.

9 See Engels on this in *Anti-Dühring*; Schmoller, 'Das Wesen der Arbeitsteilung und der socialen Klassenbildung' (a polemic against Gumplovicz). The development in the USA should be advanced against this particular theory, although North American feudalism should not be under-estimated. See also Mayers, *The History of Great American Fortunes*.

10 Sombart, in a work already cited (*Krieg und Kapitalismus*) depicts the influence wars have on the emergence of capitalism. However, Sombart's method of forcing capitalism to be born of different mothers in turn (now of war, now of love of luxury – see his book *Luxus und Kapitalismus*), depending on the honourable professor's whim, inevitably involves terrible exaggerations.

Chapter 3 The Collapse of the Capitalist System

1 Beckerath, 'Zwangskartellierung oder freie Organisation der Industrie', p. 22. The bourgeois assistant professor, as befits one of capitalism's Jesuit janitors, naturally depicts the class state using the pseudonym of 'the people'. On the other hand, he cannot see that not only do 'commodity markets' play a part, but so do raw material markets and spheres of capital investment, i.e. those very fields which correspond to the three parts of the formula:

$$M - C\frac{lp}{mp} \ldots P \ldots C' - M'$$

[M = money capital, C = commodity capital, lp = labour power, mp = means of production, P = productive capital (production process), C′ = commodity capital with an increment of value, and M′ = money capital with an increment of value. In this case C + c = C′ and M + m = M′.]

2 Feiler, the editor of the *Frankfurter Zeitung*, lays particular stress on this in his pamphlet *Vor der Uebergangswirtschaft*. See especially

211

the chapter 'Kriegssozialismus und Wirtschaftsfreiheit', pp. 33ff., where his formula reads: 'We have organised scarcity.' Lederer poses the question in much broader terms in *Der Wirtschaftsprozess im Krieg*: 'Earlier the war was a problem economically for the treasury (state funds). Today, however, the state is omnipotent. For this reason its action that is directed externally does not appear in the form of the enterprise, it is no longer a financial, no longer a money problem, but the bed-rock of the entire national economy mobilised for war' (p. 362).

3 See Hilferding, *Das Finanzkapital*, ch. 9, 'Commodity Exchange' (pp. 215ff. of the Russian edition). And, 'War economy, however, the stock-market and herewith its entire problematic ceases', was how Lederer puts the question, in *Der Wirtschaftsprozess im Krieg*.

4 In his article 'Disorganisational and Organisational Processes in the Epoch of the Transitional Economy' comrade Smit makes a distinction between 'exchange built on the capital-generating function of money' (M—C—M') and exchange 'with a view to exchanging one commodity for another', where state capitalist distribution is supposedly the transition from the first to the second type. This is an incredible muddle. In the first place, nowhere and never did or does money have a 'capital-generating function'. Second, there is no transition to a simple commodity economy (the formula M—C—M) [or, more properly, C—M—C] in a state capitalist society. There is a tendency to abolish commodity economy within a country and to modify the form of surplus value, but this is a completely different matter.

5 On the subject of state capitalism, beside those quoted above, see the following works: Pinner, 'Die Konjunktur des Wirtschaftlichen Sozialismus'; Jaffe, 'Die Militisierung unseres Wirtschaftslebens', p. 40; ves Guyot, 'Les Problèmes économiques après la guerre'; Ballod, 'Einiges aus der Utopienliteratur der letzten Jahre'; Rathenau, *Die neue Wirtschaft* and *Der neue Staat*; Bernhard, *Uebergangswirtschaft*; *Monopolfrage und Arbeiterklasse* (a collection of articles by right-wing Social Democrats). Among Russian works one can point to articles and pamphlets by comrade Larin (M. Lur'ya), particularly in relation to the organization of German industry. See also Osinsky, *The Building of Socialism* (the first chapters).

6 Clearly, this is the state of affairs in a 'pure' model of state capitalism; in concrete terms, however, it is only revealed as a trend.

7 On the subject of Germany, see the summary by Muller, 'National-oekonomische Gesetzgebung'. On France see Gide, 'The Provisioning of France and Means to that End'. On England see *The Economist*.

8 On the legal standards and forms of state capitalist relations see Professor Hatschek, 'Die Rechstechnik des Kriegssozialismus'.

9 These terms have been taken in the sense in which they are used by comrade Bogdanov. See his article on the trends of proletarian culture in *Prolestarskaya Kul'tura* and also his 'A Universal Organisational Science'.

10 Comrade Bogdanov prefers to see the whole organizational process during the war as merely one of 'coupons', i.e. nothing but a process of introducing norms, which arose because of regression of the productive forces. In actual fact, the introduction of norms is immeasurably deeper in its significance. The regression of the productive forces does not rule out the progress of the organized forms of capitalism at all. This has happened in 'normal' times, too, and in times of crisis when a temporary regression of the productive forces has been accompanied by the accelerated centralization of production and by the emergence of capitalist organizations. Engels also made this mistake – *mutatis mutandis* – when he wrote about syndicates and trusts. It is not a mistake to be repeated now.

11 There is no need, as Maslov does (*The Agrarian Question*, vol. I, 'Theory of the Development of the National Economy', and in other works) in his definition of the productive forces, to bracket together the means of production and living labour, i.e. 'to add up' the static value and the process. It is not labour which is equivalent to the means of production, but labour power. On the subject of the productive forces in Marx see *Capital, The Poverty of Philosophy*, etc. See also 'production' in *Nouveau Dictionnaire d'économique politique*, by Leon Say: 'productive force . . . the ensemble of those elements (of production) which serve as forces'. Kleinwachter, 'Die Volkswirtschaftliche Production im Allgemeinen'; Harms, 'Arbeit'; Lexis, *Production*, and *Allgemeine Volkswirtschaftslehre*; Watkins, 'Third Factor in Variations of Productivity'; Oppenheimer, *Theorie der Reinen und Politischen Oekonomie*, and *Die Productiven Krafte* (pp. 138ff.); Hilferding, *Eine neue Untersuchung über die Arbeitsmittel.* Clear formulae are to be found in Rodbertus's, *Zur Beleuchtung der sozialen Frage*, part I, 'Productive force and productivity are to be clearly distinguished. Productivity means the efficiency or fruitfulness of productive force', in other words, Rodbertus takes the productive forces *in natura*. See also List, *Die System der Politik Oekonomie.*

12 Luxemburg, *The Accumulation of Capital*, p. 31 (English edition).

13 See Marx, *Capital*, vols II and III.

14 Struve, in his book *Economy and Price*, excludes the relations of production from his analysis on purpose, so as to maintain that socio-class relations are the external appurtenances of a society. With

reference to this, see my article 'Mr Struve's Tricks' in the Marxist journal *Enlightenment.*

15 See Marx, *The Poverty of Philosophy.*.

16 Unfortunately, this has been misunderstood even by many comrades, who ascribe a super-historical absolute reality to relative laws of a definite historical significance. Even the rudimentary social book-keeping of a socialist economy 'rests' on this false impression, and this just at a time when a value and monetary expression is incompatible with the real labour process, and the latter does not regulate the distribution of the productive forces.

17 'The present war must educate us for one thing if nothing else; for a deepened economic thought. . . . Almost all economic questions seem insoluble when seen simply from the point of view of money economy . . . but became clarified when seen from the point of view of natural economy' (Goldscheid, 'Staatssozialismus oder Staats-kapitalismus').

18 On this subject see the work of comrade Lenin, *The State and Revolution,* and also our article 'The Theory of the Dictatorship of the Proletariat' [part I of this edition].

19 Hilferding's *Das Finanzkapital.*

20 Grinevetsky, *The Post-war Prospects of the Russian Economy.*

21 As befits an apologist of capitalism, whose mental horizon does not extend further than the 'Weltanschaung' of a syndicalist, Grinevetsky, in his book, examines the question exclusively from the point of view of capitalist relations of production as the eternal and universal categories of human existence. To the future historian of ideologies, the real night-blindness, which has distinguished bourgeois scholars during a period of the greatest social upheavals, will appear frankly comic.

22 Theorists of castrated Marxism, like Kautsky, have a concept of revolutionary upheavals which is truly childish. For them, the theoretical and practical problems which present the greatest difficulty simply do not exist. They scornfully brush aside empirical facts, by assigning revolutions which really did take place to the category of 'not real' and 'not true' ones, a method which, from the Marxist point of view, itself, merits the greatest contempt. See, for example, Kautsky's *The Dictatorship of the Proletariat* and his *Terrorismus und Kommunismus,* and the Foreword in *Die Sozialisierung der Landwirtschaft.* A temporary reduction in the productive forces, which objectively extends their power in the final analysis, has also taken place in bourgeois revolutions (the Great French Revolution, the civil war in America, etc.). See also Bukharin, 'The Dictatorship of the Russian Proletariat and World Revolution'.

Chapter 4 The General Pre-conditions for the Building of Communism

1 Comrade Kritsman noticed this aspect of the matter – though in a different context ('The Basic Tendencies of the Social Revolution of the Proletariat'). However, for him as for most authors, 'the capitalist organisation of the social economy is shed like a *husk* . . . by and large a simple change of leadership' (p. 13). The partial disintegration of the proletariat as a class, brought about by the drop in the productive forces, in connection with the pushing out of the proletariat and the cut-back in production, is a phenomenon of a different order.

2 Liberal professors and their conciliationist yes-men, who do not want socialism, but for decency's sake endeavour to justify this with supposedly 'erudite' reasons, therefore expound Marx after their own fashion. For example Franz Oppenheimer, the teacher of P. Maslov, writes: 'The immense superiority in numbers and strength of the proletariat . . . expropriates the expropriators, who can offer no *serious resistance* (! N.I.B.) and takes over the *completely ready* mechanism of production and distribution, that *continue to run unchanged and unshaken* . . . that is the Marxian theory of socialization' (Franz Oppenheimer, 'The Theory of Socialisation'). Dr Prange (see H. Beck's collection) calls this a 'clear exposition of the Marxist theory'. The honourable professors think that the exchange, stock-jobbing and speculation are characteristic of socialist society as virtue is of the Holy Mother of God, and that the birth of the socialist apparatus of production and distribution will not in the slightest degree violate capitalist virginity. Otto Bauer echoes them:

> It (expropriation) should not be executed in the form of a brutal (!!) confiscation . . . for in this form it could hardly end in any way other than at the cost of a mighty destruction (laying waste) of the means of production, that would immiserate the masses, and smash the foundations of the people's wealth. The expropriation of the expropriators should rather be carried out in such a way that the apparatus of production of society is not destroyed and the functioning of industry and agriculture not inhibited (*Der Weg zum Sozialismus*, p. 28).

The former 'Minister of Socialization' evidently wishes to build socialism not from earthly but from heavenly elements.

3 The monopoly of capital becomes a fetter upon the mode of production, which has sprung up and flourished along with, and under it. Centralization of the means of production and

socialization of labour at last reach a point where they become incompatible with their capitalist integument. This integument is burst asunder. The knell of capitalist private property sounds. The expropriators are expropriated (Marx, *Capital*, vol. I, p. 763).

4 'The organization of persons and things' (Dr Beck, 'Sozialisierung als organisatorische Aufgabe', in his collection quoted above).

5 In *The Poverty of Philosophy* Marx talks about 'organisation of revolutionary elements as a class' (p. 146). In the *Communist Manifesto* we find this description of the relations of collaboration between workers: 'wage labour depends *exclusively* (my emphasis N.I.B.) upon competition among the workers. The progress of industry . . . substitutes for the isolation of the workers by mutual competition their revolutionary unification by association. Thus the development of large-scale industry cuts from under the feet of the bourgeoisie the ground upon which capitalism controls production and appropriates the products of labour. Before all, the bourgeoisie produces its own grave-diggers' (pp. 41–2). It is quite clear that Marx saw the proletariat not only as the force that accomplishes the 'forcible overthrow', but also as the social embodiment of the *relations of collaboration* that grow up within capitalism and form the basis of the socialist (alias communist) mode of production. Hammacher (in *Das Philosophisch-oekonomische System des Marxismus*) concocts the idea that apparently this viewpoint was developed by Marx in *The Poverty of Philosophy* and the *Communist Manifesto contrary* to that in *Capital*. Obviously, therefore, Marx cites the appropriate passage in *Capital*! (See footnote on p. 764, vol. I.)

6 The thorough dishonesty of social-conciliatory theories lies in the very fact that they 'consent' to state capitalism, while protesting against socialism, which they are quite ready to acknowledge in *words* but not in practice.

7 Notably and primarily Kautsky. Before the war he 'was expecting' a catastrophe which 'did not mature'. During the war he warned against revolution, because the International [i.e. The Second International] is a 'Friedensinstrument' (instrument of peace) and cannot act when the cannons are thundering. After the war he is warning against socialism because the catastrophe 'is exhausted'. Well, it is an integral conception.

8 Apropos of this, see Osinsky, *The Building of Socialism*, chapter I, and also my own book, *Imperialism and World Economy*. The following prediction by Marx is interesting:

The colossal expansion of the means of transportation and communication – ocean liners, railways, electrical telegraph, the

Suez Canal – has made a real world-market a fact. The former monopoly of England in industry has been challenged by a number of competing industrial countries; infinitely greater and varied fields have been opened in all parts of the world for the investment of surplus European capital, so that it is far more widely distributed and local over-speculation may be more easily overcome. By means of all this, most of the old breeding grounds of crisis and opportunities for their development have been eliminated or strongly reduced. At the same time, competition in the domestic market recedes before the cartels and trusts, while in the foreign market it is restricted by protective tariffs. . . . But these protective tariffs are nothing but preparations for the ultimate general industrial war, which will decide who has supremacy on the world-market. Thus every factor, which works against a repetition of the old crises, carries within itself the germ of a far more powerful future crisis (*Capital*, vol. III, p. 478n.).

9 The fairly numerous 'analyses' of 'socialization', written by bourgeois professors, naturally side-step this fundamental question. See Bucher, *Die Sozialisierung*; Neurath, *Wesen und Weg der Sozialisierung*; von Tyszka, *Die Sozialisierung des Wirtschaftslebens*. See also Bauer op. cit.; Goldscheid, 'Sozialisierung der Wirtschaft oder Staatsbankrott'. From foreign communist literature we can only name the pamphlet by the Hungarian comrade Julius Hevesi, *Die Technische und Wirtschaftliche Notwendigkeit der Kommunistischen Weltrevolution*.

10 Goldscheid castigates the cowardly position of the 'leaders' very wittily:

It is really incredible how, with clearly unsubstantiated argument, one can successfully stop the acceleration of the socialization of the economy. In such a way, for instance, that one proves that the moment when all production and all traffic comes to a standstill, when there is a lack of the essential fuels, is the most propitious moment for the socialization of the economy. If, on the contrary, there were a period of high conjuncture one would no doubt declare: one should not come with experiments while everything is running smoothly. It is always easy to find reasons for opposing what one does not want. And, in any case, it is clear that in a period when production falls and where a fundamental change in the economy seems in any case to be unavoidable, that a transformation of the individualization into socialist production would be nearest to be being carried out (op. cit., p. 11).

11 Bourgeois scholars were so choked by fetishistic poison that they elevated capitalist confusion into the pearl of creation. Thus, Mr P. Struve in principle denied the possibility of rationalizing the economic process and professed a 'scientific belief in the fundamental and immanent dualism of that process' (*Economy and Price*, vol. 1, p. 60). Truly, 'the wish is father to the thought'.

12 Osinsky, 'On the Pre-conditions for the Socialist Revolution'. Marx clearly saw the protracted nature of the catastrophe and the transitional period. In *The Cologne Communist Trial* he quotes his own words: 'We say to the workers: You will have to endure 15, 20, 50 years of civil war and national hostilities, not only to change the social system, but also to change yourselves and become capable of political rule.'

13 Beck, 'Eroffnungsansprache' op. cit., pp. 10–12. Dr Beck, incidentally, treats revolutions in just the same way as the *Novaya Zhizm* did.

14 Comrade Kritsman was the first to set out this formula in a very witty article, 'On the Immediate Task of the Proletarian Revolution in Russia'.

15 Unfortunately, the latest (1918) works of Professor Vinner provide an example of this theoretical vulgarization. In the collection *The Death of European Civilisation*, which came out in the *Znaniye-sila* edition [Knowledge is Power], where there is neither power nor knowledge, the honourable professor, in failing to understand future prospects, makes generalizations about the first phases of the process and thereby says things which are downright comic. 'The belief in the unity of the workers of the world has perished. . . . The expectation of a speedy social revolution has crumbled. . . . The capitalist class is not preparing its own inevitable downfall. . . .' in 'The Downfall of the Pride of the Age', p. 75. In the article 'Socialism or the Petty-Bourgeoisie', where the gallant author criticizes the Commune and slanders it with a zeal worthy of a better fate, and where it is essentially the Russian Communists who are being portrayed under the guise of the Paris Communards [of 1871], we find for example this question:

> Why did they (the Communards; read Bolsheviks) make no attempt to urge people on to intensified effort precisely at the moment when many factory owners had left the town and hence, 'the exploiters who had oppressed the workers' had disappeared; why did they connive at idleness and endless absenteeism?

Does not this sound comic in 1920, in a year of labour armies, communist subbotniks and labour discipline? 'The salt of the earth', as the Professor modestly recommends himself, is truly bird-brained, at least in a certain historical epoch.

16 For a description of their characteristics see our book, *The Economic Theory of the Leisure Class.*

17 We say 'state economic' because at this stage 'economics' are merging with 'politics', and the state is losing its exclusively political character and becoming an organ of economic administration.

18   'Capitalism created a large class of industrial and commercial leaders' (Marx), who formed a particular category of specialists in the service of the bourgeosie. This industrial bureaucracy did not belong directly to the capitalist class, but was bound to it by the closest ties. It is educated by the bourgeoisie, receives from it ministerial salaries, shares in the profits and the distribution of dividends, invests its 'savings' in stocks and shares and as capital loses its identity in joint-stock companies. Being resourceful people who are good at using someone else's capital, gain an ever increasing influence, it sides with the capitalist 'family' more and more closely being imbued with its interests. And this is why, if they are taken into service – and this is inevitable and necessary – the ground, the surroundings with which they have inosculated must be completely removed. They must not be left in their former social relationship (Osinsky, op. cit., pp. 54–5).

See also the article by comrade Vindelbot, 'Trusts, Syndicates and Modern Production Combines', especially p. 31.

19 From this standpoint the difference in principle between the retention of the old specialists by the Noske–Scheidemann Government and their involvement in the work of construction of the Soviet Republic is quite clear. In the one case, they have taken on in their former 'social relations' and in conditions of democratized bourgeois power; in the other case they are taken on in a different relationship and under the rule of the proletariat. There they were left on the spot, here they *return* to what is only *formally* the 'old' place and to a considerable extent with a new mentality. Comrade Osinsky was quite right when he remarked: 'It is intolerable that they (i.e. the specialists) should be representatives of a hostile class, the mediator between the proletarian dictatorship and finance capital' (op. cit., p. 56). With their dialectical return this is practically excluded, since it presupposes both the disintegration of the old socio-production relations and the disintegration of the technical intelligentsia's old ideology. The reader will realize, of course, that we are not talking about narrowly defined periods, but about current processes, trends.

20 In a system of organizational science ('System des Organisations-lehre') Dr Beck distinguishes two groups of 'technical means'; means

of communication ('Verstandigungsmittel') and means of activity ('Betatigungsmittel'), particularly the increments of labour. Among the Verstandigungsmittel are: 'Zeichen, Farbe, Bild, Schrift und Sprache' ('Sozialisierung als organisat orische Aufgabe', p. 38). The practice of the Russian revolution wholly corroborates this thesis, which was arrived at by deduction. One of the oldest syndicates, the sugar syndicate, disintegrated right down to the organization of the individual factories. The same thing happened in others too. On metallurgy, see Vindelbot, op. cit.

21 Comrade Tsyperovich, in the second edition of his book, *Syndicates and Trusts in Russia*, graphically demonstrates how heavily the traditional concepts of the 'organic' epoch weigh on people, even revolutionary intellectuals. His theoretical constructions depict the economic organization of the workers' administration not as *new* apparatuses but as apparatuses whose genealogy originates in those of the bourgeoisie. And yet every *line* he himself cites as factual material blatantly contradicts this notion and *wholly* confirms *our* point of view. Logically this is also bound up with the terrible theoretical confusion which exists in most assessments of the epoch, which we shall have an opportunity to discuss in another chapter. Let us give some examples. This is what comrade Tsyperovich writes about the Supreme Council of National Economy and about the Regional Economic Councils (Sovnarkhozy) in general:

> Made up of the representatives of workers' organisations and headed only by officials from the party centres, these supreme organs of economic control of the country were in essence the successors to the Economic Councils of the Provisional Government (i.e. the government of Kerensky and Co.).

What does this mean? And how is one to understand a succession 'in essence'? Clearly, what is happening now is the complete *destruction* of the old organizations and the creation of totally *new* ones. The 'essence' lies only in their administrative function. Yet Comrade Tsyperovich talks about both syndicates and trusts in the Soviet Republic, as old apparatuses of which only 'the content itself must be materially changed' (p. 170). He completely fails to observe that our production combines are quite different organizational apparatuses and that they have grown up *on the bones* of defunct capitalist organizations which have collapsed and fallen to pieces. We invite readers to study the last chapter of Tsyperovich's book from this point of view, in order to be convinced yet again of the utter naïvety of the old concepts.

22 Social Democratic opportunists openly jeer at the revolutionary Marxist method, when they maintain that a change of functions

signifies a change in the *class* characteristic. During the epoch of the dictatorship, the proletariat does wage a class struggle, but it wages it as the ruling class, as the class-organizer and creator, the class-builder of the new society. This ABC of Marxism is nevertheless a closed book to all the apologists of 'healthy capitalism'.

23 The narrow-minded critics on the right love to scoff at our unions, newspapers and festive occasions as 'bureaucratic', diffidently passing over in silence the fact that, under the dictatorship of the proletariat, the treasury is the *workers'* treasury. This is merely a cover for the ardent wish that the 'treasury' was still in the hands of the class enemies of the proletariat.

Chapter 5 Town and Country in the Process of Social Transformation

1 Marx, *Capital*, vol. I, p. 352.

2 It does not follow from this, as Kautsky thinks (see his articles on imperialism in *Neue Zeit* [see *New Left Review*, no. 59, January–February 1970, for English translation of his article 'Ultra-imperialism']), that the roots of imperialism lie solely in this sphere. From the point of view of the conditions of reproduction, the change in the three parts of the formula $M - C\frac{lp}{mp} \ldots P \ldots C' - M'$ is important.

$$\underbrace{\qquad}_{i} \quad \underbrace{\qquad}_{ii} \quad \underbrace{\qquad}_{iii}$$

The raw materials markets and labour power correspond to the first part of the formula, the sphere of capital investment corresponds to the second, and finally, the commodity markets correspond to the third. The change occurs in *all three* branches and in accordance with this, the struggle of the imperialist bodies proceeds along three lines.

3 Lederer gives this table of the shift in profitability:

	Gross profit	Costs	Net profit
Pre-war	100	75	25
The present minimum	200	95	105
The probable average	250	95	155
The maximum	300	95	205

'The far higher prices attained through black-market dealings would have been bound to have produced higher yields.' Since the difference between prices on the 'free' market and fixed prices is increasing, it stands to reason that the real displacement is much greater. (See Lederer's 'Die oekonomische Umschichtung im Krieg'.)

4 On this subject, in the Russian language, see the pamphlet by comrade Larin, *The Utopists of Minimalism and Reality*. In this essay, comrade Larin quite rightly observes: 'In short, even if agriculture itself had not matured sufficiently *from within* with respect to its organisation, modern German capitalism proved to have a sufficient reserve of material and social organisational forces to unite and bind agriculture from above and *from without* into a single, systematically controlled organism. In other words, the material 'maturity' of a country should be examined not from the point of view of the preliminary need to bring each branch of its economy in isolation to technical and organisational maturity, but as a derivative of the general condition of all its productive forces on average' (pp. 17–18).

5 Kautsky, in his latest pamphlet says, 'The revolution in the towns was not completely lost on the workers on the land. There would also be unspeakable misfortune if they too were gripped by the strike fever' (!) (*Die Sozialisierung der Landwirtschaft*, p. 10). Kautsky is right, when he warns against *sharing out* the major estates between the agricultural workers, but to protest against 'strike fever' – this means to go cap in hand to the Russian *land-owner*. The overthrow of capitalism in the country is as essential a link in the general process as is its overthrow in the towns. In the developed capitalist states, without drawing the bulk of the agricultural proletariat into the movement ('strike fever' as Kautsky calls it, 'strike passion' as our Mensheviks once called it), the victory of the working class is impossible, for the landowner, even if it were von Tunen himself, will not voluntarily put into practice even Kautsky's programmes. Failure to understand this, the elimination of the class struggle, is the fundamental sin of Kautsky and co. See also Bauer's *Der Weg zum Sozialismus*.

6 One can draw an analogy here between the process described above and the disintegration of the relations between developed metropolitan countries and their colonies. Colonial uprisings objectively harbour the *possibility* of a new capitalist cycle of development, if you examine this process in isolation. But in the overall pattern of development this is a by-product, and at the same time, the strongest factor in the disintegration of the imperialist system, as the prerequisite for the *socialist* rebirth of mankind.

7 See the article by comrade Goykhbarg 'The Socialisation of Agriculture'. See also Milyutin, *Socialism and Agriculture*, and Bogdanov, 'The Organisation of Soviet Farms'.

8 Kautsky is therefore correct when he writes, 'For us the agrarian

question is the most complicated, and also the most important, question' (*Die Sozialisierung der Landwirtschaft*, p. 12). However, Kautsky's whole trouble lies in the very fact that he cannot see or understand precisely this whole *complexity* of the problem. For him the fundamental 'complicating' factor does not exist, i.e. the class struggle between the various social groups. This is logically connected with his failure to understand that the relations of production of capitalist society are simultaneously *both* socio-class and technical-labour relations.

9 The 'sociologist' Kautsky completely fails to understand this. In the foreword of his book (*Die Sozialisierung der Landwirtschaft*) he attacks the Bolsheviks for allowing the peasantry to lord it as it chooses (p. 10), and here reveals the full extent of his ignorance (for he does not even know about the soviet farms). But on the following page he pounces on them for 'oppressing' the peasantry by taking away the surpluses for the town and the army. The 'intelligent' Kautsky does not even understand the significance of the war against Denikin, does not understand what is clear to the most ignorant peasant. Bare-faced malice against the party of revolutionary communism dictates thoughts worthy of a grammar school boy in the second class, from a 'good family'.

10 'In the face of the predominant small-scale production this (socialisation) must be thought of more in terms of a regulation of the exchange between town and country, than in terms of an organisation of *production*' (Kautsky, op. cit. p. 9).

11 Lenin, 'Economics and Politics in the Era of the Dictatorship of the Proletariat'.

12 Ibid.

Chapter 6 The Productive Forces, the Costs of the Revolution and the Technical Revolution

1 Marx, 'The Poverty of Philosophy', in Marx–Engels, *Collected Works*, vol. 6, p. 183.

2 Compare, for example, *Capital*, vol. I, part V, also vol. III, part 1, where there is an analysis of the average rate of profit. An example:

> Along with the productivity of work the means of production increases wherein is represented a specific value therefore also surplus value of a given magnitude. The more the productive forces of labour increases the more the surplus value comprises means of pleasure (consumption) and accumulation.

Or even more positively:

> That part of constant capital, that Adam Smith calls fixed, the means of labour like factories, machinery and so on, functions always in the productive process as a totality, is, however, gradually exhausted and carries its value over to the commodities bit by bit, that it produces. It constitutes a real measure of the *advance of the productive forces* (my emphasis N.I.B.).

[There is no precise standard English text for the above two extracts, since the quotations are taken from Kautsky's popularized edition of *Capital*, i.e. Volksausgabe.] Likewise in *Theories of Surplus Value*, 'Produktivkraft oder der Kraft Arbeit'; as against this we have 'Produktivkraft' ('Poduktionsmittel') in the introduction to *A Contribution to the Critique of Political Economy*.

3 Rodbertus-Jagetzow, *Zur Beleuchtung der sozialen Frage*, pp. 60–1. Also see the literature on the productive forces cited in chapter 3 of this work.

4 Marx, *Theories of Surplus Value*, part II, p. 150.

5 The author of the present work vigorously advanced this point of view in the book *Imperialism and World Economy*. See Marx and Engels's *Communist Manifesto*: 'How does the bourgeoisie overcome these crises? On the one hand by the compulsory annihilation of a quantity of the *productive forces* (my emphasis N.I.B.); on the other by the conquest of new markets and the more thorough exploitation of the old ones. With what results? The results are that the way is paved for more wide-spread and disastrous crises and that the capacity for averting crises is lessened' (p. 33, Ryazanoff edition).

6 Marx, *Theories of Surplus Value*, part II, pp. 495–6.

7 The destruction caused by the Civil War in America, a war which was a powerful spur to capitalism, is well known, as is the devastation at the time of the French Revolution which advanced the development of the productive forces after a period of profound decline. It is also well known that the French Jacobins, who were the most active force in the revolutionary movement, were indicted with literally the same words as are contemporary communists. Here is an excerpt from the trial of Charlotte Cordet, the murderess of Marat:

> 'What were your motives for such a dreadful deed?'
> 'His crimes.'
> 'With what crimes do you reproach him?'
> 'With the destruction of France and with the civil war, which he kindled throughout the country.'
> 'On what do you base this accusation?'
> 'His past crimes are indicative of his present crimes. He it was who arranged the September assassination; he it was who fanned the flames of the civil war, in order to be appointed dictator or

the like, and again, it was he who encroached on the sovereignty of the people by having the deputies of the Convention arrested and put in prison on 31st May this year' (*The Revolutionary Tribunal in the Era of the Great French Revolution*, p. 59).

Is not this dialogue between a Jacobin revolutionary and a counter-revolutionary Girondiste the prototype of the 'dialogue' between communists and Social Democrats? Not for nothing did Plekhanov in *Iskra* predict that socialists in the twentieth century would split into 'Mountain' and 'Gironde'. This prediction has been justified with astronomical accuracy and Mr Kautsky and co. appear fully robed as the virtuous and none too clever Girondists. Once upon a time Kautsky used to defend the Jacobins. But what is to be done? 'Nous avons changé tout cela.'

8 Comrade Kritsman (see his article 'The Development of the Productive Forces and the Dictatorship of the Proletariat') is quite correct when he says:

But the proletariat differs from other productive forces (machinery, raw materials, etc.) in that it can respond to the destruction threatening it with rebellion. A time of crisis is a time of awakening of revolutionary rebellion in the proletariat. The *proletarian revolution* itself *is* in fact *the opposition of the proletariat to the bourgeoisie's efforts to mitigate waste and reduce the inertia of its won forces by destroying proletarian labour power and to overcome the crisis* caused the anarchy of the capitalist mode of production *at the expense of the sacrifices borne by the proletariat*.

9 Marx, *The Poverty of Philosophy*:

Of all the instruments of production, the greatest productive power is the revolutionary class itself. The organisation of revolutionary elements as a class supposes the existence of all the productive forces which could engender in the bosom of the old society (p. 211).

10 From this point of view it is absolutely absurd to 'blame' the working class and its party for the devastation. For it is the working class that makes the reconstruction of society possible. It is the resistance of the old order to which one must 'impute' the devastation of the transition period.

11 'Critics' of the proletarian revolution see the devastation as proof of the immaturity of capitalist relations. From our analysis it follows that even with the most 'mature' relations the devastation (temporary) is just as inevitable. The 'critics' often quote Marx's words:

No social order ever disappears before all the productive forces, for which there is room in it, have been developed; and new higher relations of production never appear before the material conditions of their existence have matured in the womb of the old society (foreword, *A Contribution to the Critique of Political Economy*, p. 12).

Marx immediately draws the conclusion:

Therefore, mankind always takes up only such problems as it can solve; since, looking at the matter more closely, we will always find the problem itself arises only when the material conditions necessary for its solution already exist or are at least in the process of formation (ibid., pp. 12–13).

The drop in the productive forces in the process of the proletarian revolution was foreseen in theoretical terms by comrade Larin in the above-mentioned pamphlet *The Utopists of Minimalism and Reality*.

12 Professor Grinevetsky – in the chapter headed 'The Revolutionary Demoralisation of Industry' – in *Post-war Prospects of the Russian Economy*, puts it down to the influence of the following factors:

1 The complete chaos in the supply of raw materials and fuel as a result of a fall in output and the paralysis of transportation. 2 A labour crisis contingent upon its general disorganisation under the influence of the revolution and the class struggle, and the drop in productivity for many reasons. 3 *Technical* disorganisation in both the physical sense and the administrative-technical areas. 4 The *extreme instability and stagnation of the market* . . . 5 *The catastrophic process of demobilisation* . . . thanks to the technical disorganisation and the financial collapse of industry. 6 *The financial collapse of industry* as a result of the increase in wages and the drop in productivity, the complete disorder in supplies and the nationalisation of the banks, etc.

It is plain to see that all these factors fit into our classification, too, but Mr Grinevetsky lays the *blame* not on the capitalist system with its war and its *resistance* to the new society, but on the working class. Of course, an apologist of capitalism, who sees 'post-war prospects' flourishing as *capitalist* prospects cannot see the matter in any other light. Mr Hoover, the 'food dictator' of Europe, says essentially the same thing:

The economic difficulties of Europe as a whole at the signature of peace may be almost summarised in the phrase 'demoralised

productivity'. It is not necessary to review at length the cause of this decrease in productivity. They are, in the main, as follows:
The industrial and commercial demoralisation arising originally out of the war, but continued out of the struggle for political rearrangements during the armistice, the creation of new governments, their inexperience and frictions between these governments in the readjustment of economic relations.
The proper and insistent demand of labour for higher standards of living and a voice in the administration of their effort has unfortunately (!!) become impregnated with the theory that the limitation of effort below physical necessity will increase the total employment or improve their conditions.
There is a great *relaxation of effort and the reflex of physical exhaustion* of large sections of the population from privation and from the mental and physical strain of war.
To a minor degree, considering the whole volume, there has been a destruction of equipment and tools, and the loss of organisation, . . . due to war diversions, with a loss of manpower.
The *demoralisation in the production of coal*. . . . It is due in a small percentage – from the destruction of manpower to the physical limitations of coal miners or their equipment. It is due in the largest degree to the human factor of the limitation of the effort.
The *continuation of the blockade* . . . had undoubtedly destroyed enterprise even in open countries.

All these causes engender 'political, moral and economic chaos' (see *National Food Journal*, 13 August 1919).

In an economic report on the post-war state of the world economy, the engineer Roedder writes: 'Everything now depends on the German worker. It sounds almost like a sneer to talk of the revival of the export trade when at home the worker is taking it easy' (*Nacht und Morgen der Weltwirtschaft*, p. 49). The testimony of the American financer Vanderlip is analogous. See also the report by Zelenko, *Memorandum on the Question of Bank Loans to Russian Co-operative Societies in North America*.

Naturally, all these gentlemen can only see the 'laziness of the working class' and do not notice the sabotage by the owners. In the simplicity of their souls they think that the class struggle being fought in the midst of the production process is a one-sided affair and that only the workers are fighting in it, whilst the capitalists sit on a 'universal' throne and sternly watch over the 'interests of production' 'in itself', 'purely for the sake of production'. In reality, however, the reasoning of 'pure production' bears all the hallmarks of an impure practical reason, which jingles a purse and bears little resemblance to the Platonic 'idea'.

13 A term suggested by comrade V. M. Smirnov (in *Ezhenedel'nik Pravdy*).

14 Marx, *Capital*, vol. I, p. 716. Usually translators naïvely translate the word 'vogelfrei' as 'free as a bird'. [Bukharin's point is that 'vogelfrei' should be translated as *outlawed*, which is not in the standard translations, the milder term 'unattached' being used. Even in the latest translation – the Penguin edition – the term 'rightless' is used.]

15 Marx clearly saw this as long ago as the *Communist Manifesto*.

16 These tasks are *technically* essential in any social model of economic revival. See, e.g. Grinevetsky, op. cit.; Gusev, 'The Immediate Problems of Economic Construction'; see also the summary of the TsK-RKP on the 9th Congress and the newspaper *Ekonomicheskaya Zhizn*.

17 Apropos of this see Marx's *Capital*; Kautsky's *Entwicklung und Vermehrung* etc.; Hevesi, *Die Technische und Wirtschaftliche Notwendigkeit der Kommunistischen Weltrevolution*.

18 See the brilliant pamphlet by comrade Krzhizhanovsky, an engineer and specialist in electrical engineering, on the electrification of Russian industry. Muller, 'Sozialisierung des landwirtschaftlichen Verkehrswesens'.

19 Bourgeois economists ascribe the cause of this to the 'natural law of diminishing returns of the soil' which has its own lengthy 'history'. There is a fine analysis of this law in the work of comrade Lenin, *The Agrarian Question and Critics of Marx*. By advancing this law, as an inherent law of agricultural production, bourgeois science has substituted the natural category for the social one, such is the basic 'method' of this 'science'. Marx gives an overall picture of the technical development from the point of view of the relations between town and country in *Theories of Surplus Value*:

> On the whole it can be assumed that under the cruder, pre-capitalist mode of production, agriculture is *more productive* than industry, because nature assists here as a machine and an organism, whereas in industry the powers of nature are still almost entirely replaced by human action (as in the craft type of industry etc.). In the period of the stormy growth of capitalist production, productivity in industry develops rapidly as compared to agriculture, although its development *presupposes* that a significant change as between constant and variable capital *has* already taken place in agriculture, that is, a large number of people have been driven off the land. Later, productivity

advances in both, although at an uneven pace. But when industry reaches a certain level the disproportion must diminish, in other words, productivity in agriculture must increase relatively more rapidly than in industry (part II, pp. 109–10).

Chapter 7 The General Organizational Forms of the Transition Period

1 Sombart, *Grundlagen und Kritik des Sozialismus*, p. vii.
2 One French writer has defined imperialism as the striving of any life form to spread at the expense of others. From this point of view a hen, not even one laying golden eggs, but just pecking grain, is the subject of an imperialist policy, for it 'annexes' that grain.
3 See our article 'Some Fundamental Concepts of Modern Economics', p. 9.
4 This, one would have thought, straightforward idea was obscure to many comrades. Thus, comrade Tsyperovich in the edition of his work, already quoted, on syndicates and trusts in Russia, writes about the post-October period: 'Even at the preparatory stage, which we are now experiencing, that of state capitalism (!!), the worker is the master of production . . .' (*Syndicates and Trusts in Russia*, p. 170). In what way the worker can be 'the master of production' in a *capitalist* system is naturally incomprehensible, for such a strange system is not different from dry water. Of course, it 'existed' only in the minds of certain people and not in 'meaningful reality'. Comrade Boyarkov – in *Vestnik Mettalista*, January 1918, Petrograd – at one time defined this system even more 'subtly' as 'full-scale capitalism', which the working class must build 'without owners'. 'Capitalism without capitalist' – this was the absurd formula to which obscurity in fundamental concepts led. It goes without saying that bourgeois and conciliatory literature is completely riddled with even more hopeless confusion.
5 See Lenin, 'Notes of a Publicist', in *Kommunisticheskii International*, no. 9.
6 A fairly large number of 'works' on socialism have recently appeared abroad which avoid this fundamental question. It is enough to take an example from the work of Franz Eulenburg who defines socialism: 'Socialization of the means of production; that includes the arrangement of production and division for and by society as a whole' (*Arten und Stufen der Sozialisierung – Ein Gutachter*, p. 5). On p. 6 he distinguishes, among others, the following 'stages': under heading ii – 'Transference of mature industry into the hands of the masses;

total socialisation (nationalisation)'; under heading iii – 'Initial participation of society in economic life: mixed economy industries (state capitalism).' It is not easy to 'contrive' in so few 'erudite' lines to write as much rubbish as the honourable German investigator has been able to. For him the 'social whole' exists in the person of the state 'in general', i.e. such a state as never was, and in the person of an obviously capitalist state; on the one hand socialism is socialization and nothing more; on the other hand 'Vollsozialisierung' (complete socialization) is Verstaatlichung (statification); complete 'socialization' differs from incomplete, according to Eulenburg, as socialization differs from state capitalism, and so on. And all this conveyed by boxes, classifications and graphs! Neither is there one iota of understanding in Rudolf Goldscheid's book, written especially on this subject. In a very interesting report Otto Neurath tries in every way possible to avoid the heart of the matter, declaring that he is not interested in the question of what *coercive means* are necessary for socialization. However, he comes close to the correct formulation of the question, and is infinitely superior to that learned gossip and coquette Sombart. Compare, for example, these lines:

> Socialisation presupposes that some authoritative central body realises an economic plan. Such administrative and economic planning does not have to be socialist, it might for instance ensure more favourable situations for a privileged group; in Sparta a sort of economic planning secured for the Spartans the fruits of the labour of the Helots. . . . That man is a socialist who stands for an *economic plan* with *socialist distribution* (*Wesen und Weg der Sozialisierung*, p. 4).

However, eliminating the question of 'Machtmittel', i.e. of the class struggle and *the classes*, obscures and diffuses the entire question.

7 Incidentally, all the 'accusations' advanced against the Communist Party by the bourgeois philistines of Social Democracy are based on a lack of understanding of this circumstance. At best, these gentlemen are protesting against 'Hottentot morality', establishing thereby a fundamental 'equality' between communism and capitalist barbarism. Indeed, can a 'democrat' really deny 'the equal right to exist' for the wolf and the sheep? Why, that would be a violation of divine justice!

8 It is characteristic of international conciliatory ideology that this term is used as a *substitute* for the term 'expropriation of the expropriators' and 'confiscation'. This is done to then to make it easier

to speak of 'socialization' in connection with the notorious 'whole', i.e. to group the measures of the state power of capital under 'socialization' too. See in particular the works of Edmund Fischer.

9 Bauer, in his pamphlet *Der Weg zum Sozialismus, contrasts* socialization with statification and sees in the former a combination of the organs of the representatives of workers, employees and officials on the one side and the consumers on another, with the state as a neutral quantity on the third. He proposes, amongst other measures, to lease out the factories to agricultural co-operatives (i.e. syndicates). The question of dictatorship is not treated as it should be; the state is 'democracy in general'. This thoroughly bourgeois viewpoint is expressed much more strongly by Walter von Rathenau, for whom 'socialization' takes place in such a way that production is concentrated in the hands of the professional capitalist groups. With regard to this 'socialization theory' Karl von Tyszka correctly observes that such a conception is a revival of the medieval guilds (*Die Sozialisierung des Wirtschaftslebens*, p. 25). However, von Tyszka himself shows not the slightest understanding of the class content of socialization. In Herman Beck ('Sozialisierung als organisatorische Aufgabe') the 'Interessenverbande der Unternehmer' appear as the subjects of the socialization process (p. 51). In a discussion at a conference of German engineers Dr Prange openly called such a structure 'ennobled capitalism (veredelter Kapitalismus) and thus showed all the cards. In E. Fischer's *Vom Privatkapitalismus zum Sozialismus*, we have a classical example of a social democratic cretin: he plays with the idea of socialization the whole time, whilst using it in two different senses and on the basis of this conjuring trick comes up with the really brilliant result that socialization already existed years ago. Oppenheimer, who knows perfectly well what the score is, defends the capitalist position with the theory of immaturity. To him, anyone striving for socialism at present is a 'putschist' and a 'Blanquist', and so on.

10 This latter term, of course, is far from accurate. In the first place it confuses 'the nation' ('the whole') with the state, i.e. the organization of the ruling class, and in the second place, it bears the imprint of the epoch of nation states. We retain it because it has completely taken root, although there are no logical grounds for it.

11 The illusion of so-called 'municipal socialism' rests on the failure to understand this. Of course, in the process of the collapse of capitalism and revolution, the proletariat could capture individual districts, in unco-ordinated actions, and there could be proletarian 'municipalizations', under the state power of capital. But any reader will readily understand that this is a very special category, in the text we are talking about relatively stable social systems.

Chapter 8 The System of Production Control Under the Dictatorship of the Proletariat

1 Cf. Lenin, Speeches at the 9th Congress of the TsK–RKP(B) [see *Collected Works*, vol. 30].

2 For example F. W. Taylor, *Principles of Scientific Management.*

3 Otto Neurath is therefore right when he says that 'Ausschusse' ('committees' or 'councils') by their structure are of little use for purely practical productive functions (see also Eulenburg, *Arten und Stufen der Sozialisierung*). But all these 'critics' completely misunderstand – or pretend to misunderstand – the social and socially *necessary* significance of these transitional forms. The engineer Beck ('Socialisierung als organisat orische Aufgabe') approaches the topic correctly.

4 If, by militia, we mean an *ideal* militia, where everyone performs his duties voluntarily, the way the members of an orchestra obey the conductor's baton, then the words of Engels are highly apposite here: 'Only a society organized and educated along communist principles can approach the militia system, but even it will hardly reach it' (quoted from the book *Karl Marx – The Story of his Life* by Franz Mehring).

5 In point of fact the term 'militarization' is quite inapplicable because both the military organization of the proletarian state and the military model of industrial organization have completely different significance here. 'Red militarism' is a truly barbarous phrase, but the poverty of the language and 'custom' force us to use the term 'militarization'.

6 Therefore, for example, the decisions of the 9th Congress of the TsK–RKP(B) was perfectly correct for that period in the life of the Russian Soviet Republic and absolutely useless, chronologically speaking, for the very same moment in other countries. We cannot discuss this system of control in detail here and would refer those who are interested to the following sources: the minutes of the 9th Congress of the TsK–RKP(B); the newspaper *Ekonomicheskaya Zhizn* for the second half of March and the first half of April 1920; the minutes of the 3rd Trade Union Congress.

7 In Russia this idea was first put forward by comrade Trotsky. Herman Beck formulates this very well:

A meeting of many people cannot make decisions, at least in economic life with its complicated relationships and consequences of every resolution. Next it must be firmly stated that it is not the job of the board of management to be poking their noses in while something is in the hands of the technical and economic staff, as little as parliament can poke its nose into the affairs of the civil service. The administration of an enterprise can also obviously not be directed by committees and advisers, responsible expertly trained individuals must be left on their own to decide it. The only point of all these organs of collective decision making is to determine the organisation, the direction and spirit of production and continuously to oversee the actions of management. . . . Over and against this we see the second important function of committees and advisers, that of specialisation.

And in another passage:

Only short-sightedness can deny that the business manager and the personnel manager are the most valuable creations of political organisation. Although today they are often still fruitless chat-circles. . . . One must, however, guard against not seeing the true meaning of this because of the functioning of early stages of this development ('Sozialisierung als organisatorische Aufgabe', pp. 52 and 58 respectively).

Despite this last remark Beck himself is a long way from understanding the specific features of the various phases of the transformation process. Hence his organization plans, which in their construction are absolutely useless for the very time for which their author himself intended them.

Chapter 9 The Economic Categories of Capitalism in the Transition Period

1 This chapter was written on the basis of a rough outline drafted by my friend, comrade Yu. Pyatakov. We wanted to write the present work jointly, but practical problems, to my great regret, distracted comrade Pyatakov from the work and upset our general plans for it. I had to partly curtail, partly amplify, and partly rework this chapter in accordance with the context of the book. In many places comrade Pyatakov's text has been wholly retained, but even in those passages which are altered the framework is his. N.I.B.
2 Marx, *Capital*, vol. I, p. 8.
3 It does not follow from this, of course, that one should not make use of empirical material. On the contrary. For, 'the method of advancing from the abstract to the concrete is but a way of thinking by which the concrete is grasped and reproduced in our mind as a concrete' (Marx, *A Contribution to the Critique of Political Economy*, pp. 293–4); see also Bukharin, *The Economic Theory of the Leisure Class*.
4 This is also reflected in the state of our practical economic literature. Let us take at random one of the numbers of the very serious

publication *Narodnoye Khozyaystvo*, no. 5 for 1919. Let us open the article by I. D. Mikhailov 'The State of Railway Transport'. Here we find figures for the 'gross revenue', 'operational expenses', 'expenditure on staff wages', 'operational expenses for one verst' and finally, 'net profit or deficit'. All the figures quoted signify a sum of *roubles* and are given to the reader in *comparative form* for 1910–18 and even for the first half of 1919. Then the author conscientiously and persistently calculates the 'cost price' – also in roubles – of one pood [36 lbs] in 1913, 1914, 1915, 1916, 1917 and 1918. Having done these arithmetical exercises, he draws the *conclusion*: 'Thus the cost price of rail freight for four years has increased more than 50 times.' Where is the sense in all these calculations? The so-called 'rate of exchange of the rouble' does pirouettes no less fantastic than does commodity in Marx's chapter on fetishism or spiritualists' tables. Can we use the rouble as the unit of measurement? And this is only one side of the matter. What do these figures indicate, if the controlling role of the rouble disappears? However, the market has not quite disappeared: a 'free market' does *partly* exist and 'free prices'; these are partly fixed 'prices' and resources are partly forthcoming 'gratis'. But he hardly mentions this. What do these figures indicate if it is quite impossible to obtain additional quantities of many articles, i.e. if monetary value ceases to have any meaning. None of these questions even occur to the author of the article. And this is not an isolated instance. This is a *typical* specimen of the singular vulgarization of our times.

5 Marx, *Critique*, p. 268.
6 Marx, *Letters to Kugelmann*, p. 73.
7 Cf., for example, *Capital*, vol. I, 'Whatever the form might be' etc.
8 Herein lies the supreme revolutionary aspect of Marxist dialectics: 'when the inner connection is grasped, all theoretical belief in the permanent necessity of existing conditions breaks down before their practical collapse' (*Letters to Kugelmann*, p. 74).
9 Marx, *The Poverty of Philosophy*, p. 167.
10 For more detail on the subject matter in the above mentioned methodological arguments see our work *The Economic Theory of the Leisure Class*.
11 See Engels's polemic with Rodbertus in the preface to Marx's *The Poverty of Philosophy*.
12 Marx, *Letters to Kugelmann*, pp. 73–4.
13 Let us consider the following extremely interesting passage from *Capital*:

But what is it that forms the bond between the independent labours of the cattle-breeder, the tanner, and the shoemaker? It

is the fact that their respective products are commodities. . . . It
is only the common product of all the detail labourers that
becomes a commodity . . . the division of labour of society implies
their dispersion among many independent producers of
commodities. While within the workshop, the iron law of
proportionality subjects definite numbers of workmen to definite
functions, in the society outside the workshop, chance and
caprice have full play in distributing the producers and their
means of production among the various branches of industry.
The different spheres of production, it is true, constantly tend to
an equilibrium: for, on the one hand, while each producer of a
commodity is bound to produce a use-value, to satisfy a
particular social want, and while the extent of these wants
differs quantitatively, still there exists an inner relationship
which settles their proportions into a regular system, and that
system is one of spontaneous growth: and, on the other hand,
the law of value of commodities ultimately determines how much
of its disposable working-time society can expend on particular
classes of commodities. But this constant tendency to equilibrium
of the various spheres of production, is exercised, only in the
shape of a reaction against the constant upsetting of this
equilibrium. The *a priori* system on which the division of labour,
within the workshop, is regularly carried out, becomes in the
division of labour within the society, an *a posteriori*, nature-
imposed necessity, controlling the lawless caprice of the
producers and perceptible in the barometrical fluctuations of the
market-prices (vol. I, pp. 254–6).

These words contain in a nut-shell the entire Marxist theory of a
commodity economy and here, too, we can see what role is played
by the principle of equilibrium tacitly assumed in all analyses. It is
interesting that Marx himself, in an off-hand way, notes that his
scientific approach:

In reality, supply and demand never coincide . . . why? To be
able to study phenomena in their fundamental relations, in the
form corresponding to their conception that is, is to study them
independent of the appearances caused by the movement of
supply and demand (vol. III, p. 186).

And this means examining social economy in a state of equilibrium.
14 Marx, *The Poverty of Philosophy*, p. 93. Another formulation of this
idea can be found there. 'Economic categories are only the theoretical
expression, the abstractions of the social relations of production'
(p. 92).

15 Marx (in *A Contribution to the Critique of Political Economy*) side by side with the relations of production distinguishes the *derived* (abgeleitete) relations of production. It is a question of their establishment.

Chapter 10 'Non-Economic' Coercion in the Transition Period

1 Marx, *Capital*, vol. I, p. 714.
2 Such as the works of Dühring, amongst later authors there is Gumplovicz and from the very latest, Oppenheimer.
3 On this subject see Engels's *Anti-Dühring*, also his 'Gewalt und Oekonomie' etc. (a conjectured fourth part on 'The Theory of Violence' published by Bernstein in *Neue Zeit*, shortly after the death of Engels).
4 Marx, *Capital*, vol. I, p. 751.
5 Kautsky and Bauer talk about 'violence, whatever its origin', with dissatisfaction and loathing. The authors of scientific communism looked at it in a different light. This is what, for example, Engels wrote about Dühring:

> That force, however, plays another role in history, a revolutionary role . . . of this there is not a word in Herr Dühring. It is only with sighs and groans (hear, hear! N.I.B.) that he admits the possibility that force will perhaps be necessary for the overthrow of the economic system of exploitation – unfortunately, because all use of force, forsooth, demoralises the person who uses it. . . . And this person's mode of thought – lifeless, insipid and impotent – claims to impose itself on the most revolutionary party that history has known (*Anti-Dühring*, p. 206).

Apropos of Kautsky's discourse on 'Bestialitat' and 'Humanitat', one cannot fail to recall Engels's brilliant lines on 'true socialism':

> A little humanity, as they have begun to call the thing, a little 'realisation' of this humanity, or rather monstrosity, a little about property – at third and fourth hand – a minor proletarian jeremiad, the organisation of labour, the formation of pitiful associations for uplifting the lower classes, plus an all-embracing ignorance of economics and the real nature of society – that is the whole business, and even then it loses the last drop of blood and the last vestige of energy and vitality thanks to theoretical impartiality and the 'absolute calm of thought'. And with this tiresome stuff they want to revolutionize Germany, to set the proletariat in movement, to make the masses think and act! These Philistine

and cowardly features of the 'true socialists' were also typical of inter-party relations. 'It is characteristic of these old women,' said Marx, 'that they are always striving to gloss over and whitewash all real party disputes' (quoted from Mehring's, *Karl Marx – The Story of his Life*, pp. 113–15).

Isn't this the true prototype of the 'impartial', 'neutral' and 'independent' theorists?

6 *Communist Manifesto*, p. 53.

7 Kautsky's view is, therefore, absurd and that of those like him, who picture the revolution as a parliamentary vote, where an arithmetical quantity (half the population plus one) decides the matter. See Lenin 'The Alternative in the Constituent Assembly and the Dictatorship of the Proletariat', *Kommunisticheskii Internatsional*, nos. 7–8, 1919.

8 In Soviet Russia a communist, who committed a crime, would on the initiative of the party receive a much harsher punishment than a 'mere mortal'.

9 The howls of the Russian Mensheviks against compulsion, during the epoch of the dictatorship of the proletariat, are just the same as the howls of the capitalists about the violation of the freedom of labour by the trade unions, which set up pickets during strikes and do not let the capitalists employ strike-breakers. It is well known that the worst infamies were perpetrated by the capitalist clique using just this slogan of the preservation of the freedom of labour.

Chapter 11 The World Evolutionary Process and the World System of Communism

1 Contrary views on the stability of the economic organisms were developed by some economically retarded ideologists. The well-known book by General Gulevich on war and the national economy is one example. On the other hand, young Russian imperialist *pur sang* saw the danger (true, within the limited framework of 'disasters' which did not overstep the bounds of capitalism). See, for example, the article by Struve in the collection *Velikaya Rossiya*. See also Prokopovich, *War and the National Economy*.

2 Of course, the text assumes that all other things are equal. There could be a simple mechanical preponderance of forces on the side of the more backward groups, if they constitute a *numerically* large quantity.

3 The most vulgar 'specimen' of the contrary viewpoint is the work of the narodnik Trutovsky (a left S.R.), *The Transition Period*.

4 The reader will find a brilliant analysis of the revolutionary situation

and its models in Lenin's work, *Left-Wing Communism – An Infantile Disorder* (a popular discussion on Marxist strategy and tactics).

5 In his book, *The Economic Consequences of the Peace*, Keynes writes about Europe after the 'peace' treaty:

> The Treaty includes no provisions for the economic rehabilitation of Europe – nothing to make the defeated Central Empires into good neighbours, nothing to stabilise the new States of Europe, nothing to reclaim Russia; nor does it promote in any way a compact of economic solidarity amongst the Allies themselves: no arrangement was reached at Paris for restoring the disordered finances of France and Italy, or to adjust the systems of the Old World and the New (p. 211).

Keynes describes the situation in the following way:

> The significant features of the immediate situation can be grouped under three heads: first, the absolute falling off, for the time being, in Europe's internal productivity; second, the breakdown of transport and exchange; and third, the inability of Europe to purchase its usual supplies from overseas (p. 216).

On the threatening social catastrophe, see p. 213; on the attitude of the ruling classes p. 222. The collapse of the imperialist system *drives* the imperialists into a love of fellowship within the unified framework of the world economy. Thus the engineer Roedder narrates:

> Just as the bricks of a great building support one another, rest on and shelter one another, so it is also with the co-operation and common striving of nations. Should one brick, however, crumble, it must then be replaced lest the whole building be endangered.

All these melancholy discourses conclude with the tragic 'To be or not to be, that is the question.' To the *capitalist* system history answers with an emphatic negative.

6 In these instances, which plainly can by no means be considered typical, the complete collapse of the system will not take place, as is inevitable in a typical case of social transformation.

7 Professor G. Ballod in his naïvety supposes that we, the Russian communists, consider communism possible at the stage of the dictatorship of the proletariat, and he upbraids us with a whole series of highly comic reproaches in which he reveals only his own ignorance. See Ballod, 'Kommunismus und Sozialismus' in *Der Sozialist* (Sozialistische Auslandspolitik).

Appendix 1

1 See K. Marx, *Capital*, vol. II, chapter 21.
2 For a full examination of Luxemburg's ideas on the role of armaments production see her *The Accumulation of Capital*, with an introduction by Joan Robinson, chapter 32. And for a critique of her ideas see K. J. Tarbuck, 'Rosa Luxemburg and the Economics of Militarism', pp. 150–67.
3 For a survey of the literature on this subject see Ernest Mandel, *Late Capitalism*, chapter 9.
4 For a very clear exposition of the relationship between value and use-value in Marx's theoretical system, see Roman Rosdolsky, *The Making of Marx's Capital*, chapter 3.
5 Karl Marx, *Theories of Surplus Value*, part I, p. 370.
6 K. Marx, *Capital*, vol. I, London, Lawrence & Wishart, 1974, p. 220.
7 Ibid., pp. 544–5.
8 K. Marx, *Theories of Surplus Value*, part I, p. 393.
9 It may appear that all 'taxation' falls upon surplus value, and for that reason some may object and point to the fact that workers also pay taxation. This objection would be confusing a value schema and one of market prices, ones that are these days computed in state paper money, not even commodity money. The method of deducting all the 'taxation' from surplus value is fully consistent with our use of the reproduction schemas, I assume – as does Marx – that workers are paid for their labour power at its value. This being the case, it is correct to show all the unproductive consumption expenditures as being a call upon surplus value. If a portion of these expenditures were drawn from variable capital, it would be an increase in the rate of exploitation and to illustrate this process would unnecessarily complicate the schemas, without any compensating theoretical or expositional clarity.

Bibliography

Bibliography

Ballod, Karl, 'Kommunismus und Sozialismus', *Der Sozialist*, no. 34, 23 August 1919.

Ballod, Karl, 'Einiges aus der Utopienliteratur der letzten Jahre' in von Gunberg (ed.), *Archiv für die Geschichte des Sozialismus*, VI year.

Barratt-Brown, Michael, *After Imperialism*, Heinemann, London, 1963.

Barratt-Brown, Michael, *Essays on Imperialism*, Spokesman Books, Nottingham, 1972.

Barratt-Brown, Michael, *From Labourism to Socialism*, Spokesman Books, Nottingham, 1972.

Bauer, Otto, *Der Weg zum Sozialismus*, Berlin, 1919.

Bebel, August, *The Society of the Future*, Progress Publishers, Moscow, 1971.

Beck, Herman, 'Sozialisierung als organisatorische Aufgabe' in H. Beck (ed.), *Weg und Ziele der Sozialisierung*, Verlag Neues Vaterland, Berlin, n.d.

Beckerath, Herbert von, 'Zwangskartellierung oder freie Organisation der Industrie' in von Schamz and J. Wolfe (eds), *Finanz und Volkswirtschaftliche Zeitfragen*, Stuttgart, 1918.

Bernhard, G. von, *Uebergangswirtschaft*, Berlin, 1918.

Bogdanov, N., 'The Organisation of Soviet Farms', *Narodnoye Khozyaystvo*, no. 5, 1919.

Bogdanov, N., 'A Universal Organisational Science', n.p., n.d.

Boorstein, Edward, *The Economic Transformation of Cuba*, Monthly Review Press, New York, 1968.

Bucher, K., *Die Sozialisierung*, 2nd edn., Tübingen, 1919.

Bukharin, N. I., 'Mr Struve's Tricks', *Enlightenment*, no. 12, 1913.

Bukharin, N. I., 'Some Fundamental Concepts of Modern Economics', *Kommunist*, no. 3, 16 May 1918.

Bukharin, N. I., 'Thesen über die sozialistische Revolution und die Aufgaben des Proletariat wahrend seiner Diktatur in Russland', *Internationale Sozialistiche Kommission Nachrichtendienst*, no. 41, Stockholm, 12 June 1918. (Also published by Verlag Freie Jugend, Zurich.)

Bukharin, N. I., 'The Theory of the Imperialist State', *The Revolution is Right*, Moscow, 1925.

Bukharin, N. I., *Imperialism and World Economy*, Priboy, Petersburg, 1918, and Merlin Press, London, 1972.

Bukharin, N. I., 'The Dictatorship of the Russian Proletariat and World Revolution' in *Kommunisticheskii International*, nos 4–5, August–September 1919.

Bukharin, N. I., *The Economic Theory of the Leisure Class*, Martin Lawrence, London, 1927.

Bukharin, N. I., 'Organised Mismanagement in Modern Society', *Pravda*, no. 147, 30 June 1929 (part is translated in Irving Howe (ed.), *Essential Works of Socialism*, Bantam, New York, 1971).

Bukharin, N. I., *Marxism and Modern Thought*, Routledge, London, 1935.

Bukharin, N. I., *Historical Materialism – A System of Sociology* (intro. Alfred G. Mayer), University of Michigan Press, 1969.

Bukharin, N. I., *see also* Luxemburg.

Carr, E. H., *The Bolshevik Revolution 1917–1923*, 3 vols, Penguin, Harmondsworth, 1966.

Clark, J. B., *The Distribution of Wealth*, New York, 1908.

Cohen, Stephen F., *Bukharin and the Bolshevik Revolution: A Political Biography 1888–1938*, Knopf, New York, 1973.

Daniels, Robert V., *The Conscience of the Revolution*, Harvard University Press, 1960.

Davies, Norman, *White Eagle–Red Star: The Polish–Soviet War 1919–1920*, Macdonald, London, 1972.

Dellbruck, Hans, *Regierung und Volkswille*, n.p., n.d.

Deutscher, Isaac, *Soviet Trade Unions*, Oxford University Press, 1950.

Deutscher, Isaac, *The Prophet Armed – Trotsky 1879–1921*, Oxford University Press, 1954.

Deutscher, Isaac, *The Prophet Unarmed – Trotsky 1921–1929*, Oxford University Press, 1959.

Diehl, Karl, 'Privatwirtschaftslehre, Volkswirtschaftslehre, Weltwirtschaftslehre' in *Conrad's Jahrbucher*, n.d.

Dietzel, Heinrich, *Theoretische Sozialoekonomie*, n.p., n.d.

Dobb, Maurice, *Soviet Economic Development Since 1917*, International Publishers, New York, 1966.

Dunayevskaya, Raya, *Marxism and Freedom*, Pluto Press, London, 1971.

Durkheim, Emile, *De la Division du travail social*, Paris, 1893.

Engels, Frederick, 'Gewalt und Oekonomie bei der Herstellung des neuen Deutsches Reiches', *Neue Zeit*, 1898 (incomplete manuscript).

Engels, Frederick, *The Origin of the Family, Private Property and the State*, Lawrence & Wishart, London, 1946.

Engels, Frederick, *Anti-Dühring*, Lawrence & Wishart, London, 1955.

Engels, Frederick, 'Dell' Autorità', *Neue Zeit*, vol. 32, no. 7, p. 32.

Eulenburg, Franz, *Arten und Stufen der Sozialisierung – Ein Gutachten*, Duncker & Humblot, Leipzig, 1920.

Feiler, Arthur, *Vor der Uebergangswirtschaft*, Verlag Frankfurter Zeitung, 1918.

First Decrees of Soviet Power, Lawrence & Wishart, London, 1970.

Fischer, E., *Vom Privatkapitalismus zum Sozialismus*, n.p., n.d.

Fischer, I., *Elementary Principles of Economics*, New York, 1912.

France, Anatole, *The Island of Penguins*.

Gide, Charles, 'The Provisioning of France and Means to that End', *Economic Journal*, March 1916.

Goldscheid, R., 'Staatssozialismus oder Staatskapitalismus', *Ein finanz-soziologischer Betrag zur Lesung Staatsschulden-Problem*, nos 4 and 5, Vienna–Leipzig, 1917.

Goldscheid, R., 'Sozialisierung der Wirtschaft oder Staatsbankrott', n.p., n.d.

Goykhbarg, 'The Socialisation of Agriculture', *Narodnoye Khozyaystvo*, no. 5, 1919.

Grinevetsky, Professor, *The Post-war Prospects of the Russian Economy*, Moscow, 1919.

Gumplovicz, *Geschichte der Staatstheorien*, Innsbruck, 1905.

Gusev, S. I., 'The Immediate Problems of Economic Construction' in *Material Relating to the 9th Congress of the RKP*, Revvoyensovet Karkayskogo Fronta.

Guyot, v. vcs, 'Les Problèmes économiques après la guerre', *Journal des économistes*, 15 April 1915.

Hammacher, E., *Das Philosophisch-oekonomische System des Marxismus*, Leipzig, 1909.

Harms, Bernhard, *Volkswirtschaft und Weltwirtschaft*, Gustav Fischer, Jena, 1912.

Harms, Bernhard, 'Antikritischer Darlegungen', *Weltwirtschaftliches Archiv*, 1914.

Harms, Bernhard, 'Arbeit' in *Handworterbuch der Staatswissenschaftlehre*, n.p., n.d.

Hatschek, Professor, 'Die Rechstechnik des Kriegssozialismus', *Deutsche Revue*, Jena, 1916.

Heitman, Sidney, 'Nikolai Ivanovich Bukharin', *Problems of Communism*, November–December 1967.

Heitman, Sidney, *Nikolai I. Bukharin: A Bibliography*, The Hoover Institute on War, Revolution and Peace, Stanford University Press, 1969.

Hevesi, Julius, *Die Technische und Wirtschaftliche Notwendigkeit der Kommunistischen Weltrevolution*, Vienna, 1919.

Hilferding, Rudolf, *Das Finanzkapital*, Verlag der Wiener Volksbuchhandlung, Vienna, 1910. (Russian edition translated by Stepanov, Kniga, 1918.)

Hilferding, Rudolf, *Eine neue Untersuchung über die Arbeitsmittel*, n.p., n.d.

Hobbes, Thomas, *Moral and Political Works*.

Holland, Stuart, *The Socialist Challenge*, Quartet, London, 1975.

Jaffe, Professor, 'Die Militisierung unseres Wirtschaftslebens', *Archiv für Sozialwissenschaft und Sozialpolitik*, 1915.

Jasny, Naum, *Soviet Economists of the Twenties – Names to be Remembered*, Cambridge University Press, 1972.

Jellinek, *Allgemeine Staatslehre*, Berlin, 1914.

Jerusalem, *Der Krieg im Lichte der Gesellschaftslehre*, n.p., n.d.

Kautsky, K., 'Krieg und Kapitalismus', *Neue Zeit*, vol. 39, no. 11, 1913.

Kautsky, Karl, *Die Diktatur des Proletariats*, Verlag Ignaz Band, Vienna, 1918. (*The Dictatorship of the Proletariat*, University of Michigan Press, 1964.)

Kautsky, K., *Die Sozialisierung der Landwirtschaft*, Paul Kassirev, Berlin, 1919.

Kautsky, K., *Terrorismus und Kommunismus*, Verlag Neues Vaterland, Berger, Berlin, 1919. (*Terrorism and Communism*, National Labour Press, London, 1920.)

Keynes, J. M., *The Economic Consequences of the Peace*, Macmillan, London, 1920.

Kleinwachter, 'Die Volkswirtschaftliche Production im Allgemeinen', *Schonbergs Handbuch*, n.d.

Kobatsch, *La Politique économique internationale*, Giard et Briere, Paris, n.d.

Kritsman, L., 'On the Immediate Task of the Proletarian Revolution in Russia', *Narodnoye Khozyaystvo*, no. 3, 1918.

Kritsman, L., 'The Development of the Productive Forces and the Dictatorship of the Proletariat' in *Two Years of the Dictatorship of the Proletariat*, Supreme Council of National Economy, Moscow, 1919.

Kritsman, L., 'The Basic Tendencies of the Social Revolution of the Proletariat', *Narodnoye Khozyaystvo*, no. 5, 1919.

Larin, Yu, *The Utopists of Minimalism and Reality*, Socialist Publishing House, Petrograd, 1918.

Lederer, Emil, *Der Wirtschaftsprozess im Krieg*, n.p., n.d.

Lederer, Emil, 'Die oekonomische Umschichtung im Kriege', *Archiv für Sozialwissenschaft und Sozialpolitik*, no. 7. 1918.

Lenin, V. I., Marginal Notes in Bukharin's *The Economics of the Transition Period* in *Lenin's Sbornik*, vol. XI, Moscow, 1929.

Lenin, V. I., 'Can the Bolsheviks Retain State Power?', *Selected Works*, vol. 6, Lawrence & Wishart, London, 1946.

Lenin, V. I., 'The State and Revolution', *Selected Works*, vol. 7, Lawrence & Wishart, London, 1946.

Lenin, V. I., 'The Agrarian Question and the Critics of Marx', *Collected Works*, vol. 5, Foreign Language Publishing House, Moscow, 1961.

Lenin, V. I. 'The Alternative in the Constituent Assembly and the Dictatorship of the Proletariat', *Collected Works*, vol. 30, Progress Publishers, Moscow, 1965.

Lenin, V. I., 'Economics and Politics in the Era of the Dictatorship of the Proletariat', *Collected Works*, vol. 30, Progress Publishers, Moscow, 1965.

Lenin, V. I., 'Notes of a Publicist', *Collected Works*, vol. 30, Progress Publishers, Moscow, 1965.

Lenin, V. I., 'The Proletarian Revolution and the Renegade Kautsky', *Collected Works*, vol. 28, Progress Publishers, Moscow, 1965.

Lenin, V. I., 'Speeches at the 9th Congress of the TsK–RKP(B)', *Collected Works*, vol. 30, Progress Publishers, Moscow, 1965.

Lenin, V. I., 'Left-Wing Communism – An Infantile Disorder', *Collected Works*, vol. 31, Progress Publishers, Moscow, 1974.

Lexis, W., *Allgemeine Volkswirtschaftslehre*, n.p., n.d.

Lexis, W., *Production*, n.p., n.d.

List, Freidrich, *Die System der Politik Oekonomie*, n.p., 1841.

Loening, 'Der Staat' in *Handworterbuch der Staatswissenschaften*, n.d.

Loria, Achille, *Les Bases économiques de la constitution sociale*, 2nd edn, Paris, 1903.

Luxemburg, Rosa, *The Accumulation of Capital* (intro. Joan Robinson), Routledge & Kegan Paul, London, 1951.

Luxemburg, Rosa, 'The Accumulation of Capital – An Anti-Critique', *see* Luxemburg and Bukharin.

Luxemburg, R. and Bukharin, N. I., *Imperialism and the Accumulation of Capital* (ed. and intro. K. J. Tarbuck), Allen Lane, London, 1972.

McLellan, David, *Marx's Grundrisse*, Macmillan, London, 1971.

Mandel, Ernest, *Marxist Economic Theory*, Merlin Press, London, 1968.

Mandel, Ernest, *Late Capitalism*, New Left, London, 1976.

Marcuse, Herbert, *Soviet Marxism*, Penguin, Harmondsworth, 1971.

Marx, Karl, *A Contribution to the Critique of Political Economy*, Kerr, Chicago, 1904.

Marx, Karl, *Critique of the Gotha Programme*, Lawrence & Wishart, London, 1940.

Marx, Karl, *Capital*, vol. I, Progress Publishers, Moscow, 1965.

Marx, Karl, *Capital*, vol. I (intro. Ernest Mandel, trans. Ben Fowkes), Penguin, Harmondsworth, 1976.

Marx, Karl, *Capital*, vol. II, Progress Publishers, Moscow, 1967.

Marx, Karl, *Capital*, vol. III, Foreign Language Publishing House, Moscow, 1962.

Marx, Karl, *Capital*, vol. III, Sarawaty Library, Calcutta, 1946.

Marx, Karl, *Theories of Surplus Value*, part I, Foreign Language Publishing House, Moscow, n.d.

Marx, Karl, *Theories of Surplus Value*, part II, Progress Publishers, Moscow, 1968.

Marx, Karl, *Theories of Surplus Value*, part III, Lawrence & Wishart, London, 1972.

Marx, Karl, *The Cologne Communist Trial* (intro. and trans. Rodney Livingstone), Lawrence & Wishart, London, 1971.

Marx, Karl, 'A Critique of Hegel's Philosophy of Right' in *Karl Marx – Early Writings* (intro. Lucio Colletti, trans. Rodney Livingstone and Gregory Benton), Penguin, Harmondsworth, 1975.

Marx, Karl, *The Poverty of Philosophy*, Martin Lawrence, London, n.d., or see Marx–Engels, *Collected Works*, vol. 6, Lawrence & Wishart, London, 1976.

Marx, Karl, *Letters to Kugelmann*, Martin Lawrence, London, n.d.

Marx, K. and Engels, F., *Communist Manifesto* (ed. and intro. D. Ryazanoff), Russell & Russell, New York, 1963.

Marx, K. and Engels, F., *The German Ideology* (ed. and intro. C. J. Arthur), Lawrence & Wishart, London, 1970.

Maslov, P., *The Agrarian Question*, n.p., n.d.

Mayers, Gustavus, *The History of Great American Fortunes*, n.p., n.d.

Medvedev, R., *Let History Judge*, Spokesman Books, Nottingham, 1972.

Mehring, Franz, *Karl Marx – The Story of his Life* (trans. Edward Fitzgerald), Allen & Unwin, London, 1936.

Mikhailov, I. D., 'The State of Railway Transport', *Narodnoye Khozyaystvo*, no. 5, 1919.

Miller, Johann, 'Nationaloekonomische Gesetzgebung' in *Jahrbucher für Nationaloekonomie und Staat*, 1915.

Milyutin, *Socialism and Agriculture*, n.p., n.d.

Muller, J., 'Nationaloekonomische Gesetzgebung', n.p., n.d.

Muller, W. A., 'Sozialisierung des landwirtschaftlichen Verkehrswesens', n.p., n.d.

Narkiewicz, Olga A., *The Making of the Soviet State Apparatus*, Manchester University Press, 1970.

Neurath, Otto, *Wesen und Weg der Sozialisierung*, n.p., n.d.

Nove, Alex, *An Economic History of the USSR*, Penguin, Harmondsworth, 1972.

The October Revolution and the Dictatorship of the Proletariat (a collection of articles), Moscow, 1919.

Oppenheimer, Franz, *Die Productiven Krafte*, n.p., n.d.

Oppenheimer, Franz, *Der Staat*, n.p., n.d. (*The State*, trans. J. M. Gutterman, Allen & Unwin, London, 1923.)

Oppenheimer, Franz, 'Staat und Gesellschaft' in *Handbuch der Politik*, n.d.

Oppenheimer, Franz, *Theorie der Reinen und Politischen Oekonomie*, n.p., 1911.

Oppenheimer, Franz, 'Zur Theorie der Vergesellschaftung' in H. Beck (ed.), *Wege und Ziele der Sozialisierung*, Verlag Neues Vaterland, Berlin, n.d.

Osinsky, N., 'On the Pre-conditions for the Socialist Revolution', *Narodnoye Khozyaystvo*, nos 6 and 7, 1918.

Osinsky, N., *The Building of Socialism*, n.p., n.d.

Parvus (A. I. Helphand), *Der Staat, die Industrie und der Sozialismus*, n.p., Dresden, 1910.

Petty, Sir William, 'Political Arithmetic' and 'Another Essay on Political Arithmetic' in C. H. Hull (ed.), *The Economic Writings of Sir William Petty*, London, 1899.

Pinner, F., 'Die Konjunktur des Wirtschaftlichen Sozialismus', *Die Bank*, April 1915.

Plekhanov, G., *A Century of Great Revolution*, n.p., n.d.

Prokopovich, S., *War and the National Economy*, n.p., n.d.

Radek, Karl, *Programme of Socialist Construction*, Communist International, Moscow, 1920.

Rathenau, Walter von, *Der neue Staat*, n.p., n.d.

Rathenau, Walter von, *Die neue Wirtschaft*, n.p., n.d.

Rodbertus-Jagetzow, Johaan Karl, *Zur Beleuchtung der sozialen Frage* (ed. Moritz Wirth), part I, 2nd edn, Berlin, 1890.

Roedder, D. O. C., *Nacht und Morgen der Weltwirtschaft*, Vogeler & Seller, Chemnitz, n.d.

Rosdolsky, Roman, *The Making of Marx's Capital*, Pluto Press, London, 1977.

Rosmer, Alfred, *Lenin's Moscow*, Pluto Press, London, 1972.

Say, Léon, *Nouveau Dictionnaire d'économique politique*, n.p., n.d.

Bibliography

Schmoller, Gustav, 'Die Tatsachen der Arbeitsteilung' in *Jahrbucher*, 1889.

Schmoller, Gustav, 'Das Wesen der Arbeitsteilung und der sozialen Klassenbildung' in *Jahrbucher*, 1890.

Serge, Victor, *Memoirs of a Revolutionary 1901–1941* (ed. and trans. Peter Sedgwick), Oxford University Press, 1967.

Shachtman, Max, *The Bureaucratic Revolution*, Donal Press, New York, 1962.

Smit, M., 'Disorganizational and Organizational Processes in the Epoch of the Transitional Economy', *Narodnoye Khozyaystvo*, no. 6, 1919.

Smith, Adam, *The Wealth of Nations*, Dent, London, 1975.

Sombart, Werner, *Krieg und Kapitalismus*, Duncker & Humblot, n.d.

Sombart, Werner, *Luxus und Kapitalismus*, n.p., n.d.

Sombart, Werner, *Grundlagen und Kritik des Sozialismus*, Verlag Askanischer, Berlin, 1919.

Spencer, Herbert, *Man Versus the State*, Williams, London, 1884.

Struve, P. V., *Economy and Price*, vol. 1, n.p., Moscow, 1913.

Struve, P. V., *Velikaya Rossiya*, n.p., n.d.

Tarbuck, K. J., 'Value and Price in Marx', unpublished MA thesis, Sussex University, 1976.

Tarbuck, K. J., 'Bukharin and the Bolshevik Revolution', *International*, vol. 3, no. 4, Summer 1977.

Tarbuck, K. J., 'Rosa Luxemburg and the Economics of Militarism' in *The Subtle Anatomy os Capitalism*, Jesse G. Schwartz (ed.), Goodyear, Santa Monica, 1977.

Tarbuck, K. J., *see also* Luxemburg and Bukharin.

Tarle, Professor E., *The Revolutionary Tribunal in the Era of the Great French Revolution*, n.p., n.d.

Taylor, F. W., *Principles of Scientific Management*, McGraw-Hilll New York, 1924.

Theses of the Left Communists (1918), Critique, Glasgow, 1977.

Trotsky, Leon, *The Revolution Betrayed*, Pioneer, New York, 1945.

Trotsky, Leon, *Terrorism and Communism* (intro. Max Shachtman), Michigan University Press, 1965.

Trotsky, Leon, *1905* (trans. Anya Bostock), Allen Lane, London, 1972.

Trutovsky, V., *The Transition Period*, n.p., n.d.

Tsyperovich, *Syndicates and Trusts in Russia*, n.p., n.d.

Tyszka, K. von, *Die Sozialisierung des Wirtschaftslebens*, n.p., n.d.

Tyszka, K. von, *Das weltwirtschaftliche Problem der modernen Industriestaaten*, n.p., n.d.

Vindelbot, M., 'Trusts, Syndicates and Modern Production Combines', *Narodnoye Khozyaystvo*, no. 6, 1919.

Vinner, Yuri, 'The Downfall of the Pride of the Age' in *The Death of European Civilization*, Znaniye-sila, n.d.
Vinner, Yuri, 'Socialism or the Petty-Bourgeoisie', n.p., n.d.

Wagner, Adolph, 'Staat in Nationaloekonomischen' in *Handworterbuch der Staatswissenschaften*, n.p., n.d.
Watkins, 'Third Factor in Variations of Productivity', *American Economic Review*, vol. V, no. 4, December 1915.
Wollenburg, Erich, *The Red Army*, Secker & Warburg, London, 1940.
Wygodzynsky, 'Staat und Wirtschaft' in *Handbuch der Politik*, n.d.

Zelenko, A., *Memorandum on the Question of Bank Loans to Russian Co-operative Societies in North America*, n.p., n.d.
Zinoviev, G. and Lenin, V. I., *Against the Stream*, Petersburg, 1918.

Indices

Name Index

Ballod, G., 212, 238
Barratt-Brown, Michael, 206
Bastiat, Fréderić, 58
Bauer, Otto, 215, 217, 222, 231, 236
Bebel, August, 205, 206
Beck, Herman, 99, 215, 218, 219, 231, 232, 233
Beckerath, H. von, 73, 211
Bernhard, G. von, 212
Bernstein, Eduard, 236
Bogdanov, N., 213, 222
Bohm-Bawerk, E., 207
Boorstein, Daniel, 206
Boyarkov, 229
Bucher, 217

Carr, E. H., 205
Clark, J. B., 207, 209
Cohen, Stephen F., 205
Cordet, Charlotte, 224

Dan, Theodor, 30; Dan-ites, 31
Daniels, R. V., 205
Davies, Norman, 206
Dellbruck, Hans, 210
Denikin, 223
Deutscher, Isaac, 206
Diehl, Karl, 59, 209
Dietzel, Heinrich, 209
Dobb, Maurice, 205
Duchene, F., viii
Duhring, E., 32, 34, 116, 276

Durkheim, E., 207

Engels, Frederick, 3, 22, 33, 34, 39, 40, 48, 67, 89, 207, 208, 210, 211, 224, 232, 234, 236
Eulenburg, Franz, 229, 232

Feiler, Arthur, 211
Fischer, Edmund, 210, 231
France, Anatole, 90

Gide, Charles, 212
Goldscheid, Rudolf, 80, 214, 217, 230
Goykhbarg, 222
Grinevetsky, Professor, 90, 214, 226, 228
Gumplovich, 32, 34, 69, 205, 207, 210, 236
Gusev, S. I., 228
Gulevich, General, 237
Guyot, ves, 212

Hammacher, E., 216
Hammerabi, 31, 68
Hatschek, Professor, 213
Hegel, G. W. F., 145
Heitman, Sidney, viii, 205
Helphand, A. I., see Parvus
Hevesi, Julius, 217
Hilferding, Rudolf, 89, 212, 213, 214
Hobbes, Thomas, 66, 210

255

256

General Subject Index

259